DRAWN TO
THE LIGHT

To Guides for heritage centres,
especially Lichfield Cathedral, who
endeavour to describe remarkable
history in a meaningful and
enjoyable way.

DRAWN TO THE LIGHT

A History of a Dark Time

ROBERT SHARP

BREWIN BOOKS

First published by
Brewin Books Ltd, 56 Alcester Road,
Studley, Warwickshire B80 7LG in 2018
www.brewinbooks.com

ISBN: 978-1-85858-580-2

A Cataloguing in Publication Record
for this title is available from the British Library.

Typeset in Baskerville
Printed in Great Britain
by Hobbs the Printers Ltd.

CONTENTS

INTRODUCTION
AND BIBLIOGRAPHY

The further the spiritual evolution of mankind advances, the more certain it seems
to me that the path to genuine religiosity does not lie through the fear of life, and
the fear of death, and blind faith, but through striving after rational knowledge.
Albert Einstein in *Science, Philosophy and Religion, a Symposium*. 1941

Traditionally Christianity started in a makeshift lodging close to farm animals and attended by visiting shepherds. Bright stars shone and the Christ child was well wrapped up and laid in a manger. Later this man from simple beginnings was baptised somewhere in the River Jordan, in the wilderness of Judea, and administered reluctantly by an itinerant preacher. He wandered in a desert, preached at many wayside locations around Galilee, performed miracles and after upsetting the temple aristocracy, ended with a horrific crucifixion at the hands of the brutal Romans. Romans ruled by terror and were upset by this man saying he had a kingdom. Except this was not the end. It continued with some kind of resurrection in which detail was given but was, and still is, beyond our critical understanding. The outcome left a group of mixed individuals fired up and commissioned to describe and explain the phenomenon to everyone. How this glorification left a marginalised country and then passed around the world was extraordinary. Eventually reaching the far shores of North-West Europe, taking several centuries. Its fundamentals became the main western religion and its teachings shaped national mores and personal values; establishing the base for common law, business and education.

It is a story that stands in marked contrast to our rapidly interconnected age in which easy global communication is taken for granted. Smartphone technology, superfast broadband, trading of equities in microseconds and the New Horizons spacecraft sending back pictures of Pluto to Maryland, USA, are now standard. Nothing could be different from the passing of data at the beginning of the third millennium, with the spreading of a belief to others early in the first millennium. Yet understanding communication in the past is as relevant as the awesome connectivity today. Just how did the foundation faith of Europe reach these shores?

Was it really inevitable Christianity became our abiding faith? How close did the so-called barbarians come to nearly stopping this belief?

Trying to understand any history of early ideas and beliefs will always be fraught with uncertainty. Neither archaeology nor documentary evidence can be used objectively to discern religious practice and understanding. Only a glimpse is possible to determine how early Christians behaved and what they thought. Indeed, when they became a Christian their expressions were simply, *accepted the faith*, *submitted to the Christian God*, or *obeyed Christ*. It is the language of obedience and seems not to be a strong personal faith. The people were usually under the yoke of an oppressor and being under the control of a God was for many not very different. Therefore, knowing how deeply committed ordinary people were to God is problematic and still is. Conversion in a life changing way appeared to be the prerogative of priests and certain kings and they were the ones who wrote it down in texts that have survived. Much of this history is therefore partisan and skewed. However, critical analysis can sometimes offer extra interpretations, provide a general understanding and tell us something about ourselves. Pope Francis, 2014, said *history is life's teacher.*

Finding how religious belief disseminated is an easier objective, but this too is fraught with anomalies. Uncovering a church building, reappraising a saint known only through folklore, or discovering a baptismal spoon with a Christian symbol says very little on their significance within the community. Much of the information can only be derived and consequently, interpretation of this early history has to be undertaken with a great deal of caution. Knowing coming to a faith is usually a parlous journey, often with setbacks following revelation, so when it comes to describing and spreading a life enhancing belief over many centuries nothing can be taken for granted. Yet with all these caveats, a wide view can be worked out and certain trends discerned. It gives an idea of the way people changed and it will say something about where we are today. It is also fascinating thinking about its unfolding and uncertain history and looking forward to what is to come.

> *O that my words were written down! O that they were inscribed in a book! O that with an iron pen and with lead, they were engraved on a rock forever. For I know that my Redeemer lives.*
>
> Job 19.23-25

Conventions and Confessions

The AD and BC designations are used for dates, but a date given without a designation is assumed AD. Most of the dates are derived and need to be held with some scepticism. Biblical references are kept short as 3.7 meaning Chapter 3 verse 7. All quotations are from the Revised Standard Version of the Bible (NRSV), unless otherwise stated. British Isles is avoided as a description of England, Ireland and Northern Ireland, Scotland and Wales and Atlantic Isles is used instead. The word Saint, or its abbreviation *St,* is avoided when possible, since it is held all people were Saints until they behaved otherwise. Romans 1.7, *To all God's beloved, who are called to be saints.* In fact, before the year 993 the entitlement of sainthood was arbitrary given to individuals by their own community. It was not until the 12th century that popes reserved the right to recognise saints. The monastic centre is called a Monastery rather than the more correct Minster or Monasteria because it has a wider understanding and usage. This does mean there is a risk of assuming an early Monastery bore a good resemblance to the modern institution, they did not, and they were very different. References within the texts are avoided and the reader is asked to accept this shortcoming for the sake of maintaining clarity.

Where images are not owned, every effort has been made to comply with a permission or acknowledgement after a courteous request. All imperfections are the sole responsibility of the author who will repent.

A book on history with strong references to faith, archaeology and traditional lore can only cover salient events and must stand accused of failing to cover every detail and discussion. Especially, one that encompasses a whole millennium in time. It is not possible to include theological discourse with a full historical narrative and it is not possible to give every historical detail and provide at the same time a balanced treatise. However, there exists a niche for an overview of these interlocking subjects. For all who want to know how a Christian faith ever progressed over 1000 years of historical turmoil the following is a contribution.

The following have been useful sources of information:

BLAIR, JOHN. *Building Anglo-Saxon England* (Princeton and Oxford, Princeton University Press, 2018)

BLAIR, JOHN. *The church in Anglo-Saxon society* (Oxford, Oxford University Press, 2005)

BRADLEY, IAN. *Columba pilgrim and penitent* (Glasgow, Wild Goose Publications, 1996)

CALDER, M. *Early ecclesiastical sites in Somerset: three case studies* (Somerset Archaeology and Natural History 147, pp. 1-28, 2004)

CAMPBELL, JAMES edited. *The Anglo-Saxons* (London, Penguin Books, 1991)

CRUMMY, NINA, CRUMMY PHILIP and CROSSAN CARL. *Colchester Archaeological Report 9* (Colchester Archaeological Trust, 1993)

CUNLIFFE, BARRY. *Who were the Celts?* (Bristol, BBC History Magazine, Nov 2015)

DE LA BÉDOYÈRE, GUY. *Roman Britain a new history* (London, Thames and Hudson, 2013)

DELAP, DANA. (et al) *Celtic Saints* (Andover, Pitkin Guides, 1997)

FLEMING, ROBIN. *Britain after Rome. The fall and rise 400 to 1070* (London, Penguin Books, 2001)

HART, AIDAN. *An introductory history of the orthodox church in Britain and Ireland (www.aidanharticons.com)*

HERREN, MICHAEL W and BROWN, SHIRLEY ANN. *Christ in Celtic Christianity* (Woodbridge, The Boydell Press, 2012)

HIGHAM, NICHOLAS J. and RYAN, MARTIN J. *The Anglo-Saxon World* (New Haven and London, Yale University Press, 2013)

KELLY, VIVIAN. *St Illtud's church Llantwit Major* (Llanilltud Fawr, 2015)

MACCULLOCH, DIARMAID. *A history of Christianity* (London, Penguin Books, 2010)

PAGE, NICK. *Kingdom of fools. The unlikely rise of the early church* (London, Hodder & Stoughton, 2013)

PALMER, JAMES T. *The Apocalypse in the early Middle Ages* (Cambridge, Cambridge University Press, 2014)

PETTS, DAVID. *Christianity in Roman Britain. An archaeology* (Stroud, Tempus, 2003)

PETTS, DAVID. *The early medieval church in Wales* (Stroud. The History Press, 2009)

PRYOR, FRANCIS. *Britain AD* (London, Harper Perennial, 2005)

RAMIREZ, JANINA. *The private lives of the Saints.* (London. W.H. Allen, 2016)

RODWELL, WARWICK. *The forgotten Cathedral.* (London. Current Archaeology. 205, Sept/Oct 2006)

ROESDAHL, ELSE. *The Vikings* (London, Penguin Books, 2016)

SEABORNE, MALCOLM. *Celtic crosses of Britain and Ireland* (Oxford, Shire Archaeology, 2012)

SHARP, ROBERT. *The hoard and its history. Staffordshire's secrets revealed* (Studley, Brewin Books, 2016)

STENTON, FRANK M. *Anglo-Saxon England* (Oxford, Oxford University Press, 1989)

STEPHENSON, PAUL. *Constantine* (London, Quercus, 2009)

VENNING, TIMOTHY. *The kings and queens of Anglo-Saxon England* (Stroud, Amberley, 2013)

WILKEN, ROBERT LOUIS. *The first thousand years* (New Haven and London, Yale University Press, 2012)

WOOD, MICHAEL. *In search of the Dark Ages* (London, BBC books, 2005)

ZALUCKYJ, SARAH. *Mercia. The Anglo-Saxon kingdom of central England* (Logaston, Logaston Press, 2011)

A collaboration. *The story of Jesus* (Washington D.C., National Geographic, 2016)

Image acknowledgements and thanks

Jesus the Good Shepherd. Jesus and the healing of a bleeding woman. Both catacomb images. Public Domain, Wikimedia Commons.

House of Peter. Berthold Werner, Public Domain, Wikimedia Commons. Desaturated and cropped from original.

Wirksworth Stone. Permission St Mary the Virgin. Wirksworth.

Ivory panel with Saint Peter. 5th to 6th century. Frankish. The Metropolitan Museum of Art, New York.

Bodmer Papyrus 66. Wikimedia Commons. Desaturated from original.

Dura Europos house church. Wikimedia Commons. Desaturated from original.

St. Helens church cross, Kelloe, Durham. Permission *www.jameswoodward.info*

Coin of Ezana. Permission *www.EdgarLOwen.com*

Magnentius coin. Permission wildwinds.com, ex Freeman & Sear.

Wycliffe Bible with permission from Dean and Chapter of Lichfield Cathedral.

Latinus Stone taken at Whithorn Priory Museum.

Grave marker stone taken at Dumfries Museum, Dumfries and Galloway.

Clovis 1. Wikimedia Commons. Arnaud 25 Public Domain. Cropped and desaturated.

Skellig Michael. Wikimedia Commons. Jibi44 CC BY 2.5. Desaturated from original.

Gundestrup cauldron taken at Copenhagen National Museum.

Inishmurray Monastery. Permission Martin Byrne, *www.carrowkeel.com*

Eileach an Naoimh Monastery. Permission Gordon Doughty, *www.geograph.org.uk/photo*

Dunbarton Rocks. Permission from Gordon Doughty, *www.geograph.org.uk/photo*

Icon of Betti at St Mary the Virgin, Wirksworth. Permission from Aidan Hart, Aidan Hart Icons, *www.aidanharticons.com*

Tonsures. From 'The history of Romanism', c1845. Flickr Commons.

St Chad's window. Permission from Wardens of St Chad's church, Hanmer.

Patrick's bell reproduced. Metropolitan Museum of Art, New York.

St Augustine's Gospel. Scenes from the Passion, Folio 125. Wikipedia Commons. Public Domain. Desaturated from the original.

St Luke. Lichfield Gospels, Wikimedia Commons. Anon. College of Arts and Sciences, University of Kentucky. CC BY-SA 3.0. Desaturated, refined and cropped from original.

Appollinaris Mosaic Ravenna kindly taken and given by Ivor Gough.

Marcian coin. Permission *www.cngcoins.com* and *www.wildwinds.com*.

St Chad's Gospel with permission from Dean and Chapter of Lichfield Cathedral.

Auroch. Ur-painting, Wikimedia Commons Public Domain.

Codex Amiatinus with Christ, Apostles and Archangels. Wikimedia Commons. Desaturated from the original.

St Marks symbol from Lichfield Gospels, Wikimedia Commons. University of Houston. Desaturated, refined and cropped from the original.

Wirksworth Stone. Permission St Mary the Virgin, Wirksworth.

Bede image is Robert at St Dunawd's Church, Banger-on-Dee. By permission of the church committee.

Repton stone. Poliphilo, Wikimedia Commons CC0. Desaturated and cropped.

Charlemagne. Wpclipart, Public Domain.

Saxon warrior. Viking warrior. Credit Shaun Campbell, Scamps.

Winchester Cross painting. Wikimedia Commons Public Domain. Desaturated and cropped from the original.

All the many heads and sculptures, some stained glass and floor roundels were taken at Lichfield Cathedral by the author who is grateful for the kindness shown by all who look after this wonderful Church Cathedral.

Chapter 1

THE NAZARENE CHURCH
c7-4BC – 311

I am the light of the world. Whoever follows me will never walk in darkness but will have the light of life. Spoken by Jesus at the end of the first day in the Court of Women where candles were lit for the eight day Jewish Feast of Tabernacles taken at the time of harvesting the fruit crop.

John 8.12

Jesus probably spoke with a Galilean dialect of Aramaic. The Hebrew priests in Jerusalem also spoke in Aramaic, as did most people in the Middle East. The Romans conversed in Latin and some communities spoke in Greek. There was no contemporary record of the words of Jesus and the events of his life. Instead, 40 to 45 years later there was a recalled account of his life, death, resurrection and glorification. Matthew, Mark, Luke and John between the years 70 to 100 wrote full accounts in Greek. Matthew being a tax collector and so educated would have had no difficulty writing in Greek. Probably Peter could only speak in Aramaic, so it was translated into poor Greek by

Matthew dressed like a Greek.

1

the young Mark. Luke was educated and a much travelled man. He took many eyewitness statements and turned their language into his Greek. Finally, John appears to have read the three Synoptic Gospels and so must have understood Greek. Whether Jesus knew Greek or Hebrew is unknown, but he visited Greek-speaking communities and conversed with educated people who knew Hebrew.

Dating derived by interpretation

Mark wrote his Gospel in Rome between 68 and 70, Matthew in Antioch between 75 and 85, Luke probably wrote between 80 and 90 on his many travels, though his Gospel was much changed later on. The identity of John is uncertain, but he wrote at the turn of the century, 90 – 110, and appears to have belonged to a Jewish-Christian community.

Corroboration for the events

According to scripture over 500 people saw Jesus after the resurrection.

Josephus, an unsympathetic Jew, mentioned Jesus 5 times, c93. He described him as a wise man, as the so-called Christ and as a Jewish High Priest. His earliest surviving manuscript is an 11th century copy and has been altered. Authenticity has been much argued and the consensus view is part of the text is credible.

Tacitus, a Roman antagonist, mentioned a *Christus* executed by Pontius Pilate, c116. He described this new belief as a *deadly superstition*.

A papyrus dated somewhere between 80 and 140, and written possibly by Clement, 4th Bishop of Rome, referred to Paul of Tarsus and asked the reader to remember the words of Jesus.

The Didache is a short, anonymous description of baptism and Eucharist written late in the 1st century. It described Jesus as the servant of God.

The existence of John the Baptist was corroborated. Also Pontius Pilate. An ossuary incised with *son of Caiaphas*, found 1990, might indicate Caiaphas the high priest, but this is tenuous and has little acceptance.

It took 2 centuries before a tract is known that trivialised Jesus, his teaching and mission.

Therefore, there is no known evidence denying the existence of Jesus. There is little disagreement on his baptism and crucifixion. Differences of interpretation come with trying to understand his nature, human and divine, and with aspects of his mission.

The birthplace anomaly

Mark identified Nazareth as the birthplace for Jesus. In contrast, Matthew and Luke described a 100 mile (160km) long southwards journey of expectant Mary on a donkey to Bethlehem in Judea. John 7.41-43 described a crowd doubting Jesus was the Messiah since he came from Galilee. This disagreed with scripture that said the Messiah will be of the House of David and he will come from Bethlehem in Judea – Micah 5.2

There is no evidence of a census at the time of his birth and it would be most unlikely for people of outlying Galilee to have one. Also it is very questionable people had to trek to their ancestral home, especially since many would not know where this was following all the turmoil of exiles. Indeed, there is no archaeological evidence Bethlehem in Judea existed at the time of Jesus's birth. Throughout the New Testament Jesus is always Jesus of Nazareth, never Jesus of Bethlehem.

Around 9 miles (14km) north-west of Nazareth lies a small hamlet called Bethlehem-in-Galilee and the place was mentioned in Joshua 19.15 so it has an ancient ancestry. Some overheated suggestions have been made that this was the real Bethlehem. Mary, it is suggested, went there to avoid criticism of having a baby out of wedlock, but then surely gossip would reoccur on her return? Instead, it could have been Joseph's homeland.

Readjustment of the incorrectly fixed calendar now indicates the birth of Jesus was sometime between the years 7 and 4BC. King Herod of Judea died in March or April 4BC, so the birth of Jesus must be before this date. A bright star at the time of the nativity might have been the conjunction of Jupiter and Saturn in 7BC. A supernova appeared in March or April 5BC. There are other calculations.

The humanity of Jesus

- Around the age of 30, he became a wandering teacher and sage visiting many towns and villages around Galilee. He spoke in towns on the north and east side of the River Jordan where Roman and Greek cultures thrived. He visited Jerusalem in the south several times. This ministry lasted 3 years at most.
- He said much on what gives value and purpose to life. He urged his listeners to strongly obey the will of God and keep his commandments. There is no evidence he baptised. He healed people on 16 occasions, and used miracles to improve lives.
- He visited synagogues, celebrated Jewish festivals, kept to the food laws, approved of offerings to the temple and urged others to obey the conventions

on purity. Despite keeping to the Jewish conventions, he spoke little on the current religious topics. He said nothing on the political reality of Roman oppression.

- Much of his teaching was by parables and figures of speech which invited the listener to interpret and respond. Sometimes they were confounding. His own responses were often sharp and critical. To young, old, sick and those wanting to learn he expressed great kindness. He wanted others to show mercy, meekness and humility.
- He was not a solitary person, but on occasions sought solitude. There are a good number of occasions where he enjoyed eating with the company of others.
- He was not an ascetic, did not own any property and had friends with low status and little wealth. He depended much on the hospitality of friends.
- He surrounded himself with a small group of friends, male and female, who loved him greatly. He tried to explain to them how his earthly life would end.
- He forgave all who harmed him.
- Physical descriptions of people in the New Testament are rare and absent with regard to Jesus. Based on the appearance of males in mosaics of the 1st century there is a good probability Jesus would have had olive hued skin, short, curly hair and a Semitic nose. He was most likely clean-shaven. If dressed like other Graeco-Romans, he would have had a knee length tunic and over this was a woollen, undyed mantle. Flat-soled sandals protected the feet. His appearance, often unflattering, was mentioned in later texts. Later still, drawings gave him features considered good and imposing.

Left, Jesus the Good Shepherd with sheep painted on the ceiling of a cubicle in the Priscilla Catacomb, Rome, and late 3rd century. The analogy of a poor, wandering shepherd looking after all his sheep was a common way to depict the humanity of Jesus. John 10.7 Jesus said, "I am the gate for the sheep." Right, Jesus in a catacomb of Marcellinus and Peter, Rome, 4th century. Note the similarity of pose; it was drawn again in other paintings.

Galilee

The Romans knew the modern state of Israel as a province called Palestine. The northern area, Galilee, was very different from the southern Judea. Galilee was isolated by being mostly surrounded by mountains. To the north were Greek speaking people. Larger townships were to the south and east. The Jewish writer Josephus, c37 – 100, stated there were 200 villages in Galilee, giving an estimated population of 150 to 200 thousand. King Herod never made improvements to Galilee; it was largely ignored.

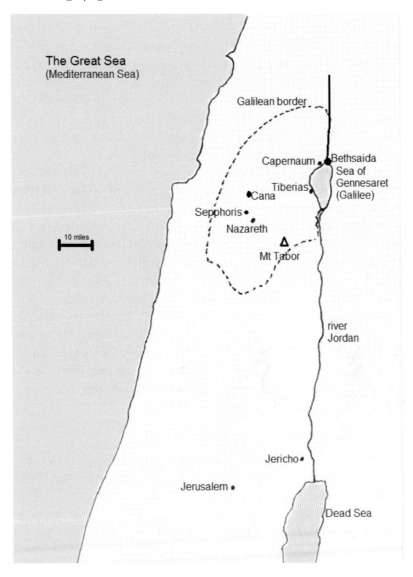

Nazareth was built on a ridge 366m above sea level. It received the cool breezes coming from the Great Sea. This moisture helped the growth of crops. It was 16 miles (26km) from the Sea of Gennesaret and 6 miles (10km) south-east of the large town of Sepphoris. The hamlet of Nazareth probably had no more than 500 residents at the time of Jesus. There has been much discussion on how many inhabitants were Jewish and how many were Gentiles and the common view is it was a Jewish enclave. It was comparatively poor, but Jesus came from a family that appeared to have a relatively comfortable life. The rural peasant subsistence farmers, mostly illiterate, were Jewish and the few educated wealthier individuals who generally supported and benefited from Roman occupation were Gentiles. Acts 4.13 described Peter and John as uneducated and ordinary. They fished on the Sea of Gennesaret supplying salted fish to prosperous markets. The wider community was markedly ranked by status. Responsibility for the village's water supply, roads, housing and markets lay with the inhabitants. The majority of people married within their family or tribe and worked together as a cooperative. Despite this self-reliance and some isolation, the governor of Galilee still severely taxed the population.

The house where Jesus was brought up could have had walls made by piling up local rocks and then mortaring with mud coated with a clay. The roof would be made from beams and tree trunks filled in with a lattice of branches and then covered in palm fronds. In 2015, it was reported a different sort of house partially hewn out of a rock might have been his childhood home. All furnishings were self-made. Boys were obliged at an early age to learn a trade and help with building and maintaining. Girls had to learn how to weave. Mary has been associated with weaving and sowing. It has been conjectured both Joseph and Jesus were conscripted into working in wood, metal and stone in the local town of Sepphoris. Later in the 1st century, boys were taught by rabbis in the rudiments of the law, but this does not appear to be available at the time of Jesus. However, at sometime in his early life he must have received instruction on the Hebrew bible. He would know about the long history of occupation by Babylonians, Persians, Greeks and now Romans.

Recent speculation on Joseph and the first heresy
The Greek Gospels called Joseph a *tektōn* which meant a craftsman. The equivalent in Hebrew is *naggara* also meaning a craftsman. In 1983, these words were speculated to mean a craftsman of words, which made Joseph wise and literate in the Torah. In 2006, it was pointed out the word was used in later texts to be a metaphor for someone knowing the word of God and in

2007 this was interpreted as being a scholar or even a rabbi. By itself, it is not significant, but it has been used to explain Luke 2.49. Unknown to his parents, Jesus, aged 12 and a young man, was in the temple listening and asking questions with teachers, and amazing them with his knowledge. When his anxious parents found him, Jesus could not understand their frustration and said *did you not know that I must be in my Father's house?* Was this the house of his rabbinic father? If so, it feeds in to the idea Jesus was unaware of his divine nature until around the age of 30 when he was baptised and a heavenly voice spoke to him. Becoming divine late in life is known as Adoptionism. It was declared heresy at the end of the 2nd century. Luke is very clear on why this was wrong. He said, *the child grew and became strong, filled with wisdom and the favour of God was upon him.* Jesus at all times was both divine and human.

The royal Herodian family were tyrannical and one of Herod's sons was so bad he was replaced by the Romans with one of their own, namely Pontius Pilate. Later Pontius Pilate was recalled to Rome with complaints of excessive violence. It is with this oppressive and marginalised background that makes it surprising so much is known on the ministry of Jesus. It also helps to explain why much of his ministry was outside of the larger settlements around Galilee. Jesus and his disciples focused on the immediate Jewish community; *the lost sheep of the house of Israel*, Matthew 10.5-6.

Archaeology in Nazareth has revealed remarkably little, apart from granaries, olive presses and wells dating to the 1st century. Elsewhere tombs and burial caves have been uncovered. On the spot where Mary was said to have lived, now occupied by the third church to celebrate this location, excavation has revealed parts of walls, storage pits and cisterns to collect rainwater. A small house nearby was considered to be of the time of Jesus and has revealed two rooms, a courtyard, a water cistern, fragments of 1st century pottery and chalk vessels.

For much of his adult life Jesus lived in Capernaum, Matthew 4.13. He moved to Capernaum after hearing John had been arrested. In 1921, Franciscan archaeologists found a 5th century octagonal church in Capernaum close to the synagogue. New excavation in 1968 uncovered an apse and baptistry. Beneath this church, was found a 1st century house consisting of 6 small rooms and two open courtyards. The date was ascribed by finding coins, oil-lamps and fish hooks characteristic of 1st century homes. Interpretation suggested this was a crude, single-storey house to begin with, which had drystone, black basalt rock walls and a roof of tree branches filled in with straw and earth. It was conjectured to have been Peter's house where Jesus could have stayed.

Excavated house and reconstructed plan of house under the church at Capernaum.

Later the walls were plastered and decorated and a stone roof with supporting arches was added. Graffiti scratched on the walls, mostly Greek with some Syriac and Hebrew, was Christian. Many crosses were also incised. This was explained by the house being turned into a Christian meeting place, an early church, thought to be 2nd century. In the 5th century, an octagonal church was built over this accepted sacred space and then destroyed in the 7th century with blame attached to the Muslim occupiers.

Jesus accused the organisers of the temple in Jerusalem of being thieves. The temple was run by a *high-priestly family*, Acts 4.6. This priesthood, known as the House of Hanin (sometimes Annas), was a cabal that paid for their lucrative position in the year 6 and every year afterwards paid the Romans for this privilege of making money. After the crucifixion, the family business made sure Christ's followers did not trouble them. Nearly all the attacks on Christians in Jerusalem in the following years can be traced back to a grudge from the House of Hanin. This malice resulted in arrests, stoning, beheading and widespread persecution. It also meant the disciples could not preach in the temple and had to secretly find homes to assemble for meetings. Perhaps this was the same *Upper Room* on Mount Zion, where the disciples and many others met Jesus for the Last Supper. To begin with, they thought Jesus would return immediately and bring in a new world. When it became evident this was not going to happen, they *proclaimed the Lord's death until he comes*, 1 Corinthians 11.26. Exactly when they realised the historic Jesus was the true God, Jeremiah 10.10, varied with each follower. For those disciples close to Jesus this realisation came early in the 50 days from resurrection to Pentecost. For others it would take longer. As time passed, their understanding circulated to other tribes and sects. The Apostolic Mission also began to move away from troubled Jerusalem.

Here are some of the ways this Mission was accomplished. Four passages from the Book of Acts show four ways Christianity was proselytised in early times.

Discussion and homily, speaking and preaching, curing and enabling, and finally by providing an exemplar to follow. Explanations were gradually reinforced with written accounts and texts made available.

1. Discussion and homily

One of the early roaming apostles was Paul of Tarsus. Not much is known about him apart from being born a Roman around year 1. Perhaps he studied in Jerusalem, was a wandering preacher for at least 35 years and died aged 68. His home town of Tarsus had a harbour, a system of good education and was a commercial centre, all of which would have helped Paul write in Greek and travel. Paul spent 14 years on three peregrinations around the Mediterranean. The first journey in the year 44 was to Cyprus and then Turkey, the second in the year 49 to Turkey and Greece and the third again, in the year 53, to these countries but taking in many more towns. His last journey

Paul with his letters.

ended with capture in Jerusalem in the year 58 and being shipped to Rome two years later. His relics ended up in a shrine called St Pauls-outside-the-Walls in Rome. In contrast, the relics of Peter were interred under the altar of a large St Peter's Basilica.

His importance comes from his letters sent to various churches which gave a great insight into the thinking of the first missionaries. The letters or Epistles of Paul were written very early between c51 and 62, and so 20 to 25 years after the crucifixion. The first was a letter to Christians in Thessalonica, now the second largest city in Greece, and is the earliest Christian writing to survive. (The dating of the Epistle of James is uncertain).

In the year 57, probably mid-April, on his third journey, Paul stayed for 7 days in the town of Troas on the north-west coast of Turkey. On the Sunday night before he left, he led a meeting in a small room on the third floor of an apartment building. This was the earliest church meeting described in the New Testament. It was marked by a young man called Eutychus falling asleep whilst sitting at an open window and then dropping from the window to his death. Paul miraculously brought him back to life. It was likely, the individual was a poor slave who had worked for 7 days and this was his only time off, so he fell asleep exhausted. This incident typified the way the Christian message was given in the early years of the

Church. Meetings were long conversations with much of the time taken up by questions and answers. Good length sermons delivered by churchmen were unknown for another hundred years. In Acts 20.11, it stated the upper room meeting continued until dawn. From early times, converts, now called *Nazarenes*, took their time to accept the new teaching and much dialogue was needed. It was a process of homily and was never doctrinal. The teaching was in the control of everyone attending. Indeed, in 2 Timothy 13 we learn Paul left behind books and parchments for the church members to continue their own conversations.

2. Speaking and preaching

The first lengthy speech mentioned in the Bible has always been attributed to Peter at Pentecost when he addressed a crowd. Peter standing with the eleven disciples told the very mixed gathering of people of the gift of the Spirit. Individuals asked what they should do to receive this gift and Peter said, *repent and be baptised in the name of Jesus Christ so that your sins may be forgiven*, Acts 2.38.

Left: Peter. Right: The end panel of the Wirksworth Stone at St Mary the Virgin church, Wirksworth, Derbyshire. 1 and 2 are male and female onlookers, Joseph and Anne have been suggested. 3 is Mary holding Jesus 4 on her left arm. Jesus holds a scroll in his right hand and points with his left hand to Peter 5. Peter possibly stands in a boat representing the church. It is teaching the idea of Jesus sending out the word of God by making Peter its custodian and the church its mediator.

This way of conversion was direct and for many would have been immediate. It was the preacher standing on a platform or small hill, addressing many and being unequivocal. Seeing many converts, sometimes called *The Way Sect*, standing close to the speaker, must have been encouraging for onlookers to join in. In Acts 3.13, it stated; *now, when they saw the boldness of Peter and John and realised that they were uneducated and ordinary men, they were amazed and recognised them as companions of Jesus.*

3. Curing and Enabling

One afternoon Peter and John visited a temple and found a man lame from birth at the gate, Acts 3. The man asked for alms. Peter told him he did not have silver or gold, but instead from Jesus of Nazareth the power to cure. Peter made the man stand up and he began to walk into the temple to the astonishment of onlookers. Peter said faith through Jesus had given the man perfect health. He asked them to repent and listen to the prophets. Seeing a miracle would have meant the audience came to know there was something very special being said and there was an urgent need to heed the message. It was summarised in Acts 4. 29, *Lord grant to your servants to speak your word with all boldness, while you stretch out your hand to heal.*

Peter with his key to heaven. From an ivory panel, 5th to 6th century, probably from France.

4. Teaching by example

Acts 2.43 described very many baptised followers taking communion and listening to the prophets in awe of their *wonders and signs*. The text then stated they so embraced the new faith they went on to sell their possessions and goods and distribute the proceeds to all as any had need. Attendance at the temple for more instruction and prayer was necessary and repentance was ongoing. The apostles were now teaching by example and the new *Christians* were making the same sacrifice. The word Christian was mentioned for the first time in Acts 11.26 and applied to worshippers at a church in Antioch.

Yet despite all this herculean effort by a small band of apostles, inevitably by the middle of the 1st century novel versions and distortions of Christianity emerged. One rejected the inclusion of Gentiles and another believed Jesus had always been divine so his earthly presence was an illusion. A third cult thought the opposite with Jesus always being human. Greek scholars tried to reconcile

Christianity with the teachings of Plato. Sceptics took exception to the resurrection and others tried to remove the Jewish foundation. Gospels were written which merely stated the events and teaching of Jesus without any theological structure. Debate was intense when attempting to connect the four Gospels and even more so when trying to bring together the corporeal and spiritual sides of Christ. There never was a perfect time when Christians could claim a unified understanding guided with a single corpus of teaching.

The Jewish – Christian division

It was apparent to very early Christians that there were differences with the Jewish tradition. It has been suggested John's Gospel was written within a Jewish Christian community that was beginning to break from the Jewish synagogue. Nevertheless, for two centuries many Christians continued to worship in synagogues. One problem arose with dates. Jews celebrated their Sabbath on Saturday and Christians met on the Lord's Sunday. Jews fasted until the Passover, but for Christians it extended slightly longer to Easter Sunday. As the Christian liturgical calendar was worked out, so the rift widened.

Another problem came with seeing the Old Jewish God speaking through the prophets and now a New, transcendent Christian God speaking through Jesus. It gave the impression the New was doing away with the Old and nothing could be further from the truth.

A further division resulted when Christians failed to support Jews in a revolt, 132 – 135.

Jews and Judaism did not disappear because of the rise of Christianity. The destruction of Jerusalem by the Romans in the year 70 was a huge setback, but Jewish life and worship continued in a renewed form. Indeed, their leaders laid out a post-biblical Judaism which satisfied the estimated 5 to 6 million Jews in the Roman Empire (compared with a mere 200 thousand Christians). It can be argued the contrasting of the two religions helped both to develop. This was despite certain Roman Emperors who tried to play one religion against the other, though never succeeded. Similarly, certain preachers tried to blame the other religion for misfortunes, but again most Christians knew the Jewish books were the foundation for the Christian belief and it started as a movement of Jews for Jews. Although difficult to date precisely, it took until the 4th century and the building of Christian churches before the two religions claimed a separation of organisation.

Despite these many divisions, Christianity gained converts in Turkey, Greece, Egypt, Syria, India and North Africa. This dissemination of the faith was remarkable and is a history in itself. The leading churches with teaching centres were at Alexandria in Egypt, Antioch, now in Turkey, and Rome in Italy. Tradition has it that Alexandria was visited by the apostle Mark, Antioch was visited by Peter, Barnabas and Paul, and Rome received both Peter and Paul. Through these visitations, the chief centres claimed early linkage with Jerusalem. Later relics removed from Jerusalem help maintain this linkage.

Often the early churches had a difficult beginning. One example was recorded in 112, in Bithynia the Roman province in northern Turkey, when the governor described religious unrest, obstinate Christians who worshipped Christ as their God, and citizens who refused to take oaths to the Emperor. It took three centuries before a kingdom, Armenia in 301, accepted Christianity as the state religion.

Earliest Scripture

The Bible of Judaism or Old Testament began in the 8th century BC and continued until the 1st century AD. The oldest surviving texts are the Dead Sea Scrolls found in the Judean Desert in the 1940s. In the 3rd century BC, the Hebrew texts were translated into a Greek version and some of these papyri scrolls have survived. It was originally thought to be the work of 70 scholars working in Alexandria, Egypt, and therefore called the Septuagint. In fact, it was a translation by a smaller number of scribes working in various libraries.

By the 1st century, the Old Testament was being written in a leaf-book form and not as a scroll.

The *Books* which eventually became the Christian Bible began c51 and finished around 110. The Greek scripture to begin with was in sections and written to satisfy the needs of the local Christian communities. The Gospel of Matthew was the most widely circulated. Other books were also written, but ultimately were not added to the collection. Unknown books have been speculated to account for later known writings. Who wrote the Gospels was recorded by Papias c95 – 120. A kind of anthology of 27 books might have been completed no later than the year 150, though some say it was much earlier. This New Testament (or Covenant) was not constructed solely by fathers of the church wisely picking out scripture that was trustworthy. Instead, it arose by knowing which books were favoured by the Christian communities and deemed to faithfully witness the apostle's story. Time, use and opinion selected the books.

It now meant the events that occurred in an outpost of the Roman Empire were able to be read about in the wider Graeco-Roman world in a comparatively short time. The Christian story became available within 150 years of the resurrection to people who could read Greek. It took another 200 years before Latin readers had a full account. It took another 3 centuries to bring a final collection of texts together that was agreed and accepted, and in the form known today. The New Testament has to be the most peer-reviewed book.

The University of Manchester Library has fragments of papyri of both the Old and New Testaments. They believe a small piece of St John's Gospel (Papyrus 52) dated between 125 and 175 is the oldest surviving fragment of the New Testament. It is displayed at the John Rylands Library.

Bodmer Papyrus 66 is one of the oldest Testament manuscripts. Its dating varies from 2nd century to the 4th. It contains much of St John's Gospel. It is one of 22 papyri discovered in Egypt in 1952. It is held in the Bodmer Library, Geneva, Switzerland.

Justin Martyr c100 – 165

He was born in Nablus, 30 miles (49km) north of Jerusalem in the West Bank, and probably had Roman ancestry. On his way from Judea to Rome, he met a stranger who persuaded him with the truth of a Christian philosophy. He subsequently set up a school in Rome, 138 – 161, and taught this morality within a Greek framework. Particular Romans took exception to his teachings and eventually had him beheaded. One of his works was a petition to the Emperor, c155, explaining why it was unnecessary to persecute Christians. It is a very long plea arguing the importance of Christianity giving opinion on atheism, immorality, loyalty, paganism, hell and much more. He quoted at length from the Old and New Testament and did not hide differences between Roman Gods and his Christian God. He ended the long polemic with a description of how Christians worshipped and it is summarised here to show how little has changed over 2 millennia. This early worship in a temple or church would have been very similar to the Jewish tradition in the synagogue. On arrival, shoes would have been removed.

We worship the Fashioner of the Universe praising him by the word of prayer and thanksgiving for all that he has given us. Singing can be accompanied by instruments, especially for the special services. We offer up prayers and hymns to God for creation. If you believe, then you are instructed to pray and beseech God with fasting for the remission of past sins. You are reborn by being washed in the water in the name of God the Father and Master of all, and of our Saviour Jesus Christ and of the Holy Spirit. This washing was called illumination, since those who learn these things were illumined within. We offer prayers to all those who have been illuminated and all others everywhere. On finishing prayers, we greet each other with a kiss.

Then bread and a cup of water and mixed wine were brought to the president of the brethren and he sent up praise and glory to the Father through the name of the Son and of the Holy Spirit. An explanation for transformation of the elements was given and the whole congregation assented by saying Amen. Deacons gave to those present the bread and water with wine. Afterwards we constantly remind each other of these things.

On Sunday, we meet in one place and read the memoirs of the apostles and the writings of the prophets. This was followed by the Eucharist. Finally, we stand together and offer prayers. Offerings are made by those who prosper to help others, such as orphans, widows, sick individuals, enslaved people and visitors travelling by.

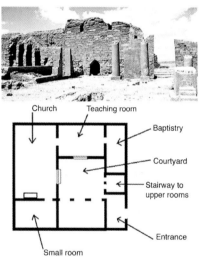

An old photograph from Dura Europos, an ancient city in Syria abandoned in 256. It contained numerous temples and this could have been a very early Christian House church. It was targeted in the Syrian war. The church had been converted from a courtyard and had a room without an altar. Wall paintings included Christ as the Good Shepherd and Three Marys investigating Christ's tomb.

Apostolic Tradition

Fragments of a Greek manuscript were found in the 19th century detailing early church orders and together with other versions in different languages is known as the Apostolic Tradition. It has been dated to 235, but parts could have been added later. There is a description of the procedure for baptism, though whether it was followed cannot be discerned. The candidate was given much instruction heavy in moral teaching. They then bathed, fasted and were presented to the bishop, who exorcised any sin. During the night, more instruction was given accompanied by following certain readings. At daybreak they took off their clothes, were oil anointed followed by full immersion and oil anointed again. Finally, Eucharist was taken. There was no question of this being repeated at another time, once baptised the individual would belong to a church and expect to be faithful at all times.

The Other World – 1st century

Jews accepted the Greek idea of a body and soul, and after death, the soul was returned to God. In your life, you needed to fulfil God's commandments in order for the soul to return.

> *The dust will return to the ground as it was, and the spirit (breath) will return to God who gave it.*
>
> Ecclesiastes 12.7

It has been claimed the early texts and the Torah had little to say on life after death. The Torah does, however, indicate the righteous will be reunited after death with their loved ones, while the wicked will be excluded from this reunion. After death, you are firstly judged by God and then moved to a place called Sheol. It is a kind of temporary netherworld. If you have repented and all sins are purged, then your soul goes to a heavenly place that has been called a *Garden of Eden*. Those still with sin enter a dark place called Gehinnom and has even been ascribed to a valley just south of Jerusalem where unspeakable sacrifice occurred. This is not the same as hell because most can leave this place to eventually reach heaven. Not all Jews at this time accepted the idea of the resurrection of the dead.

> *Many of those who sleep in the dust of the earth shall awake, some to everlasting life and some to shame and everlasting contempt.*
>
> Daniel 12.2

The full detail of funereal customs of Jews in early Christian times is not understood. Psalms were said at the time of burial and in later centuries, a Eucharist was given. Up to the end of the first century, the body was buried, but after a time it was disinterred, cleaned and bones kept in an ossuary. The baptised body was seen as the temple of the holy spirit, 1 Corinthians 6.19. This practice continued in many regions including in Jerusalem, but it was not universal.

Jesus emphasised the need to follow the commandments in life in order to reach heaven, but added little on the nature of heaven. He described a place prepared for you where there is joy, justice, treasures and rewards that will be forever. In this figurative *house*, there are many rooms and the entrance is narrow; it is a gate. Your approach must be like a child. The first to enter will be last and the last will be first. All people will be eligible for the feast.

He said the Kingdom of God is close, in the midst of us, at hand and yet much has to happen before it is revealed. Matthew 13 contains many parables showing how this Kingdom is attained. He never spoke of disembodied souls. Jesus's resurrected body was seen and touched before the 40th day of Easter when he ascended into heaven. Marking his ascension with special worship was mentioned in an early 4th century text.

In the Christian narrative, the passage from death to heaven was immediate. According to Luke 23.43 Jesus on the cross, told one criminal, also being crucified, *today, you will be with me in Paradise.* It was not mentioned in Matthew and Mark's Gospels, but that does not detract much from the message. Furthermore, God raised Jesus in less than 3 days, according to all three Gospels. This is in stark contrast to the belief of those who were not Christian. They held to a belief of the dead going on a protracted journey in which they would be tested. Therefore, they were encouraged to bury their dead with goods to accompany them on their exacting journey and to show the sort of person they were. Many held to the idea of an intermediate destination, even a holding location, before there was passage to Paradise and this is still taught by some churches. These great differences need to be kept in mind in the following chapters, especially when considering burial practice and 'world to come' beliefs. There was much variation in the thinking in the early church and there is still variation today.

Jesus said to Martha;

I am the resurrection and the life. Those who believe in me, even though they die, will live, and everyone who lives and believes in me, will never die.

John 11.25-26

It is a mystery. It invites you to understand it in the best way you can. To do this it is vital to know the character and background of Jesus.

Chapter 2

THE ROMAN CHURCH 312 – 407

About the time of the midday sun, when the day was just turning, (Constantine)
saw with his own eyes, up in the sky and resting over the sun, a cross-shaped trophy
formed from light, and a text attached to it which said, 'In this sign you will conquer'.
Eusebius, *Life of Constantine the Great*. 4th Century

At sometime in the years 26 to 33, (Pontius Pilate was governor of Judea 26 – 36) Jesus of Nazareth was murdered by the Romans. The Gospel writers laid much of the blame on a scheming Jewish temple aristocracy demanding compliance, a callous Pontius Pilate looking for a scapegoat, and a rigged crowd bellowing for a victim and sacrifice, but this was not the whole story. The Romans believed Jesus was a potential Jewish leader and the charge against him was political and had little to do with Temple machinations and his teachings. The Romans nailed a sign stating *Jesus of Nazareth King of the Jews* in Latin, Hebrew and Greek, John 19.19-20, to the cross and that was a warning for anyone thinking they could question Roman supremacy. The Romans only cared about keeping a grip.

Scheming Emperor Nero Claudius Caesar killed Christians in the year 64, after blaming them for a great fire that destroyed much of Rome. Amongst his martyrs were Peter and Paul. In the years 66 – 70, there were riots and much of Jerusalem, including the temple, was burned and destroyed by the Romans and after another revolt, 132 – 135, it was finished. Jerusalem was replaced by a new Roman city called *Aelia Capitolina*. Judea stopped being a Roman province. Many Jewish Christians fled to Pella, Jordan, 17 miles (27km) south of the Sea of Galilee. Thereafter for almost 200 years, persecution was local and spasmodic. Despite this terror and subjugation, by the end of the 2nd century, there were significant numbers of Christian communities. It had even penetrated into the Imperial household. The problem was Christians stood out in many small ways which still encouraged oppression. Anyone avoiding pledging allegiance to the Emperor was seriously offending the Romans. Secretiveness and not taking part in communal practices like bathing raised attention. Writing on sheets of parchment (codex) and not on a scroll looked peculiar. The Eucharist with bread and wine, body and blood, was easily misinterpreted. Avoiding conscription could be lethal. Over a long period of time resentment turned to hatred. Then Decius killed Christians over a period of a year and a half, around the year 250, with many victims becoming saints. The Roman's bloodiest persecution of Christians was under Diocletian in the years 303 to 305. He wanted to turn the clock back to the glory days of Rome and the worship of many Gods. One Christian victim was George the Greek, later becoming Saint George of England. Diocletian's *Great Persecution* varied across the Roman Empire and did not appear to impact much on Britain, apart from a few uncertain exceptions. In 304, Julius and Aeron were martyred at possibly Caerleon, South Wales and Amphibalus at Verulamium, St Albans. Alban was beheaded according to an account written a long time afterwards and much doubted. Augulius, Bishop of London, was another possible martyr. A story of 1000 Christian martyrs being slaughtered by Diocletian Romans at Lichfield was folklore. Considering this bloody history, it was astonishing Emperors then had a very sudden and complete turnaround in their relationship with Christians. In 311, Emperor Galerius issued a proclamation recognising Christianity as a legitimate form of worship and asked Christians to pray to their God for the safety of his Roman Empire.

What followed was remarkable; a Roman Emperor became a Christian. Varying accounts tell us how this turnabout happened. On October 27 in the year 312, the Roman Emperor Constantine had a vision before he was about to fight, or it might have been when he was on a long march. The vision from the Christian God was interpreted as giving him protection from his enemies. He then, according to one

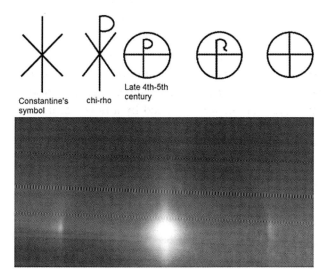

Constantine's symbol   chi-rho   Late 4th-5th century

From the left, Constantine's shield sign, a chi-rho in a way normally seen, a chi-rho surrounded by a halo of the sun. Next is a chi-rho seen in mosaics from the 4th century. The last Greek cross sign was often incised on stonework. Below shows a parhelion caused by refraction of sunlight through ice crystals high in the sky. It is a cross within a circle of light.

account, carried a standard with Christ's monogram, a chi-rho, or was it an X with a vertical line through it? A chi (X) and rho (p) are the first two letters of the Greek spelling of Christ, and the two letters are usually joined together.

God was believed to help Constantine defeat his rival at the battle of Milvian Bridge over the Tiber, north of Rome, but in one account, there was no mention of using an army displaying a Christian symbol. A witness claimed at sometime in Constantine's quest to be Emperor in 310 he saw a cross of light above the sun (parhelion?) and took this to be divine protection. It was a common experience for war leaders to receive supernatural signs before battles. These events led him, and his fellow Emperor Licinius I, 308 – 324, a year later to grant total religious freedom, *Peace of the Church*, within their Empire.

Cross at St Helens church, Kelloe, Durham with 3 scenes portraying Helena finding the True Crosses. Constantine also is shown. It is late 12th century when this story was much liked. Indeed, some wanted to believe Helena was born in England.

Monument to Constantine I outside York Minster. He was made Emperor by his supporters on the death of his father in July 306. York can claim to be where his elevation started and subsequently led to the official acceptance of Christianity.

Constantine might have encouraged his mother, Helena of Constantinople, c250 – 330, to be a Christian. She journeyed in 327 on a pilgrimage to Calvary, Palestine, and saw, or learned about, some wood from the original cross.

From the 340s, a fragment of the cross was kept in a silver gilt casket in the basilica church at Calvary. It was opened on each Good Friday and the fragment removed for pilgrims to kiss. This continued until 614 when the Persians captured Jerusalem and took away the cross relics as trophies. The Romans supposedly retrieved the cross fragments in 630, but this claim came without any convincing corroboration.

What caused the *Constantian Shift*?

Constantine's transformation was not as sudden as is often made out. Coins minted in his name still showed Roman Gods for 8 more years after his battle victory. The victory arch erected in 315 in Rome has no Christian depiction. Around two thirds of his government in Byzantium, later Constantinople and Istanbul, Turkey, were non-Christian. In 325, he organised the Council of Nicea at Iznik, Turkey, when the relationship between God and Christ was established with the words that Jesus was the true Son of God brought into being from the substance of the Father. (Amendments were made later). Yet Constantine probably held the heretical view of God and Jesus were not of one substance. Shortly before his death, he was baptised by a follower of this heresy. He also allowed pagan temples to be built, though started to remove them and their treasures near the end of his reign. Perhaps the real reason for his shift was Constantine was following the popular appeal of the people of Byzantium, including his mother, who were Christian. He was also giving freedom to the church and bishops and in return expected total loyalty. God apparently was also protecting him in battle and he made his soldiers pray before each occasion of conflict. It is easy to see the conflict for Constantine of being an almighty Emperor and knowing about an almighty God. It did not stop him shrewdly taking opportunities in his self-interest.

Vague and doubtful references to how early Christianity arrived in Roman Britain

Hippolytus, c170 – c235, stated Aristobulus was Bishop of Britain. Tradition claims he was the brother of the disciple Barnabas and accompanied Paul on his journeys. He possibly died, perhaps martyred, in Britain in the 1st century. Glastonbury has been claimed to be his church.

In c198, a Carthaginian in Tunisia called Tertullian, c155 – 240, became an early Christian and ten years later wrote about the many places that were subjected to Christ. It included *the haunts of the Britons, inaccessible to the Romans*. It is not easy to know precisely what he meant, but has always been taken as Christians being present where the Romans had not settled. Since he knew very little about faraway Britain, it might simply be a statement of Christianity reaching all corners of the world.

In 239 Origen, c185 – 254, a Christian from Alexandria, Egypt, claimed the Christian light now reached even the Isles of the Sea and this has been interpreted to mean the Atlantic Isles. It could also be a straight reference to Isaiah 24.15.

Eusebius, 263 – 339, Bishop of Caesarea, 260 – 339, claimed in 314 some apostles passed over the ocean to the British Isles. A Bishop of Tyre writing c300 claimed this was Simon. Later writers refer to the possibility of Paul being this apostle.

A 9th century book referred to the visit of Joseph of Arimathea linked with Aristobulus. Abbot Chinnock, 1375 – 1420, at Glastonbury Abbey promoted the myth. William Blake added to the fable. A hawthorn cultivar planted on the site helped to mark the legend.

King Lucius of Britain invited Bishops Fuganus and Duvianus to Christianise Britain in the 2nd century. It was fiction, but repeated by Bede and quoted much in medieval England.

The unglamorous truth for the first arrival of a Christian on the shores of the Atlantic Isles was most likely an unknown 3rd century merchant or Roman soldier, who had previously visited an eastern Mediterranean country.

The legacies of Constantine
- The fish and anchor signs were frequently used to sign for a Christian, but from Constantine onwards the chi-rho symbol was commonly used.
- Constantine paid for the production of 50 bibles to be written in Greek in the scriptorium at Caesarea. The two oldest known Greek bibles, the *Codex Vaticanus* and *Codex Sinaiticus*, were somehow connected with this project.
- Downgrading the Empire's religion at Rome and firmly placing it in Jerusalem started pilgrimage to the Holy Land. A thriving Christian presence in Jerusalem returned. This was much enhanced when Helena's visit to Jerusalem was associated with some wood said to be from the true cross. It also meant the cross symbol now became an icon to possess.
- Constantine raised the status of bishops and gave them various privileges. Over the next decades, they became identified with large metropolises and by the 6th century, area bishops became metropolitan bishops. Bishops

began to sit on a central seat and reside in a way seen in the administrative centres of the Roman Empire. The Latin for seat was *sedes* and from this came *see*, meaning the area covered by the bishop. Another Latin word for a seat is *cathedra* and from this came *cathedral*. Only Cathedrals could have bishop's chairs, not Minsters, Monasteries or Abbeys.

• Rome had subdivided the Empire's administrative regions into provinces. Later, under Diocletian, they were made into larger areas he called *dioceses*. The church copied this civil administration and often the clergy worked alongside the governors. In time, the area under pastoral care in the church came to be also called a diocese.

• The Bishop of Jerusalem in 325 was given instructions to build a church on the site of Christ's crucifixion. It was probable the location had always been known to a few Christian residents, but it was now under a temple to Venus deliberately built by Emperor Hadrian in the 2nd century to hide the tomb. This temple was reduced, rock removed from the front of the tomb and a double church built over Calvary and the burial place. It became the prime site for pilgrimage. Strangely, other sites in Jerusalem associated with Jesus were largely ignored. Whether or not the exact burial tomb for Jesus was found has since occupied many studies. There are over a thousand rock-cut tombs around Jerusalem, many with scratched crosses and Christian paintings, but the one at the Church of the Holy Sepulchre fits the location from the biblical description. Around 5 rock-cut tombs exist below this church. No alternative site is now seriously suggested.

Constantine built many churches and the ground plan was often similar and based on the basilica building used for meetings, especially the basilica where law was established. That is, they were rectangular with a semi-circular apse. Lawmakers and priests occupied the head shaped apse. Christians moved from the outside world along the nave to the altar. Nave means ship and symbolised this Christian journey. Laity would have to stop at a barrier separating the nave from the chancel. Chancel means lattice and this was sometimes used as a decorated barrier. Priests could not be interrupted once worship had begun. It also protected the Blessed Sacrament from the Eucharist so that the body of Christ is always looked after in the church. Similarly with relics kept in the chancel.

The churches were aligned west-east, not because they were looking to Jerusalem, but because of several references in the Bible. For example Genesis 3.24 and the position of the Tree of Life in the Garden of Eden. This preferred axis almost certainly goes further back in time and probably relates to the sun's rising and waning orientation. The ground plan changed at some point with

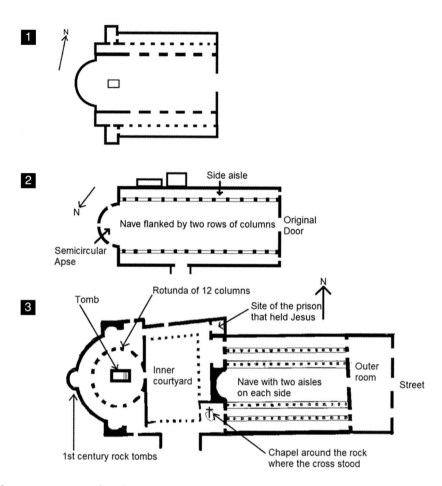

Three Constantine churches.
1. St John Lateran archbasilica built 324 for bishops of Rome. It is 2.5 miles (4km) to the south-east of the Vatican City. It was similar in shape to St Peter's Basilica.

2. Basilica of Santa Sabina, Rome, built in 432. It was the archetypal shape for many churches and is the oldest church still with this basic plan. The wooden door displays carved scenes including an early crucifixion scene.

3. Church of the Holy Sepulchre built around Calvary and Christ's tomb, finished in 335. The plan is derived from a 4th century description and some archaeology. The church has been destroyed several times and only a small part of the early church remains. In 2016, the tomb was opened revealing a limestone burial bed clad in grey marble for protection and laid in the 4th century.

the apse now being at the east end of the rectangular building. The entrance was now in the west end and the visitor would be greeted with a long view towards an altar and cross with a seat close by. You were in God's house and needed to journey to the cross towards the domed end where the sun rose and there was light. More so at dawn on Easter Day.

By the end of the 4th century, the liturgy expressed by the Bishop was controlled. Exact wording was important. Being seated showed he was an authority in every way as an Emperor sat on a throne. Therefore, distinctive vestments started to appear with copes, chasubles, mitres (not like those worn today shaped like a flame of fire, an allusion to Pentecost, Acts 2.3), maniples, bells, censers and staffs. All designed by imitating and adding to the ceremony shown by Emperors.

Baptism was often outside of the church and although fonts began to appear it took a long time for them be used widely. Burial was managed and occurred outside of the city walls or deep underground in catacombs. Death was not part of the church, only resurrection.

Those who had not been baptised were kept in a separate room of the church close to the west door.

There was an obvious graduation of authority from the low west door, where the sun went down, to the high east end altar, where the early light entered. From all this, the shape of large churches was worked out over 1600 years ago. They were modelled on Roman ideas of grandeur, ceremony, administration and authority. It is remarkable many churches have largely kept this structure and tradition, despite adversity and a natural inclination to prefer simplicity and occasional change.

Coin of Ezana, ruler of a kingdom, c320 – c360, stretching from the Middle East to North Africa. He was the first king in the world known to be a Christian having been converted by a Syrian head of the church in Ethiopia. This is the earliest coin to show a cross.

Roman Britain

At the 314 Council of Arles called by Constantine to settle disputes in his Imperial Church, there were at least 33 bishops and 16 other clergy. Three bishops were from Britain and included, Restitutus Bishop of London, Eborius Bishop of York, Adelphius probably Bishop of Lincoln (Caerleon or Colchester have been suggested), and alongside were Sacerdos a priest and Arminius a deacon, possibly representing Cirencester. Some might have attended the abortive Council the year before and held in Rome. Similarly, they could have been present at the important Council of Nicea in 325 which for a time settled an argument on the nature of Christ. It is unclear whether British bishops attended the Council in Bulgaria, c343. They were definitely present at the Council in 359 in Italy, because we know all the British bishops, except three, declined expenses. After these Councils, Athanasius c363 wrote *with this faith all the churches throughout the world are in agreement.* In a long list, he included Britain.

In each of the 1st, 2nd and 3rd centuries over 60 bishop's names are known. In the 4th century, this increased to 165. The Latin Roman Church included the Atlantic Isles, France, Spain, Italy and North Africa and the Greek Roman Church had Greece, Balkans, Syria, Egypt, and kingdoms along the River Nile. It is thought 800 priests from the Western Church and 1000 from the Eastern Church were invited to the Council of Nicea in 325.

Possible churches in Roman Britain

When the elite of the Roman Field Army left Britain, starting in 407, to help fight the Vandals in France, it was said there was a church named St Pancras at Canterbury, Kent.

There is a basilica shaped building at Colchester, Essex, now accepted to have been a church. It was surrounded by a cemetery with 371 graves, located in a west-east direction, with the head to the west. It had a screen and aisles. It was in use between 320 and 340 and an apse was added c380.

A hall like building with aisle and apse was uncovered in 2013 at Maryport, which is at the west end of Hadrian's Wall. This site has yielded many Roman altars and it is not too much of a surprise to suggest a Christian church was later built on the site.

Roman centres where it is now thought there was a Christian presence.

At Icklingham, Suffolk, a possible church has been identified. It was a rectangular, 7m x 4m, building with a possible apsidal end, next to a cemetery and not far from a pit containing parts of a lead tank having Christian imagery.

At Richborough Roman Fort, Kent, a brick font has been uncovered and is thought to have stood close to a timber church.

A suggested church at Silchester, Hampshire, has a nave, vestibule and aisles and yet is in reverse orientation with the altar at the west end. It has some doubt. There has been a claim at Wroxeter, Shropshire, of a very large church, 30m x 13m, with an apsidal east end built above its baths in the 5th century. This has not had wide acceptance and it is more logical for an early church to have been built a short distance down Watling Street and closer to the ford across the River Severn.

At Verulamium, St Albans, Hertfordshire, two sites for possible churches have been fixed. Several small buildings with an apse and interpreted to be early churches have been found along Hadrian's Wall at Vinolanda and Housesteads; though some are in a north to south orientation and need more confirmation. However, stones with Christian marks have been found nearby. At Birdoswald, also close to Hadrian's Wall a remodelling of a centurion's quarter with a rounded west end added has been conjectured to be possibly a church.

At South Shields, Durham, a table altar was found that suggested a church was close by.

It is logical there were early churches at Lincoln, London and York knowing they had early bishops.

A very large building has been uncovered in Walbrook, London and has a similar layout as other supposed churches. It lies west-east, has an apse and aisles. However, it was built in the 3rd century and has been identified as a mithraeum with worship to the Roman God Mithras. There is evidence of later damage and it might have suffered pagan intolerance. The similarities show the difficulty of confidently labelling an uncovered building as an early church.

All Roman churches have been suggested to be early 4th or 5th century and so resulted from Constantine's Shift. Within their localities have been found certain artefacts with Christian symbols. Therefore, in recent years, the evidence is accumulating for the existence of Roman churches on Roman sites, but it is still an open question without full proof. There is no idea of what their altar was like. Maybe there were church/temples with Romans worshipping Christian and Roman Gods together. Surprisingly no objects used in the Eucharist have been found. Also, documentary evidence is virtually absent. Location of the church in the forts varies greatly. Much more needs to be established.

Left: Hadrian's Wall at Housesteads. An apsidal building described as a possible church could be post-Roman. Right: Stone found at Vinolanda with incised Christian crosses. It could be a grave marker, or even a portable altar.

Two Roman churches

1. Colchester 4th century.

It is alongside a cemetery suggesting a Christian church. Normally, Romans would have buried well away from a building since they held corpses polluted a site.

It had a rectangular basilica shape with a small apse, radius of 5 metres, and is west to east.

Two burials were found near the altar, another Christian feature.

Coffins depicted Christian motifs, such as scallop shells. A few Christian symbols were found on objects in the locality.

N ←

Apse

Chancel

Post holes for timber posts and arches

75 metres

Nave

Doorway

25 metres

2. Silchester Church.

A building 13 metres x 9 metres uncovered at Silchester in 1892 was re-excavated in 1961. Strangely, it is orientated with the altar in the west. The nave had a red tessellated floor and the apse had a square mosaic of black and white pieces showing an equal armed cross. There appeared to be two very separate chambers at the end of the aisles. 3.5 metres out- 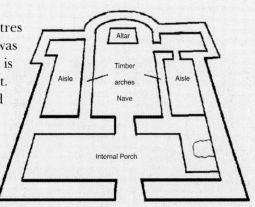 side of the porch was a base which could have been a baptistry. No Christian artefacts were found. A pottery sherd and mosaics have been dated to the late 2nd century and this is a problem because it predates Constantine. The unusual layout is similar to early churches in North Africa.

Arianism – the second heresy

Arius, a priest in Alexandria, Egypt, c256 – 336, taught that Christ was subordinate to God. Thus, he was not part of the Creation and there was no Trinity. God created Jesus. In John 14.28, Jesus stated *the Father is greater than I*, and this was taken literally to reach the conclusion of a separate God and Christ.

To settle this deep dispute a Council of Nicaea was held in June 325. Nicaea, now Iznik, which is 130km south of Constantinople, now Istanbul. Between 250 and 318 bishops attended bringing many other priests. It was the first Council for all the church. Constantine chaired the discussion, said it was trivial and hurried the outcome. The result was a rebuttal of Arianism, but it was not the end of the argument. 17 bishops continued to support the Arian interpretation and the doctrinal argument was not finished until the 7th century. Some large towns even had one bishop who was orthodox and a second one who was Arian.

Gregory of Nazianzus, 329 – 390, who became Archbishop of Constantinople, argued against Arianism. Also known as Gregory the Theologian; he wrote much that is now accepted Christian theology. As time passed, ordinary Christians eventually resolved the issue and determined the truth causing Arianism to fade. A variant is still believed in certain churches today.

To help counter this heresy, as well as lay down a core of belief, a Creed was established in 325, amended in 362 and fixed in 381 at the Council at Constantinople. This Nicene Creed is still repeated in services as the essence of Christian belief. The oldest surviving copy of this Creed is a partially damaged papyrus from the 6th century held in the John Rylands Library of Manchester University.

There is also an Apostles' Creed, which is a simpler statement. Some believe it was agreed by the Apostles, but its earliest date is 390. Indeed, the Creed used today might not have been completed until as late as the 7th century. For exact and full detail of core beliefs tag *Creeds and authorized affirmations of faith* into a server.

The death of Constantine resulted in the Roman Empire being split between his two sons. Constans ruled in the Latin West and accepted the orthodox belief. Constantius II ruled in the Greek East from Constantinople and believed the Arian notion of Christ being the Son of God, separate and not divine. Theology was dividing the bishops and separating brothers. In 350, Constans was killed in a coup and replaced by Magnentius and three years later, he was killed by Constantius II. The *Arian heresy* now took hold across the Empire and beyond.

Constantius II sent Paul to be his representative in Britain and give an Arian creed. He proved to be vicious. From Diocletian times, Britain had been divided into 4 provinces under the direction of a *Vicar*. The current Vicar, Martinus, tried to kill Paul, but failed and then killed himself. When Constantius II died in 361, he was succeeded by Julian II who was pagan. From then on Roman rule in Britain was ever changing. Occasionally the Picts and Scots (Irish) raided and damaged border communities with a serious incursion in 367. Saxons also attacked the south-east coast. Theodosius I, 379 – 395, quelled all the uprisings on the continent as well as in Britain and brought back orthodox Christianity, but the church was in as much turmoil as the Imperial house. It deteriorated further when in 406, the Vandals devastated Gaul and the path between Rome and Britain became very difficult. To retrieve Gaul, the Romans withdrew from Britain most of its army and administrators in 407. One writer described a major Saxon invasion in 408, which was repulsed in 409, but little is known about this event. Bede gave a lurid account of Irish and Picts taking over the north; *the enemy with hooked weapons never ceased from their ravages.*

Conventionally the year 410 was the time Britain was now freed of the Empire. Rome had created a unified mainland Britain, though they had never invaded Ireland, and now the Empire gradually fragmented. In comparison with the rest of Europe, Britain came out best in this crisis of Roman retrenchment. Unlike most parts of Europe, Britain was not invaded during this time and it still possessed and kept its own indigenous administration. Some Britons might even have been thankful for the end of a military dictatorship instituted from a distant land. Christians would know the Book of Revelation 17.1, in which Babylon is *the great mother of whores and of earth's abominations* and see Babylon as code for Rome.

They saw it as another fulfilment of scripture. There were others, expecting at a future time Rome would rise up and return, as had happened several times in the past. With all this uncertainty it is understandable why some think the full breakaway from Rome was over a protracted period, say 60 or 70 years.

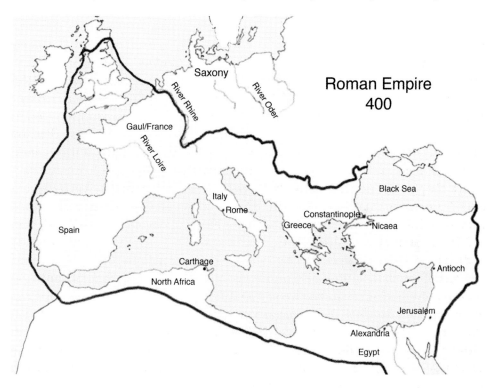

The Germanic Goths – the lesser-known story

Constantine's conversion is frequently cited as a pivotal moment. It was well recorded and ultimately led to a Roman Church in West Europe. There is a lesser understood story of similar conversion, at a similar time, within the Germanic countries. Around the year 300, there were Christian settlements along the Danube River flowing into the Black Sea. Coins with a Christian cross have been found in the Crimea region on the north side of the Black Sea. When Goths raided these settlements, they took away Christian captives and it is thought they introduced the Arian religion to the Germanic Goth kingdoms of East Europe. It must have spread westwards along the Danube valley.

In The Netherlands in the 2nd century, the Romans built a line of 25 forts extending 60 miles (100km) from the North Sea, through the Low Countries to where Bonn is now located. This northern frontier mostly followed the River Rhine. Known as The Limes, it also became a trading border with people, goods and ideas freely crossing it. There is increasing evidence that Christianity also crossed over in Constantine's reign to the Germanic tribes north of the border. If true, it changes the idea of tribes immediately north of the Roman Empire being non-Christian and barbaric. However, the people to the north, later known as Franks, together with the Lombards, were still labelled pagan. The many different tribes known as Saxons and occupying the northern part of modern Germany, from the Rhine to the Oder, were still worshipping *Herthum* or Mother Earth.

Ulfila, c311 – 383, was born in Cappodocia, central Turkey, and was made a bishop at Constantinople in 341. He was probably the first bishop to be sent outside of the Roman Empire and began the conversion of the Goths in what is now Ukraine, Bulgaria and Romania. After introducing a Gothic alphabet based on Greek, he used it to translate the Bible. This bible was one of the earliest Germanic texts and it was widely disseminated.

In the 6th century, a wonderful *Silver Bible* or Codex Argenteus containing Ulfila's translation was made. Gold and silver ink on high quality purple stained vellum bound ornately testifies to the highest level of devotion. It can be seen in Uppsala, Sweden.

Early missionary work led to many Germanic people on the northern borders of the Eastern Roman Empire becoming Christian with an Arian slant. It is thought this conversion between 370 and 390 was relatively rapid. It is often assumed these *barbarians* were pagans or followed a heretical Christianity, but they were no different from many Roman Emperors and citizens in the 4th century. They also significantly influenced the tribes of Poland (Gepids, Vandals and Burgundians) who went on to conquer other lands. In the 4th and 5th centuries, the Goths occupied territories in Northern Italy, Spain and Southern France. When an Arian Christian Goth took over Rome in 476, it was a minor coup, but it is still presented as marking the end of the Western Roman Empire. In reality, much of the Roman form of governance continued. The story of Christianity with the Goths and the Romans follow similar trajectories and seeing one Empire as wholly Christian and the other as barbaric Pagan is a Victorian generalisation.

Second translation of the Bible

The switch to Latin in Rome might have been made by Pope Victor, 189 – 199, but this was exceptional. The first major writer in Latin was a Berber from Roman Carthage called Tertullian, c155 – 240. His school in the Roman province of North Africa predated Rome whose writers stayed with Greek. Tertullian has been called the *Father of Latin Christianity and the founder of Western Theology*. He was the first to use the word *trinity* (trinitas) and for him God was the founding member of a threesome in one.

Jerome, c347 – 420, was a gifted Italian teacher and historian. The pope invited him to stay in Rome between 382 and 385 to revise the Old Latin version of the Gospels. Later he was in Antioch and Bethlehem and between 390 and 405, he translated the Hebrew Old Testament into Latin. A Psalter was finished in 392. Jerome's Latin Bible was called the Vulgate and was widely used. It meant many Latin speakers could now access the Bible.

Jerome showing his new Bible.

It probably took another 50 years before the Vulgate was used widely in Britain. Its use meant the liturgy was now almost entirely expressed in Latin irrespective of the local language. Even in Ireland, where the Romans did not invade, their worship was conducted in Latin with Jerome's Bible. Around 392 an Irish monk wrote in the margin of a Jerome manuscript, it is in the nature of every man to do good and to avoid doing evil.

House churches

Some early Christians met secretly in houses and it is even possible there were Romans meeting in secret before Constantine. One writer has claimed that by 300 the Christian population had risen to 10% of the Empire. This would never show in the documentary or archaeological record. After Constantine, there were rooms set aside in villas for worship and a few are known.

At Lullingstone villa, Kent, a suite of 4th century rooms, probably with exterior access appeared to be a house church. One wall had a frieze of 6 well-

Roman Britain has arbitrarily been divided into 3 zones of settlement. The numbers refer to the quantity of villas in each zone. The ovals show where the greatest intensity of occupation and therefore farming occurred. There was a clear dividing line running down the Pennine and Peak District chain of hills, along the River Severn and on the Dorset-Devon border.

dressed, red haired figures who were holding out their hands in an ancient orant posture for praying. The orant's costume had large crosses sewn on the front and this suggested they were priests, possibly bishops. If the opposite wall originally had another 6 figures, they would have been the disciples.

There was also a painting with a chi-rho sign and with alpha and omega letters, an allusion to being the first and the last, a description used by Christ.

Drawing of a possible Christ in Roman attire in a mosaic roundel dated c350. Unfortunately, only the roundel is on display at the British Museum, the rest is now in bits.

In a villa at Hinton St Mary, Dorset, a mosaic 8m long and 5m wide was found in 1963. It had a roundel showing a head and a chi-rho sign behind. The figure had two pomegranates by the head. It has been suggested the figure was Christ and therefore was his earliest depiction in Britain.

Pomegranates were associated with several Greek and Roman Gods who if they ate the seeds might or might not return from the dead. It therefore could be a symbol of resurrection. The floor roundel was in a small room with no underfloor heating, with the figure looking eastwards and having room for a small altar. Thus, it has features expected for a villa-church. The roundel was surrounded by Roman mythical creatures and the mosaic was therefore a mix of myth and faith which is, perhaps, to be expected in the 4th century. Not everyone agrees it shows Christ and placing it on the floor to walk on seems suspect. Also, there is a similarity to this motif on coins belonging to the Christian Emperor Magnentius, ruling 350 – 353, and therefore the figure could be him, or indeed another Emperor.

Magnentius coin minted in Lyon. The chi-rho symbol has a similarity with the Hinton St Mary roundel. Similarly, Magnentius had a large chin, thick neck, long nose, and tightly waved hair like the figure in the roundel. Here he appears to be wearing a pleated cuirass.

At Frampton, also in Dorset, a mosaic was found in 1794, but later destroyed in 1850. However, lithographs show the mosaic had both pagan and early Christian symbols. Those who have tried to interpret its meaning have found many ambiguities. It could have been a 4th century idea of sharing Christian and pagan motifs in a time of great uncertainty.

Pewter, found at Lakenheath, Suffolk, was very lightly marked with a chi-rho and might have been used in a house-church service. Similarly, the early 4th century Water Newton hoard found in Cambridgeshire contained possibly the oldest church vessels known. Some are marked with the chi-rho symbol and have Christian wording. They were found far from any possible church so were they used in a villa-church?

At Carrawburgh, on Hadrian's Wall, a possible clay incense burner was found.

The Mildenhall silver treasure buried in Suffolk, between 380 and 420, has three spoons with the chi-rho and alpha plus omega symbols inscribed in the bowl. Two more have names with *vivas* accompanying, which might be a Christian idea of giving spiritual life.

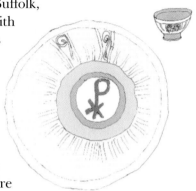

A silver spoon found at Biddulph in Staffordshire also had a chi-rho mark, as does a bowl found at Caerwent. A small bronze bowl, said to be found in a priest's grave, at Wall Roman mansio in Staffordshire in 1922 had a chi-rho on its base. Its manner of discovery was uncertain and it is now lost. It could have been 4th century.

Drawing of the Wall bowl with a chi-rho on the base.

A good number of finger rings with Christian symbols have been unearthed. The earliest was recently found at Binchester Roman fort, Durham and it showed two fishes and an anchor. Rings are also known from Brancaster and Swaffam in Norfolk, Brentwood in Essex, Bagshot in Surrey and Richborough in Kent.

Buckles and strap ends with fish and peacock symbols have been discovered and construed as being Christian, but since these can be lost anywhere, it says little of the find area.

It is likely many more objects with inscribed Christian marks will come to light. The difficulty is many are chance finds and cannot be connected with their surroundings. This makes it impossible to say with any confidence how and when they were used. Indeed, some time ago it was thought they were mostly strays imported from the Continent and were lost with travel, but this is no longer being considered. At the very least there must have been isolated Christians feeling free to worship the Christian God now that Constantine had decreed acceptance. Perhaps, the only safe conclusion can be the pieces were mostly personal and private. It is plausible their owners, who could have come from any part of the Empire, were praying alone or in a villa-church without any attendance to a dedicated church.

How widespread was Christianity in 4th century Britain?
It is thought at least five bishops were in place at the end of the 5th century (London, York, Lincoln, Cirencester and Carlisle) together with senior clergy in the smaller towns. One writer has gone as far as stating 25 bishops existed and if so would compare well with France.

The possible construction of small churches at some Roman forts and the suggestion of some rooms in a few villas being house churches gives little idea of how much Christianity had penetrated culture in post-Constantine Britain. The discovery of hoards in which plates, bowls and cups are inscribed with Christian symbols gives further verification of some people worshipping the Christian God, but it has to be judged with caution. This evidence could easily be misinterpreted. It is odd the best portable Christian artefacts have come from East Anglia and the East Midlands where there is also a strange lack of church buildings in the archaeology. All discovery has to consider possibilities such as the Roman soldiers and citizens might have been worshipping several Gods. Perhaps, they took on the new religion because the Emperors deemed it. Indeed, it would have increased status and be mixed up with power games. If it is accepted at face value, it still could be a religion deformed by heresy, especially Arianism, and be affected by local tendencies and particular brands of worship. When seen with these qualifications it is not surprising for most historians to conclude Christianity was a minority religion in Roman times. The predominant cult was a Romano-Celtic polytheism and this too varied greatly.

There is another aspect concerning cemeteries. Archaeologists have found many managed cemeteries in small Roman settlements with graves orientated west to east and clearly lacking pagan grave goods. If it is accepted this is a situation identifiable with Christian burial, and again this has to be said with some caution, then it seems Christianity, especially at the time of death, was well established in the 4th century. The problem is Christian graves in the large Roman towns are strikingly absent. There are towns like Colchester where there is a mixture, but it is exceptional. There are many graveyards where the orientation is varied and even confusing. It is still work in progress and a confident view cannot yet be given.

Guy de la Bédoyère has said that religion in Roman Britain is a subject we barely understand and this needs repeating. It is not possible to say whether the Christian communities in Britain were small or large, isolated or in communication, truly orthodox or malformed and ephemeral or persistent. It is possible to claim Christianity in Italy and France after Constantine, became organised and evangelising and this must have spilled over to Romans travelling to Britain. It is easy to believe its spread was slow and sporadic given it was replacing many local deities with a God making himself known in a faraway land. It was a religion of a high ranking individual or at best a small group of foreign converts. Therefore, the picture glimpsed for the 4th century is naturally one of a nascent religion gradually taking hold. The conclusion of Nicholas Higham and Martin Ryan was Christianity was probably highly variable, concentrated in the towns, mostly among officers and administrators as well as in families of the landholding elite.

The Bible

The greatest outcome of the first 4 centuries was an officially agreed and accepted canon of Christian texts known as the Bible. By 367, the Bishop of Alexandria had set out the books to form a New Testament. In 380, an Emperor declared alternative sects illegal and in 393, repeated in 397, the Bible in its current form was made the true book to define Christianity.

The Bible is remarkable in many ways. Written in pieces over 16 centuries, involving over 40 main writers and very many more minor contributors and going through numerous amendments and translations, over 2000 are known, it is the most critically examined and changed canon of works.

The first translation into English was by John Wycliffe, 1382. After the Black Death of 1348, he thought the end of the world was due near the end of the century and all should prepare for the final days. For this, they needed a bible which could be read.

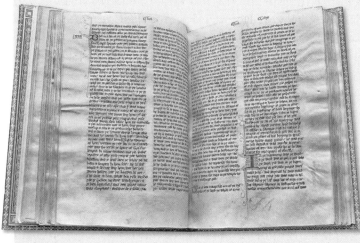

Wycliffe Bible, 1410, in the library of Lichfield Cathedral.

Reading the Bible

Four out of five UK citizens describe the Bible as the Word of God, or a book of guidance and advice, or a source of beautiful literature with very many phrases and idioms now used in everyday language. There are critics who want it to be a textbook which can then be faulted for apparent contradictions, historical inaccuracies and raising story into fact. Many dip into the book looking for events and holy words to justify their own prejudices; they use it as a voice of original authority. Worst of all sceptics search the Bible for answers to big questions, such as; How did the world begin and how will it end? What will happen when I die? Why is there so much death and destruction? What should be our response to the varied sexual mores in the world? What is the nature of the true church? How should I behave? Inevitably, they do not find a definitive answer and jump to the conclusion it is an ineffective book of wisdom. How anyone can believe a book 2 thousands years and more in age can answer precisely modern day technical and cultural questions and then dismiss it, is deeply troubling.

The Bible can only be read prayerfully. That is, by yourself, or better still in a small group, listening to the words, taking note of context and thinking about the work as a whole. It is much the same as understanding a poem, a symphony or nature reserve. Examination of bits will not work since it has to be seen holistically. Give time for the poem to sink in, judge the symphony at the end and consider the interdependence of creatures. Be imbued, but give it time and prayer. It is not a book to be rushed.

Early Christians must have realised a document summarising the life of Jesus was inadequate. It would have been very easy to teach about his mission and present it like a diary. They must have known it is necessary to know the whole picture of where he was coming from, why he behaved in the extraordinary way he did, and why his followers taught others their conclusions. Therefore, an eclectic collection of various texts with different genres, written by a very diverse number of individuals and recorded from 3 continents in greatly varying circumstances was much more likely to persuade minds. No wonder it took 4 centuries to sort out what was appropriate and meaningful.

Augustine of Hippo
Augustine was born in 354 in Algeria. When aged 17 he received a good education at Carthage and later moved to Rome and then Milan to teach rhetoric. He was baptised in 387 and in 395, aged 41, he became the Bishop of Hippo, now Annaba in Algeria. Augustine wrote much on a wide range of topics and many consider him to be the best Christian thinker of the first millennium. Whilst a bishop, he had to deal with a Donatist cult which believed in a *rigorist* interpretation of faith that held the church community had to be all saints and there was no room for sinners. They did not accept Christians who had acceded to Roman oppression and particularly the persecution under Diocletian. Some Donatists killed Christians who they saw as collaborators. Augustine argued strongly against this cult. By the end of the 4th century the thinking was the church and Empire were one polity. It consisted of one God, one Christ, one Emperor and one Church. The Roman Church and the Empire were holy,

eternal and of one mind. To begin with, even
Augustine believed Rome had positioned itself
entwined with God's grace and control. Then in
410, the Goths sacked Rome and terrorized its
citizens. The holy city was now considered
vulnerable and gradually the idea grew that its
decline was all the fault of the Christian God. In
426, Augustine wrote a massive book in defence
of Christianity called *The City of God against the
pagans*. He broke the bond between the Empire

and the Church by writing about an earthly city and a separate City of God
(taken from Psalm 46.4). This separation was discretely phrased knowing the
citizens could honour both, but the two places were contrasted and defined. The
earthly city would always be provisional, whereas the City of God was truly
eternal. This state-church relationship was now described and referred to many
times over the centuries to follow. It has been argued the relationship was not
broken until modern times.

Between 429 and 438, Vandals, an East German tribe, entered and took over
North Africa. Augustine's people became answerable to yet another culture,
sympathetic to Arianism, and violent to those who were Trinitarian. Augustine
died in 430 aged 76 and it was recorded he spent much time weeping and asking
for forgiveness before he died. He possibly died of starvation during a siege. It
demonstrated Augustine's personal belief of a life spent in a state of helplessness
assisted only by God's mercy.

The Other World

The Romans believed in a very elaborate journey of the spirit after death. Both
burial and cremation were used. Proper burial was necessary before the spirit
could be escorted to the River Styx, a mythical boundary borrowed from the
Greeks. Here a coin had to be given to a ferryman to take the spirit across the
river where it would then be judged by three Gods who were part of a multi-God
complex. Outcome of the judgement could be entrance to paradise, especially
if you had been a good warrior. Alternatively, you moved towards a Plain, if you
had been a good citizen. The third possibility was to be forever tormented by
joining the God Hades. A precious few could be allowed to return to life.

In 3rd century Rome, underground burial chambers were built. Callixtus,
Bishop of Rome, 218 – 223, gave land outside the city walls, now known as the
Callixtus catacomb, for Christian burial. Dark corridors lit by oil lamps led to
decorated chambers for burial. There might also have been a small room to allow

prayer and to even have an agape meal. Their sacred necropolis was a Christian communal complex in which the dead, represented in bone, were still with them. Martyrs had special chambers, which were much visited. Somehow, the steadfastness of the martyr could be accessed and perceived. The attributes of the dead would be sensed.

Plaster decoration depicted Christian symbols, especially the fish, anchor, chi-rho, alpha plus omega and a ship. Biblical scenes and favourite mythical images were commonly painted on ceilings and walls. Occasionally certain words or acronyms were written. It is now thought these early Christians had no objection to images. They were expressing love for a deceased. It was also the beginning of Christian art.

St Paul's catacomb, Malta. Left image shows a prayer room with a stone table for an agape meal to celebrate a recently deceased. Note the recesses in the walls for oil lamps. There might have been an altar. Right image shows an incised symbol, date unknown but possibly 4th or 5th century. If it is a trident, it has several interpretations, with one being a symbol for the Trinity, which was a most important issue for the 4th century.

Chapter 3

THE ROMANO-BRITISH CHURCH 407 – 577

There are two powers by which this world is ruled, the sacred authority of the priests and the royal power of the kings. The power of the priests is weightier, since they have to render an account for even the kings in the divine judgment. Kings must bend their neck to the bishops and await from them the means of their salvation.

From a letter by Pope Gelasius, 494, to a
Roman Emperor putting him in his place.

This historical period is often written as a short postscript to the Classical Roman era or a simple preamble to the arrival of the Medieval Saxons. It is a twilight time in history – the darkest of ages. Paucity of prime historical evidence and scarcity of archaeological remains give it minor importance in many books. So, often it is described simply in terms of migrations of people and an emphasis on their heathenism. The Roman builders have left and the Saxon organisers have still to arrive so the people in between, so it seems, were culturally deficient and parochial in outlook. They were also tribal, hostile and forever skirmishing. Furthermore, there was a north-south prejudice. The north was barbaric, the south was post-Roman and increasingly Christian and the midlands was a dark middle-world. Added to this were the ideas of Saxon migration sending the indigenous Britons westwards and the Christians in the south-east moving in the same direction to evangelise Cornwall, Brittany and Wales. Most of this is now considered implausible and a fundamental reassessment and correction is underway.

The historically pivotal time of around 407 saw not only the loss of Roman military and therefore a weakness in defence, but also the removal of Roman administrators and a finish for the regular issue of Roman coins. There was a slow decline in the use of Latin, except in the church, with a corresponding rise in speaking Old English (Germanic with Frisian added and some Latin mixed in) or a Celtic variant. Regions differed and it might just be some people did not notice a difference. Indeed, it is also possible, it all happened gradually over a couple of decades or more, it is unrecorded. There were around 30 *civitates*, or centres of administration, with each run by a large number of men. Their locations were like the tribal centres in pre-Roman times. Therefore, it is quite possible with the withdrawal of Roman administration these centres took over without much of a hiatus. It is not known, if there was a national primate or ruler who led all of these local *civitates*, but that might have been unnecessary. The King Arthur exploits have been added to this dilute comprehension and they do not help.

The only documents available to find what really changed are fragments of chronicles, a small number of poems and opinions given in Continental narratives. All are historically insecure and especially contentious when it comes to dates.

One example of a foreign account involved a monk from Britain or Ireland, called Pelagius, c354 – c418, who travelled abroad and was in Rome around 380. He caused, or unknowingly started, a controversy which can still surface in theological discourse.

Pelagianism – the third heresy

Pelagius became well known for his persuasive oratory. He was said to take Deuteronomy 24.16 literary; *only for their own crimes may persons be put to death.* This was used to advance the idea everyone had free will and was answerable to themselves. The path to salvation and heaven did not involve divine will; it was simply open to those who strived for a perfect life. Poor Pelagius suffered much abuse, being called a *bloated Celtic yokel.* He was labelled a heretic.

After the sacking of Rome in 410, he fled to Carthage and by 415 was in Jerusalem. Here he claimed he had never said individuals could achieve salvation by their own efforts. He explained God was necessary for salvation because every human was created by God. He had either recanted, or truthfully claimed his detractors had made up and distorted his ideas. The outcome, however, was he was expelled from Jerusalem in 417 and went to live in Egypt where he died three years later.

Pelagius has split opinion with some believing he was much maligned. Whatever the truth, the name of Pelagius was used to split the church during the next two hundred years.

Pelagianism became such an issue that in 418 in the presence of possibly as many as 200 bishops at the Council of Carthage it was branded heresy. It disappeared quickly in the eastern Greek Church after another Council in 431, but smouldered on in the west for a long time particularly in France and Britain. A mission sent to Britain by the pope and led by Germanus of Auxerre and Lupus of Troyes came and stayed between 429 and 431. They travelled around preaching on the flaws of Pelagianism. Germanus returned in 447 with Severus, which suggested the original mission was not wholly successful. A century later Wales became embroiled in the argument and it needed David, Bishop of Mynyw, and now St Davids, to visit and correct the heretics. Eradicating this heresy showed a close communication between bishops and the pope. The church appeared to be determined to restore and maintain an orthodoxy. After his intervention, the reputation of Germanus increased and this was seen by the many clergy who visited him, or moreover claimed to have visited him. He became the authority to follow and was the bridge between Britain and Rome. His biographer was Constantius of Lyon and in 480 wrote that Britain had essentially a Roman administration and orthodox worship, and surprisingly was a very wealthy island. If true, this showed the Roman withdrawal was not as damaging or reshaping as many might have thought. However, that was soon to change.

The Great Schism
Many differences led to a split in the church with the formation of two popes, one leading from Rome and another from Constantinople. The disagreement was complicated with differences in culture, politics and language; all entangled with theological standpoints. No specific date for the origin of this division can be given, but it was evident in the 4th century and coloured most of the discussions in the 5th. In 445, Pope Leo the Great strengthened and established papal authority by reminding the church it was mediated through the apostle Peter at Rome and he was supreme. This was accepted by the Church in the west of Europe, including Britain without question and again showed how much the church was in line with Rome. However, this has to be qualified with the apparent absence of British bishops at the Church Councils. The schism between a Latin speaking Rome and a Greek conversing Constantinople did not end until the sacking of Constantinople in 1204 by mutinous crusaders. It was totally finished in 1453 by Ottoman Turks.

A fourth schism occurred over the nature of Jesus. In 451 at a Council of Chalcedon held in Turkey and convened by the Roman Emperor in Constantinople the nature of God and Jesus being both divine and human (two natures coexisting) was settled for most churches, but some orthodox oriental churches saw Christ as having a perfectly united Godhead and manhood (one nature) and could not accept the outcome and separated. In 553, an attempt at reconciliation was made, but bishops in Syria, centred at Antioch, and bishops in Egypt, centred at Alexandria, continued to maintain the view of an inseparable divine and human Christ. This split between Syriac- and Coptic-speaking Christians and the Roman church still exists. Again, it showed there never was a completely united church.

The most significant Christian Romano-British text to survive was by Gildas and called *On the ruin and conquest of Britain,* dated c500 to 550. It is now thought to have been written in Wales, though some place him in Dorset, between 510 and 530. Gildas, c482 – 570, came originally from Scotland and probably taught at Llanwit Major, South Glamorgan, and it is there he became a monk. His often inaccurate and vague diatribe pretending to be history was full of scorn for allowing barbarians to penetrate into Britain. For some unknown reason he described the immigrant Saxons as *the scourge of God.* There was a special anger for the leaders of five kingdoms, including some from his homeland. His lambast was substantiated by quotations from the Bible and there was much reference to the apocalypse and the Book of Revelation. He appeared to believe Christianity entered Britain with the Roman incursion and their retreat was to be regretted. He was not the only one to think this way. A strong belief in a providential retribution fired his excoriations. The newcomers were unwanted.

There is a section where Gildas heavily criticised the clergy for being shameless fools and wily plunderers. Since he did not name any particular clergy this has become open for all kinds of interpretation. One such is that Gildas was held to be an ascetic and angry with those in the church who embellished their church and adorned themselves. He also disliked elitism in the priestly class. Another version sees Gildas as a prophet charged by God to call the kings and clergy back to being a chosen people of the covenant. This call was based on the Christian scriptures and he was the new Elijah.

There is one part of his excoriating sermon where he listed the misfortunes of the people. He mentioned obstinacy, subjection, rebellion, harsh servitude, persecuted religion, martyrdom, and heresy, and this might be a description of the state of the church. He then added there were two plundering races; he could not bring himself to name them so it was not certain whether he was referring to

Saxons, Picts or Scots. Finally, the woes of the people were increased with hunger, a *memorable plague* and crime. Clearly, there was much unrest with both natural disaster, incursions of armies and oppression. If this was not the ranting of an alarmist with personal grudges and a hatred of foreigners, but was instead a plea for God's help in a fractured world, then it gives us some idea of why there was so little evidence of an organising church and growth of Christian settlements. Maybe it explains why there was little recorded on the state of the kingdoms.

It was also a time when the environment was hostile and there is good evidence there was a severe depopulation. One estimate of 3 million reducing to almost half this size has been given. Reasons for this decline can only be tentative.

Climate change and disease

At the start of the 5th century, there was a shift to wetter, colder weather in Britain and this deterioration worsened over the next hundred years. Deforestation and grazing must have increased the chances of the rain causing soil erosion and flooding. Annual average temperatures dropped, perhaps by as much as 1.5°C. Colder weather would have shortened the growing season, reduced the hay crop and made it difficult to feed animals throughout the winter. Wet land would have become impossible to manage. All of this must have affected survival, settlement, migration and possibly taxation.

Two volcanic eruptions in 536 and 540 possibly blocked the sun with dust and for a time lowered the global temperature by as much as 2°C. If this *volcanic winter* was as bad as reported, it would have caused widespread famine.

There is no other direct reference to a plague beyond the one given by Gildas. It has been suggested the plague in Gildas' polemic occurred between 410 and 440. If this is true, it could be another reason why the Roman elite left and did not return. It could also be why he hated immigrants. Around the 540s, a plague bacillus from China decimated populations around the Byzantium Empire stretching around the Mediterranean. Analysis of DNA from skeletons has shown it was a variant of bubonic plague and has been named the Plague of Justinian. One writer said the pandemic was worldwide. It severely weakened the Byzantine church with perhaps a quarter of many populations perishing. There is only anecdotal evidence it reached the Atlantic Isles, but rats on merchant ships must have carried it far. Some have suggested it did weaken Britain and in its aftermath allowed Saxons to invade from the 550s onwards. The demise of Silchester in the 560s has been connected to the disease. Mutants of the bacterium caused further plagues, especially in the 7th century, and its consequences were much the same as seen with the Black Death, 1347 – 1351.

There is a dearth of archaeology to show the progress of Christians in this time. Excavations in and around the Roman towns show life continued after 407, even though there was a movement by the elite to build villas in rural areas. Did they avoid the plague-infested towns? Occupation of post-Roman settlements has been indicated at Caerwent, Caistor, Canterbury, Chester, Colchester, Cirencester, Dorchester, Dover, Dunstable, Exeter, Gloucester, Ilchester, Leicester, Llandough, London, Northampton, Rendlesham, St Albans, Silchester, Southampton, Southwell, Wells, Wroxeter and York.

Occupation for some time after the exit of Romans has been identified at many sites, such as at Canterbury until the middle of 5th century. Unfortunately, no early hall has been found, though two buildings were dated to c450. The next buildings uncovered were mid-6th century. The Roman theatre might have been in continuous use.

A similar story occurs at Lincoln with the St Paul in the Bail church being rebuilt in the 5th century and possibly demolished in the late 6th century.

A burial ground at St Martins in the Field, Westminster, revealed high status individuals being buried till the 5th century. Some were aligned west-east. The oldest church in London is All Hallows by the Tower and dates back to 675. In the crypt is a Roman pavement and the church still has an original Saxon arch.

It is likely occupation at Whitchurch, Shropshire continued from Roman times. There is no discernible continuity at Roman Buxton, Chesterfield, Coventry and Worcester, but with late Saxon occupation, it seems plausible. The same can be said about the Cotswolds and Vale of Evesham areas where many Roman settlements have been found and later there were many wealthy monastic centres.

There was a cemetery in Northampton with grave goods dated 450 – 550 laid next to a Roman settlement by the River Nene. Later in the 7th century there was a Saxon Hall built not far away. The upper Nene valley clearly showed much Roman and Saxon activity.

Leicester and at least 6 Roman settlements in Leicestershire, showed Saxon cemeteries and burials close by. Medbourne particularly stands out as having had occupation in this transitional period and it is likely more sites will be added to this list. Similarly, a Saxon cemetery at Saffron Walden, Essex, was on or near a Roman fort.

At Poundbury, near Dorchester, a Roman cemetery appeared to be used into the 5th century by Christians. Billingford, Norfolk was Roman and nearby at Spong Hill an enormous Saxon cemetery with possibly as many as 3000 burials has been excavated. This area around the River Wensum was not far from the Saxon cathedral at North Elmham. Many artefacts were found and they show a connection with objects known from Scandinavia and North Germany.

Archaeologists excavating at Wells, Somerset, revealed a late Roman burial chamber in the gardens of the current Cathedral. Above this was a Saxon mortuary chapel and the buildings were more or less in the same west-east alignment with the current cathedral. This led to the idea of continuous worship on the site, but subsequent writers have doubted this.

Similarly, at Exeter, Devon, graves found close to the current Cathedral suggest post-Roman occupation. Boniface c675 – 754 might have had early training at a monastery in Exeter and this is marked with a special chapel in the current cathedral.

Southwell Minster has a section of the floor of the original Saxon church, c956, showing and a painted plaster from the wall of a nearby Roman villa. A very large field and adjoining gardens on the south-east side is thought to have extensive Roman remains, possibly walled and defended. Not far away could be a large harbour connected to the River Trent. If ever the area was excavated, it could show a long history of occupation and maybe worship on the site.

At Uley, Gloucestershire, a hilltop Roman temple was abandoned in the 4th century, then replaced with a wooden one in the 5th century and finally a stone church in the late 6th or early 7th century and again this has been questioned. A similar takeover occurred at Lamyatt Beacon, Cadbury Hillfort and Henley Hill, all in Somerset. South Cadbury hill fort, Somerset, was destroyed by the Romans, but then rebuilt in the 5th century and again improved in the 6th century. At Aylesbury, Buckinghamshire, an early 4th century hillfort was settled. By the 8th century, it was surrounded by a palisade and ditch and finds like a glass having a cross suggest it had a monastery.

The hill at Breedon, Leicestershire, was also an iron-age fort and it is thought it later had a Romano-British temple or shrine. Close-by was a Roman villa. In the early 8th century, land was given to build a monastery which survived until Norman times. A priest from the monastery in 737 became Archbishop of Canterbury. This is one of the best examples for expecting continuous occupation, but it is not entirely conclusive.

Bede said the church at St Albans, Hertfordshire, still to be identified, remained in use until his time.

Both Nennius and Bede mentioned Roman Bath and the hot springs. Bath is a Saxon name and so points to some continuity.

Bede also recorded an Irish monk called Dicuil landed at Bosham, Sussex, in mid-7th century and joined 5 or 6 others at a monastery, but they apparently had no effect on the local people. At Bosham, many Roman objects have been found and it is close to the Roman villa complex at Fishbourne. Its position in Chichester harbour strongly indicates it could have had a continuous settlement from early times.

Bede also described a royal centre at Rendlesham, Suffolk, in the 8th century. Ongoing archaeological excavation has shown a rich Saxon site with a possible hall, 23m long and 9.5m wide. Artefacts suggest Saxon occupation from the 5th to 8th century and the discovery of late Roman finds pushes the date back to at least the late 4th century. This site might be where Roman-Saxon continuity is eventually established.

The Roman port of Dover probably never stopped being used. At Buckland, near Dover, a Saxon cemetery with 170 graves has been excavated. It contained mostly pagan burials dated from the late 5th century to the 8th century.

At Llandough, 2 miles (3.5km) from the centre of Cardiff, a 2nd century Roman villa existed until the early 4th century. Historical evidence showed a monastery was built on the site in the mid-7th century. Less than a mile away was a defended hillfort at Dinas Powys where Roman amphorae were found. It was probably reoccupied in the 5th century. Nearby a cemetery was excavated and sherds of amphorae indicated activity into the late 5th century. The cemetery was mostly west-east burial and 122 white quartz pebbles were found associated with the early graves. This is linked with Revelation 2.17: *and on the white stone is written a new name that no one knows except the one who receives it*. A white stone is left for the departed to hand in when they reach heaven. So it could show a Christian presence from the 5th or 6th century right through to the current church on the site.

Similar white quartz stones have been found in burials at Whitesands, Pembrokeshire. Excavation at Whitesands has exposed an early chapel, named St Patricks. Unfortunately, more than half of the stonework has been lost to the sea eroding the dune site. More than 20 infant burials were found and they frequently had white stones alongside or over the top of the remains. Some of the burials could have been newborns and were never given a Christian name. Whitesands is close to St Davids which has been connected to a Roman station though its precise location has still to be determined.

At Llanwit Major, Glamorgan, a Roman villa existed immediately north of the settlement and later a 5th century school was set up in the middle of the current town.

A large late 4th to 6th century cemetery at Queenford Farm, outside Dorchester, Dorset, had 2,400 graves estimated to have served a community of 200 to 300 people over a time span of 100 to 150 years. Most were lying west-east, but no grave goods were found. It is suggested to have been a Christian community, but this conclusion is tentative. Larkhills cemetery at Winchester was probably Christian. At Highdown near Worthing, Sussex, a grave contained a glass vessel with a Christian inscription. Many more cemeteries have revealed small finds showing Christian burial. All are not far from Roman settlements.

The tombstone found at Vinolanda, by Hadrian's Wall, has the name of Brigomaflos and the words *here lies* in Latin. This could be a Christian phrase and dates from 5th or 6th century. A strap end has also been recovered from this location and it depicts a figure that might be priestly.

At the church of St Mary de Lode, Gloucester, excavation revealed a substantial Roman building. This was demolished in the 5th century and another built with the same alignment. It contained a number of west-east burials. In the 9th or 10th century, a Saxon church was built on the site. Similarly, at Cirencester, Gloucestershire, a 9th or 10th century church was built with the help of Roman stone and it was then rebuilt as an Abbey in 1117. The reuse of a site suggests continuous occupation and perhaps worship, but again it cannot be confirmed.

A wooden stoup was found in a grave at Long Wittenham, South Oxfordshire, and on a bronze plate was decoration with biblical scenes. It is thought to be late 5th century and from France. To the north-east of the village was a Roman settlement.

The wonderful Hoxne hoard from Suffolk is dated to sometime after 407 and it contained an eclectic mix of coins and jewellery, including a necklace with a chi-rho on the clasp. There are also spoons showing several sorts of Christograms. However, there are other depictions resembling late Roman decorative art. The general view is the hoard came from one or several Christian households.

An attempt was made to locate a number of pre-Saxon religious centres in the Midlands with later Saxon churches and included Worcester and Lichfield, but like Gloucester and Wroxeter there is nothing substantial to support this. In a similar way certain monasteries, such as Flawford in Nottinghamshire, Frocester in Gloucestershire, Much Wenlock in Shropshire and Wimborne in Dorset, have been connected with possible Roman villas.

It is hard to believe the salt, tin and lead mines stopped because the Romans left. For example in the Hope Valley, North Derbyshire, lead was mined by the Romans. A Roman fort called Navio had a name change to the Saxon word Brough. Not far away there could have been a Christian presence at Bakewell and Wirksworth in the 7th century. Between the early 8th century and the late 9th century, the lead mines around Wirksworth were controlled by the monastery at Repton. However, proving continuity of occupation as well as Christian worship has not been possible.

On the opposite shore of the River Alde to the village of Iken, Suffolk, recent excavation has shown a 1st to 3rd century Roman site where salt processing occurred. Over 6,400 pieces of ceramic trays used for salt evaporation were found. In the early 7th century and later, it was re-occupied by Saxons and burials show a Christian presence. Iken could be the Icanhoh where Botolph built a monastery in 654.

Stray Christian objects from this time include the Latinus stone at Whithorn on the Solway Firth. It could be the oldest Christian monument in Scotland, dating from the mid-5th century; a Kilmadrine stone might be of similar age.

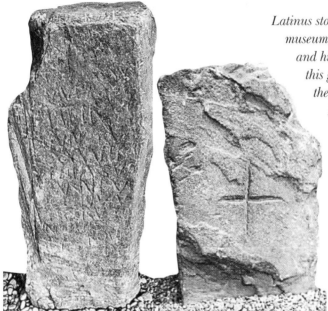

Latinus stone (left) at Whithorn Priory museum, South Scotland. Latinus and his daughter were incised on this gravestone found in 1890 in the wall of the medieval church. Latinus stated he was descended from a local native, had taken on a Roman name and learnt Latin and was apparently a Christian. Above the lettering might be a faint chi-rho sign. Grave marker stone (right) from Ruthwell churchyard, Dumfriesshire thought to be around 550.

The priest's stone found at Kirkmadrine, on the Rhins of Galloway, has the names of three priests plus a ringed cross and chi-rho mark. It could be as early as 450. Two more stones at the church also have Christograms incised. It is not far from the huge Roman marching camp at Glenluce and the Roman station at Stranraer.

Amongst the best finds are large lead tanks, with many having Christian symbols, which are believed to be portable and used for baptism or foot washing, though it has still to be verified. Around 23 tanks and other caskets are known

Drawing of the Ashton Tank, Northamptonshire. It has been estimated to have held 220 litres (6 gallons) of water. Made of three layers of lead sheet, it would not have been easy to move around.

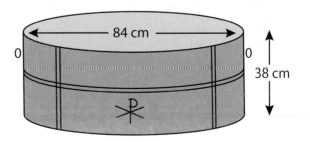

and about half have chi-rho marks. Fragments of lead that might be part of a tank have also been found. The tanks appear to be peculiar to Britain, since none have been found elsewhere.

The Walesby tank from Lincolnshire might have been deliberately broken up after usage ended. This tank showed a scene that has been interpreted as a baptism, but not everyone agrees. Dating these tanks is also problematical. Some could be Roman and others might even be as late as Middle Saxon. The majority come from the East Midlands and East Anglia and because much baptism was conducted by itinerant priests, it raises the question of why they have not been found more widely. If they were Christian objects and Romano-British, it emphasises the existence of the religion in Middle Eastern England and follows on from the rich Roman finds in the area.

All this very disparate evidence shows there is still a need to find a Roman site that in time becomes a Christian site and convincingly continues until the 7th century. There are cathedral grounds and gardens which invite archaeological inspection in pursuit of this missing evidence. One difficulty, however, is obtaining precise dates for each phase of building and, perhaps, this will always be beyond any archaeology. Nevertheless, the religious centre that first claims continuous worship for 1700 years will have a great distinction.

Saxon Incursion

From where, why and where to the Saxons migrated has occupied much thought, without any certain conclusion. Bede gave the too neat idea of Old Saxons from Saxony, Germany, occupying the Sussex and Wessex area, Jutes possibly coming from Jutland, mainland Denmark, and occupying Kent, the Isle of Wight and its adjacent coast, and the Angles possibly from Schleswig-Holstein and occupying East Anglia, Middle England including Mercia, sometimes pronounced *Murshia,* (or Mierce pronounced *Miercha),* as well as Northumbria. Bede's description of migration has to be treated with great caution. All were Germanic people in origin. It is also likely people came here from Frisia, mostly in the Netherlands, and from Gaul or northern France. Where they settled must also have varied and Bede's concise colonisation pattern has to be seen as an approximation.

Why they came can only be speculative, but ideas like a rise in sea level took away their coastal homelands, climate change was pervasive, population increase meant the farms could not support everyone, there was a trading gap when the Romans left, and it was tempting to sail across the sea and enter the rivers Thames, Trent, Tyne, Tees and Tweed. They could also have wanted to plunder. Added to this list must be the idea of people migrating away from areas suffering from plague. The general view accepted now is the migration was incremental, started early in the 5th century and continued for two more centuries. Early genetic studies of a comparatively small number of excavated skeletons found in Yorkshire, Cambridgeshire and London support the view Saxon migration was significant and the newcomers mixed with the indigenous people. It is too early to say anymore.

Nevertheless, the long accepted view is they were heathens, so the bigger question is to what extent did they practise this cult and how quickly did they assimilate the form of Christianity already here? Did they bring with them a nascent Christianity? This is a pivotal question, yet to be answered and accepted.

Paganism and Heathenism

Julius Caesar in the 50s BC described a cult labelled druidism which has no written record and no supporting archaeology in the Atlantic Isles. It was claimed it disappeared after a Roman campaign in Anglesey, but it was likely there were isolated communities in other parts of Britain with similar practices. The northern tribe, known as Brigantes, were Druids, but were destroyed by the Romans in the year 80. The Roman pagan pantheon was equally mysterious with deities in almost every natural setting. These spirits had to be placated. Surprisingly the super classical Roman Gods were virtually absent from Britain explaining why their altars have rarely been found. Often the honouring of a God was tied up with reinforcing Romanitas and pledging loyalty to the Emperor. For some, it was a tradition and not a tightly held belief system.

The Romans made public pagan rites illegal in 391, so any paganism in Britain afterwards was rare. There is no reference to paganism in West Britain after the 5th century. Gildas in the 6th century claimed paganism had been eradicated.

Finding cow bones thrown into the Sulis Minerva temple at Bath has often been given as a pagan cult continuing, but it now seems this was over by 430. Similarly, the many pagan inscriptions in the Thetford hoard have been used to state paganism survived to the end of the Roman occupation, but it is now dated to the middle to late 4th century.

The subject of Saxon Gods and their worship is murky, even opaque. There is very little information recorded and much has been warped by Christian distaste. Perhaps, the most important aspect of paganism and folk magic is how seldom it was mentioned. The old Gods were known, such as Woden, Thunor, Tiw, Frige and others, a few ceremonial rites were understood, but the extent of pagan worship in early Saxon England is guesswork. It is known that augury, taking omens from changes in the environment and the behaviour of animals, was widely used. Healing rites went with plant nostrums and could have been genuine herbal medicine, but still seen by some as heathen. The customs were localised, folk based, varied regionally and were never transcendental.

A remarkably few burials were accompanied with amulets and items thought to have given magical power, but these are modern interpretations and hesitation is needed. *Ritual* and *Votive* are words too easy to use for explaining the weird.

Today there are only around 20 towns or places with names connected to Saxon Gods and only 27 locations with names that were derived from heathen or pagan words. Almost all are found in central and South-East England. Many place names have been interpreted to derive from pagan entities, such as springs, wells, stones, dragons (dragon stories in Saxon mythology were rare), demons, pits, mounds and other natural features, but proving they were places where pagan rites existed is entirely another matter. For example, an early name for Lichfield was Letocaiton, which meant *grey wood* and this was more likely to be a description of the area rather than a reference to dark deeds. The Saxon name was Licetfeld and Bede used Licitfield. In fact, many of the topographical place names were present by the 5th century and thus could have been in place well before the arrival of the Saxons. Early Saxons undoubtedly knew heathen ideas, but labelling them pagans worshipping alternative Gods cannot be substantiated.

The outcome of this Saxon migration is also uncertain. Did the Saxons ethnically cleanse the resident Britons and either remove them or cause them to move on? Did they intermix with the local tribes changing their ways and language? Did they live together and gradually the Britons and Saxons merge in most ways? In reality was it a mixture of all three progressions and it varied from area to area? This aspect has caused much to be written and it might be resolved with DNA studies. In 2006, a book on the origins of British people claimed only a small fraction of the English gene pool was traceable to a Saxon invasion. Similarly with a Celtic influx of people. Three quarters of the gene pool came as a direct descent from Neolithic settlers. Another book with evidence from mitochondrial DNA supported the view the overwhelming gene pool came from Neolithic people. The contribution from Celts was also minimal. The Saxon contribution was less than 20% and the Normans around 2%. A 2016 study of rare genetic variants concluded between 25 and 40% (median of 38%) of DNA in people living today in North-East, Central,

East and South England is traceable to the Saxons and there is little difference in their genetic profile. 21% was Celtic and only 9% Scandinavian. The low level of Scandinavian derived DNA has very recently been questioned on linguistic and archaeological grounds with a doubt expressed on being able to differentiate between Saxon and Viking DNA. To date only a small number of individuals have been determined archaeogenetically and there is still more to learn before agreement is reached. One conclusion at this early time for the subject is the Saxons gave more to the gene pool than Celts, Scandinavians and Normans. That must be a reflection of the numbers of immigrants. Equally, it could be a reflection of levels of intermixing with the indigenous Britons descended from Neolithic people.

At West Stow (Suffolk) and Mucking (Essex), evidence suggested the Saxon settlers were welcomed, but allocated marginal land next to an already existing Romano-British settlement. The West Stow village was then abandoned in the early 7th century and it is thought the people moved (allowed?) to Icklingham where an established settlement with a church thrived. By then they would have been fully integrated.

Wroxeter is another example of what might have happened to many Romanised settlements once the Roman army left. For Wroxeter this was early in the year 90. It was then taken over by civilians and it became the fourth largest Roman town with an estimated population of 15,000. It appeared to never have had any kind of defence wall. By the end of the 5th century, the bath complex was finished. Around the years 530 to 570 the basilica area was levelled, covered with much rubble and up to 70 timber buildings erected, including a very large winged hall 38 metres long (125 feet) and 16 metres wide (52 feet). Also built were council chambers, shrine, record office, market, food bars and shops, workshops and a large bath complex.

Wroxeter archway (left) from the basilica, built in the foreground, to the bathing area, behind the wall. It is the largest standing Roman wall in England. The basilica was an enclosed exercise area and after exercising Romans visited the various baths. Underfloor area (right) of the baths showing how extensive it was. Part of the baths was used for grain storage in the 4th century. Wroxeter is a remarkable site with much more to reveal.

Recently, this extensive post-Roman development has been questioned and the interpretation should be considered still unfinished archaeology.

Such a development, together with the numerous houses, and many still to be uncovered, was on a large scale. The best houses faced the Shropshire hills and the worst received the fumes from the workshops with a prevailing wind. In all around 260 buildings have been identified by geophysical surveys and still to be investigated. This was not the work of a demoralised or defeated Romano-British tribe, probably the Dobunni from the Malvern area, especially considering the coins and pottery. The settlement was gradually abandoned from the middle of the 6th century. Some think it was the arrival of hostile Saxons claiming land along the River Severn, which might have ended the site. Many of the buildings appeared to have been dismantled deliberately and sadly, all useful materials were taken away. It has been heavily speculated Wroxeter was the seat of Vortigern the British leader who, according to Gildas, let Saxons into Kent to help its defence and then found they wanted to have more and more land. Another much-loved idea for some is it was King Arthur's base. Whoever led Wroxeter led a very successful town, almost certainly diverse in makeup, with all the amenities needed for a comfortable life. They appeared to be so secure there was little concern about its minimal defence. It stands as potentially the best site to show Roman into 7th century Saxon continuous occupation. Its location on Watling Street and close to the River Severn would assist in new tribes arriving and being accommodated.

At Catterick in Yorkshire, is another fort where similar timber buildings were added to the Roman site.

Another picture is seen with the Gewissae tribe of west Saxons moving into and inhabiting the upper Thames area in the early 6th century. Their leader was Cerdic, c494 – 534, and this was a Briton's name. Archaeology does not show such an advance of people across Hampshire and into the Home Counties and some have doubted the whole story. Nevertheless, their metalwork shows a mixing of Roman, Celtic and Germanic characters and could be because there was a mixing of people, or was it simply a mixing of ideas. Their ancestry has been connected with the later Wessex Saxons, but again this might be fiction. Disentangling early times in this region has been fraught.

Extraordinary Migration
Procopius of Caesarea c500 – 554, was a Palestinian who became the legal adviser to a Roman Emperor and wrote a kind of history for the 6th century whilst based in Constantinople. There is much confusion with claims that Britain was ruled by three tyrants and its geographical position was placed further south. He also wrote that people migrated to France and this has been explained by missionaries travelling to

Armorica, now called Brittany. Large numbers of people were said to have migrated and this is either an exaggeration, or there was a large return of Saxons back to France. Similarly, if an 8th century German document is believed there was a migration of disaffected Saxons in c531 back to the port of Cuxhaven, Germany.

There has been much reference of pilgrimage to Rome. Bishops were compelled to make this journey and on the route take detours and visit French bishops having a saintly reputation. There were shrines on the way where homage was important. Jerome spoke of British pilgrims in Jerusalem as early as around 385.

In the 6th century a British bishop, Mailoc, had a British Christian settlement in Galicia in North-West Spain. It must have had a pilgrim's route from Britain or Ireland, possibly passing through Brittany.

Columbanus, an Irish monk, together with 12 companions, travelled to France and founded a monastery at Annegray and nearby Luxeuil, c585 – 590. He then moved to Bregenz on Lake Constance in 610 and finally founded Bobbio Abbey in Lombardy, Italy in 614.

In 508, Clovis I king of a region that is now part of Belgium, following a plea to Christ for help in a battle, was baptised at Reims. He became the king of most

Some missionary routes (right).

Clovis I (below) at Cathedral St Denis near Paris.

of France, started the Frankish dynasty and caused Nicene Christianity to replace the Arian heresy. This conversion to the Roman Church set in motion a similar conversion to most Germanic people north of the Alps.

The Visigoths in Spain converted in 589. His realignment of the church in France set the foundation for missionaries to move farther northwards and to realign Britain. 508 can be considered a significant year for the progression of Christianity across Europe. Clovis died in Paris in 511. He was equal in significance to Constantine in his rehabilitation of orthodox Christianity and its dissemination.

In 581 Bertha, the Christian daughter of the ruler of Paris, crossed the Channel and married Aethelbert, King of Kent. This brought baptism to the first Saxon king in Britain. Bertha's chaplain, Bishop Liudhard, accompanied her to Kent and help found and dedicate to Martin of Tours the first Christian Saxon church in England, St Martin's at Canterbury. It is the oldest church in the English-speaking world.

Monasticism

From very early times, certain individuals chose a solitary life, eschewing drink, exotic food, cohabitation and instead devoted time to prayer and worship. Indeed, the Bible mentioned widows and virgins helping to make a house of prayer. They, in time, were called the *Spouses of Christ*. Maybe, some found this was a way to escape from Roman oppression. Living an ascetic life was mentioned in Syria in the 2nd century. It is often said this solitary existence started in the desert, but undoubtedly, it grew from loners in the towns and villages across the Christian world. Indeed, both Jesus and Paul intimate the need to avoid distractions in order to pray.

Paul of Thebes, c227 – c342, fled to the Egyptian desert to avoid Roman persecution in 250. He is sometimes credited as being the first Christian hermit. Another recluse called Anthony lived for around 20 years in the Egyptian desert and his story was written down. The reality is he had mental issues and his self-imposed confinement helped him to recover and recover he must have done for he lived for 105 years. An early church, dedicated to Anthony, was built in the eastern Egyptian desert in 356. These and many more desert recluses are sometimes said to be the founders of monasticism, but this downplays John the Baptist, the sect called Essenes and many other isolated Christians.

Pachomius, an Egyptian, together with over 100 others, including women, set up the first recorded monastery in the Egyptian desert between 318 and 323. A papyrus found in the Egyptian desert, dated 324, first referred to an individual as a *monachos*, or monk/nun. John Cassian, c360 – 435, after visiting the monastery was invited by the pope to found an Egyptian style monastery in France and it became the Abbey of St Victor, dated c415, near Marseilles. Many visitors saw the principles of how this mixed sex monastery worked and copied it. When Benedict of Nursia in central Italy, 480 – 550, framed his Rules for monasticism, around 540, many were borrowed from Marseille. This was a set of precepts describing the ethical and spiritual ways a monk or nun should live in a community under an abbot or abbess. It was the result of a collaboration of many ascetics and it soon became a rulebook for monastic life. It brought order and common sense back into religious houses that had become autocratic because of their leader's personal ideas. It breathed a fresh perspective and attitude to monasteries and helped them to flourish. Obedience and discipline now became a way of life.

1. Fear God
2. Subordinate one's will to the will of God
3. Be obedient to one's superior
4. Be patient amid hardships
5. Confess one's sins
6. Accept oneself as a worthless workman
7. Consider oneself inferior to all
8. Follow examples set by superiors
9. Do not speak until spoken to
10. Do not laugh
11. Speak simply and modestly
12. Be humble in bodily posture

Benedict's Rules with 12 ways to be a good monk.

Notable women eremites included Macrina, c330 – 379, from Caesarea, Turkey. She led a life of prayer, simple diet and household work, but was noted for looking after orphan girls. It led to others setting up hospitals for the sick and hospices for looking after weary pilgrims. During the 4th century a rudimentary service for helping the sick developed. The monasteries built an infirmary and both monks and nuns provided natural potions, good food, comfort and even primitive surgery. An Egyptian papyrus mentioned Didyme who in the 340s appeared to belong to a group of ascetic women actively making sandals and cakes to help the less fortunate. The earliest nunneries were often built not far from the earliest monasteries. The monastic life was unisexual but co-existed. Early writers described women and men being equal in their devotions.

Monasticism grew independently of the bishops and priests. This meant they had to be self-supporting and work to sustain themselves, which then became a necessary part of their devotions. It led to great tensions with criticism centred on their menial, poverty-ridden ways and recruiting loved ones from rich families to become poor monks or nuns. Nevertheless, monasteries grew everywhere, monks proved to be resilient and certain bishops continued to see them as a threat to authority.

Skellig Michael is a steep sided rocky crag extremely difficult to access, 7.2 miles (11.6km) off the coast of West Ireland. It has six beehive buildings, two oratories with wells and a cemetery. They were built in the 6th to 8th century and abandoned in the 12th century. It is a distinct example of extreme monastic isolation and stoical religion. Each building housed one monk who would spend most of his time in prayer and isolation. A little time was spent as a community which included young children according to skeletons excavated.

In the 1930s, a possible monastic site was excavated at Tintagel, Cornwall. It was said to have begun sometime between 470 and 500. Pottery sherds and glass fragments of this date were linked with Egypt and Tunisia. A cross on a sherd resembled one found near Marseille. It was said the monastery had some kind of communication with a Mediterranean equivalent. Recent re-evaluation of the site now concludes the Christian artefacts were stray imported items and a convincing monastic centre has still to be found.

Another very early monastic site in England was possibly Beckery Chapel, next to Glastonbury, Somerset and another could be St Patrick's chapel at Heysham, Lancashire. It is plausible to think many early monasteries started in the late 5th century, mostly sited around the coast of the Atlantic Isles, and archaeology might eventually show this movement over time. So far, too few sites have been uncovered to show conclusively a coastal migration.

In 577 the West Saxons led by Ceawlin, and his son Cuthwine, fought the Britons killing three kings and taking control of Gloucester, Cirencester and Bath. It opened land in the lower reaches of the River Severn to colonisation by the migrating Saxons. Moreover, it separated the South West Britons of Devon and Cornwall from those in Wales. It has even been suggested this caused the Cornish and Welsh languages to diverge. The battle was fought close to the hill fort at Hinton near Dyrham, 6 miles north of Bath. Ceawlin fought another battle in 584 against the Britons at a site probably in North-East Oxfordshire. In 592 and 593, there were further battles. All these mark the ascendency of the Saxons and the historical disappearance of people loosely labelled as Romano-British.

Conclusion

A seminal book on the Anglo-Saxons written in the 1940s stated that between the end of the Roman government in Britain and the emergence of the earliest English kingdoms stretched a long period of which the history cannot be written. This has since changed and, largely through the work of archaeologists, more is known. The importance of working out what happened in this critical time was emphasised by Michael Wood. He wrote, *In spite of their obscurity the years following the year 500 were some of the most important in the 2000 years of recorded British history. It was then that the key racial and linguistic alignments of Britain were defined.*

There was no measureable deterioration in the progress of people simply because the Romans had left, though this has been questioned. Most of the Roman settlements continued although construction was now mostly in wood. For reasons not fully understood dykes were dug across many areas throughout Britain. The economy, at least to begin with, flourished despite not having coinage. Old coins were clipped and recirculated. Ports like Tintagel, Cornwall, Hamwih (Southampton), London, Ipswich and Dommoc or Dunwich, Suffolk, continued to import and export goods from as far away as the Mediterranean. Saxon infiltration was often accommodated by resident Britons and artwork became hybridised. Tribes were led by local councils at *civitates* and comparatively little warfare, mostly minor battles, were recorded. Small invasions were reported, but this was nothing new. Christian worship appeared to flourish in many areas and heathenism more or less disappeared. A variety of languages was spoken, but this did not hinder travel and even migration. Loyalty to a chief was important and a way of holding together a small kingdom. Overall, it was a time of consolidation in which settlements with a small number of related families grew to become very large hamlets with mixed races, cultures and having mobile workers. Yet, there was some evidence of a population decline. It is a great pity we do not know more of this developing and significant culture.

The Other World – early Saxon era

There is no known document, and very little archaeology, that described the post-death belief of the early Saxons. It has been deduced the Germanic belief for the other world was a pleasant place somewhere where the dead went for healing. The word *hell* comes from the Saxon word *hel* and from this is derived healing, health and whole. Saxons did not believe in an afterlife of torment, but instead had a notion of people coming together for everlasting health. Since their heathenism was localised and probably very fluid varying from tribe to tribe, it would seem plausible that their idea of what happened at death would also have much variation. One writer has described their belief as concerned with the here-and-now, a folk-religion concentrating on survival and prosperity in the world. If this was true, it explains why their religion is invisible to anyone trying many centuries later to determine its essentials.

There is a 9th century *Life of St Gildas*, c482 – 570, which claimed the Welsh saint instructed his body to be cast adrift in an open boat and to reach its final resting place determined by the tides and God's will. This chimes with the ship burials in the early 7th century found along the east coast, including Sutton Hoo, and in northern Europe. The ship is taking the deceased on their afterlife journey. Burials in Scandinavia, northern Germany and around the Baltic were common in which the body was surrounded by a ship shape in the ground marked with stones. It is odd these stone ship-shaped burials have not been seen in Saxon Britain. This all points to the other world being reached by a voyage. It is easy to conclude coastal residents would believe the voyage was beyond the horizon where no one living knew what would be encountered.

There is a wonderful folk story concerning Brendan of Clonfert, 484 – 577, in which he goes on a great voyage after his death. With 15 other monks, he was supposed to have reached a paradise island off the coast of Africa. It is a story of reaching the Garden of Eden. Overtime, the fabled island was believed and thought to be real. The non-existent *Isles of the Blessed* and the *Isle of St Brendan* appeared on Hereford's Mappa Mundi as well as other early maps.

Archaeologists have uncovered a wide variety of graves containing objects which clearly show the journey of death. The list includes burial with whole animals, shellfish, eggs, nuts, fruit and grain for food, bottles of liquids for drinking, dogs and cats which could only have been pets, horses for riding the journey, flowers, miniature scissors, tweezers, combs and knives for keeping up appearances, beads, rings and brooches to maintain a good dress, gaming pieces to while the time away, and weaponry for the deceased to fight off the demons. It is difficult to ascribe some objects to be useful in this travel in death, for example, buckets, coins, body parts of wild animals, severed horse heads and small bags containing collections of ephemera. Knowing the entire 4th to 6th century mind at the time of grief is far too ambitious. The words *ritual* and *pagan* have been used to summarise this behaviour, but it is only a small step away from modern practices seen at gravesides and elsewhere. It is all part of the need to look after people in life and in death. No Christian text or tradition is critical of this behaviour. It is only when a multi-God entity is overlaid on the burial, Christians backed away and bishops objected.

It might not be quite the same, but Christians were also buried with grave goods. A list of gold crosses, baptismal spoons, consecrated wine, books, white stones, wooden cups or chalices, rich garments and possibly workboxes attached to belts and containing bits of cloth can be construed as more to do with a long journey carrying loved tokens than being Christ like. It could also be a preparation for a Eucharist as soon as heaven is reached.

Chapter 4

THE CELTIC CHURCH?

See in each herb and small animal, every bird and beast, and in each man and woman, the eternal Word of God.

Attributed to Ninnian

The most popular word to describe the early tribes of Ireland and West Britain is *Celtic*, but this is a slippery word to define. Celtic is a catchall title for a very varied mix of peoples who possessed certain myths and beliefs, displayed artwork in which certain tropes appear again and again (whorls, spirals and triskelion), and spoke a common root language.

Spirals and whorls at centre of Aberlemno Cross, Angus, Scotland.

Consequently, there is no pan European, or specific British folk-type, that can be identified. Many writers ascribe them to the Iron Age period and so avoid placing in any particular culture.

Between the 6th and 1st century BC, over a dozen Greek and Roman writers loosely referred to the *Keltoi*. Roman leaders saw them as barbarians, meaning they spoke the babble of babies. They were the enemy and labelling them savages was good propaganda. Furthermore, Celtic oral traditions were never recorded and so no alternative is known. All this has contributed to a poor understanding of their origins.

The artwork was once thought to be typical for Iron Age people who originally came from Hungary, Austria, and Southern Germany. They settled around the Danube and later the Loire rivers. In the 5th century BC, they migrated out of their homelands and moved westwards and eastwards. Doubt is now being expressed for these people ever reaching the Atlantic Isles. Much has been made of similarities of motifs on stonework found in Southern Germany and Ireland, but this can be explained by the ideas travelling and the people did not.

Gundestrup cauldron in Copenhagen's National Museum, dated 150BC to 1BC. The incomplete silver vessel might come from South-East Europe. It has Celtic symbols not easy to explain, which are mixed with artwork from the Near East. It typifies the difficulty of connecting Celtic artwork to particular regions and tribes.

An alternative hypothesis is based on the idea the Celtic language originated in or near the Iberian Peninsula. Stonework from Southern Portugal has inscriptions of a language that could have evolved into the Celtic language, but this would have been early in the Bronze Age, a 1700 years span that ended around 800BC. Therefore, it is now thought these people gradually migrated along the Atlantic Coast, including around the Atlantic Isles, perhaps searching for copper, silver and tin, bringing similar pottery skills and having a distinct language. Whether this migration was primarily northwards (old theory) or southwards, (a recent suggestion) has still to be worked out.

If Ireland, Western Britain, Western France, Portugal and Western Spain had this common Celtic language, it must have been some kind of isolating event which then split it into its current Celtic forms. Perhaps, the tribes had settled, were self-sufficient and had no need any more to mix with foreign tribes. There might have been some new difficulty crossing the seas. At some time, the language split into Irish and British versions. It now has three Gaelic languages, Irish, Scottish and Manx. Plus three Brittonic languages, Welsh, Cornish and Breton (Cumbric and Pictish have died out). Today speakers of each of these languages would have great difficulty following the spoken word of another. Within the languages are dialects which do not help. This, however, would not be the case two millennia ago, but it is uncertain how easy a resident of Ireland would be able to communicate with a traveller from Wales or Cornwall. A barrier of language has not been mentioned in historical narratives.

With recognition of a unique language and a distinct art, the peoples of the Western Atlantic Isles are best described as Insular Celts, but not everyone accepts this label. It follows their church is best called Insular Celtic, but again, there is disagreement with some believing churches generally did not differ from the catholic mainstream. It is a continuing debate and is unfinished. This nuance is avoided for simplicity. Dates of a common Celtic church c450 – 630 have been given. Others have said it continued to c900 with a distinct tradition and some claim it continued into Norman times, but this dating ignores the impossibility of defining such a church.

Those who entered the church would have learnt Latin and this would have been necessary for those travelling to Rome. Therefore, Latin would have been the first choice of language when educated churchmen travelled and conversed.

Ogham – an alternative language

Ogham has an alphabet of 20 standard characters written as lines usually along the edge of a stone pillar or wood. The origin of Ogham is uncertain, but a date between the 1st and 4th century is often assumed, with the later date generally preferred. Welsh ogham is thought by some to have come from Southern Ireland and the earliest dates given are early 5th century. It was much used in the 5th and 6th century and is mainly written in Old Irish or Old Welsh with a few having Pictish and Latin words. A few stones show Christian words.

Almost 400 stones are known with Ogham, of which over 300 are in Ireland, mostly concentrated in the south, about 40 occur in Wales and there are 8 in South-West England. Those in Scotland are mostly within the Pictish kingdom on the east coast north of the River Forth. They are seen in the Orkney and Shetland Isles. The majority of inscriptions consist of individual's names and they are read from the bottom to the top of a stone.

It is possible early missionaries were responsible for these inscriptions and used Ogham as their special way of communication.

Kenfig stone (left) displayed in the Margam Stones Museum. It was discovered in 1578 by a road. It has a Latin inscription and on the right edge in Ogham is the name together with two others. On the right is a drawing from a stone at St Kew, North Cornwall, with a Latin and Ogham name of 'Justi', a possible saint of the 5th century and therefore very early for Cornwall.

Probable features of a *Celtic Church*

Primarily there was no central authority. Instead, there was respect for influential monastic figures who in time became saints. Scripture and the apostles gave authority and so other theologians and their writings were minimized. Salvation could be gained by strict obedience to scriptural laws. There was an ambivalence to the Eucharist, a unique ceremony for infant baptism, a different way to calculate the date of Easter, an alternative form of monastic tonsure, a special way to consecrate a bishop and a tendency towards a kind of Pelagianism. Many valued isolation and engaged in journeys to convert others. Some were married and had families. The pain of hell was emphasised more than the joy of heaven. Icons such as showing Christ on the cross did not appear until the early 8th century. All of this varied regionally and most likely, did not constitute a separate and different church, but in many ways, it was distinctive.

The origin of the *Celtic church* is unknown and is shrouded in folklore. For example, someone called Bran, who was a captive in Rome for 7 years, brought his son Caractacus to Wales and both began the spread of Christianity as well as fighting the Romans in the 1st century. This myth is equal to the Joseph of Arimathea legend.

The Welsh Chronicles claimed a colony of Christians settled at Caer Worgan, a part of Llanwit Major in the Vale of Glamorgan, where they set up a school. Dates of 388 and 395 have been mentioned because they are within the last years of the Christian Emperor Theodosius I, 347 – 395. Theodosius I in 380 had issued decrees that effectively made orthodox Trinitarian Christianity the official state church of the Roman Empire. It is said a man called Balerus from Rome supervised the school and Padrig was the first Principal. It was reputed to have burnt down in 446 when Irish pirates raided South Wales. The setting within the reign of a Christian Emperor seems appropriate, but the story comes from a collection which is much doubted. If there is any truth in this, it is the first record of Celtic Christianity in the Atlantic Isles.

The chief teaching centres were, Clonmacnoise and Clonard in Ireland, Iona and Whithorn in Scotland, Llanwit, Llandough and Llancarfan in Wales and Padstow and Bodmin in Cornwall. The major monastic centres in France were in the south, but St Gildas de Rhuys stands out in Brittany. There is an estimate of more than 800 church centres in Ireland by the year 600. Around 30 early medieval ecclesiastical sites have been recognised in South-West Wales and an estimate of 500 for the whole of Wales has been given. It is now thought many, perhaps most, were community centres with a small church served by a priest, possibly peripatetic, and were not strictly monastic. Early local centres were

Celtic region showing the main centres for early Christian worship.

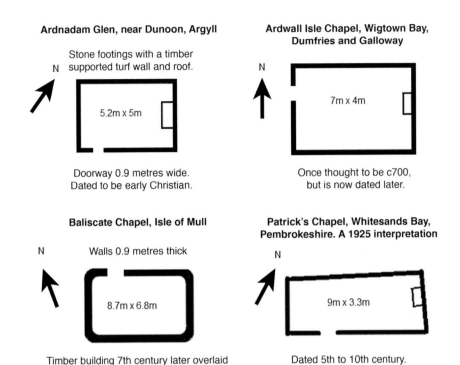

Ardnadam Glen, near Dunoon, Argyll

Stone footings with a timber
supported turf wall and roof.

5.2m x 5m

Doorway 0.9 metres wide.
Dated to be early Christian.

**Ardwall Isle Chapel, Wigtown Bay,
Dumfries and Galloway**

7m x 4m

Once thought to be c700,
but is now dated later.

Baliscate Chapel, Isle of Mull

Walls 0.9 metres thick

8.7m x 6.8m

Timber building 7th century later overlaid
with a stone building in 8th century.

**Patrick's Chapel, Whitesands Bay,
Pembrokeshire. A 1925 interpretation**

9m x 3.3m

Dated 5th to 10th century.
Much has been lost to sand dune erosion.

Four early chapels. Some think Saxon churches were built to a particular plan, often with a 2:1 scale, length to width, but early Celtic chapels grew as the community increased and changed. Also, their altar slab was always against the east wall.

probably placed close to where heathen practices once had been accepted. It is thought the mother churches of Ireland and Wales had bishops who would have owned a house and estate. Their diocese was essentially the local kingdom. This is all based on limited documentary evidence and archaeology.

Scotland

Colm Cille, known as Columba, 521 – 597, aged 42 sailed in a small wicker and animal skin currach boat from the River Foyle in Donegal to the North-East Isles of Scotland, a journey of around 100 miles. Eventually settling on the small island of Iona. This perilous sea journey has been frequently cited as the start of Christian history in the north.

Columba's possible journey (right) through the Gaelic kingdom of Dalriada.

Donegal currach (below). Possibly 4 to 5 metres long and 1.5 metres wide; though it is said it carried 12 disciples! It had a wooden lattice frame of willow and hazel rods with stretched tanned hides around it. Melted fat was poured on to the hide to give waterproofing. A sea-going boat could have a crude sail as well as paddles. It might also have been double-skinned and

Iona

Staying on the
island of Eileach
an Naoimh

20 miles, (32km)
crossing to Kintyre

Garton, Donegal,
Columba's birthplace

had seats. It is thought it took a day to sail from Ireland to Scotland and Wales, but it has been said Spain could be reached in 3 days and Iceland in 6. In 2016 a similar, but larger, currach, with 6 rowers, crossed the dangerous Pentland Strait, 10 miles (16km) in 5 hours. Success depended greatly on knowing precisely the tides and weather.

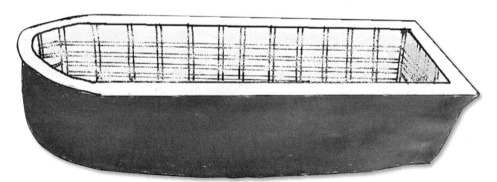

In his twenties Columba studied in two monasteries before entering the large monastic school at Clonard led by Finnian. In 544, bubonic plague reached Ireland and this caused Columba to retreat to Ulster. He later entered the monastery at Derry and planned a visit to Rome, but only got as far as Tours. Around 560, it is said he quarrelled with Finnian and this was the spur for his sea voyage to Iona in 563. There are several differing accounts of why Columba left Ireland. One writer described it as a pilgrimage and another suggested it was a forced exile, though he did return to Ireland on at least two occasions.

According to his biographer Columba had wide interests. He explained parts of the Bible to many others, was a poet, loved singing, took an interest in the law, calculated the seasons and the cycles of the moon and probably wrote original verses on spiritual issues. There is a poem, almost certainly written by another monk, which described Columba's daily routine. It tells us how Columba

Left is the monastery on the island of Inishmurray on the west coast of Ireland. In the foreground is an altar platform with round stones of which some have circles and crosses incised. Folklore says the stone is spun clockwise for a blessing and anti-clockwise for a curse. The left gable is the Church of the Fire where it is said an eternal flame was held. The turf-covered church is that of Molaise who built it c520. It is said Columba came to the island for penance and Molaise sent him off to Iona.

Above is double cell beehive monastery on Eileach an Naoimh known as the Island of the Saints in the Garvellachs on the west coast of Scotland. It is said to have been founded by Brendan in 542. He came from Tralee, County Kerry. Columba probably visited this monastery on his way to Iona. Also Cormac a monk on his travels, c560 – 580, when visiting Columba at Iona.

searched in all books to help his soul, knelt and sang the Psalms, contemplated God, worked diligently, plucked red alga called dulse from the shore rocks for eating, fished, distributed food to the poor and stayed in his hermitage. In the last days of his life Columba travelled around Iona in a cart visiting brother monks working the fields, attended Sunday Mass, had a vision of an angel, blessed the grain in the barn, climbed the hill overlooking the monastery and blessed the island, returned home to copy out a Psalm, then went to vespers before returning to sleep. He then summoned his brothers and told them to love one another and when the bell rang for midnight prayer he ran into the church which was filled with light and died. He had lived for 35 years on the island. The cult of Columba was known throughout the Celtic church and many of the saints who followed also had lives filled with the same discipline.

An excavation in front of the current church on Iona on a rocky knoll revealed in 1957 a 5 metre square foundation for a wattle and daub shelter. In 1997, it was reexcavated and found to have an internal size of 3.8m x 2.8m. A stone bench and slabs that could have been a table were found. The floor was covered in turf. This was suggested to be the home of Columba, but few believed this. Very recent radiocarbon dating of burnt hazel wood recovered from the site gave an age of 540 to 650 which now supports the idea. The carbonised remains were covered in pebbles and a post hole for a possible cross adds to the site being special. There is now the thinking the whole area, enclosed by a deep ditch, has a resemblance to the layout of the church of the Holy Sepulchre at Jerusalem. Further archaeology could prove this.

Another pupil of Finnian was Brendan of Clonfert, 484 – 577, and he too was said to have gone on long voyages, such as to the Hebrides, Orkneys, Faroes and possibly Iceland. If true, this must have been a hazardous mission.

The church at Iona trained numerous monks who later moved on to found many monasteries around Western Scotland. Aporcrosan Monastery at Applecross, Kildonam Monastery at Eigg, St Blanes at Kingarth and Lismore Monastery are examples. At least 65 early monasteries have now been identified in Scotland.

According to Bede, a son of a northern king travelled to Rome for his education and returned as Bishop Nennio, Ninnian, or Ninian.

Recent work has identified this missionary as a British monk who became Bishop Uinniau of Moville, County Donegal. He later crossed the Irish Sea and taught at settlements around the Solway Firth. He was buried at Whithorn. It is now presumed later writers

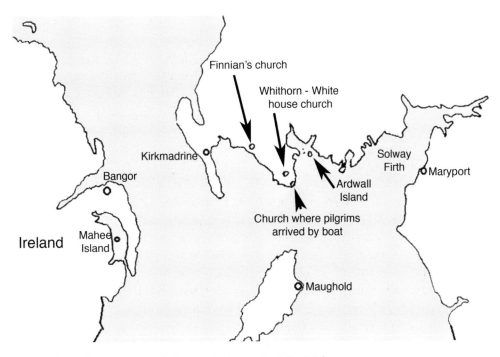

Monastic settlements around the north channel of the Irish sea.

wrongly translated his name to Finnian and Finnbar. It then got corrupted to Ninnian.

Ninnian was supposed to have set up a *White Church*, so named because it was painted with lime, much like early monastic centres in the Egyptian desert. The name Whithorn derives from this white church. His church became a centre for teaching and included initiates from Ireland including Columba. Therefore, Ninnian, c360 – 432, appeared to be a very early missionary who brought Christianity to Southern Scotland. Today there are many churches throughout Scotland dedicated to him.

Archaeologists have failed to find an early white church at Whithorn though they have found evidence of Christian practices. The current view is Whithorn Abbey was a burial ground for the secular elite and a major feasting location for possibly a royal site. The largest collection of imported glass drinking vessels has been uncovered. Attention has now turned 30 miles, 48km, north-west to Kirkmadrine, where early 6th century burial stones have been found and this might be the large *monasterium*, known as Ninnian's centre, mentioned in Irish documents. There is much uncertainty in the Ninnian story and old ideas are still being rehearsed.

Remains of a Chapel (left) on the headland of the Isle of Whithorn where pilgrims arriving by boat might have been met by a priest before travelling on to the church at Whithorn, 4 miles (6.5km) inland. It is thought to have been built c1300 and it replaced an earlier, narrower chapel. Right is the supposed foundation for the White Church at Whithorn where Ninnian had a school. It is now known to be part of a royal hall.

It would have been possible to cross the Solway Firth from Maryport, Cumbria, to Isle of Whithorn, a distance of 35 miles (56km), and enable pilgrims from North-East England to visit Ninnian's church. There was a Northumbrian Saxon presence all along this south coast of Scotland. At Ardwall Island, an 8th century stone chapel with carved stones has been found. Under the stone church was a 3m x 2m post-hole structure that might have been an early timber oratory.

South-West Scotland (Rhinns of Galloway) is 25 miles (40km) from Ireland and the monastery at Bangor set up by the monk Comgall in 552. It is a little farther from Mahee Island in Strangford Lough which had Nendrum Monastery set up by Maughold. This was a very early monastery and possibly had links with Patrick.

The life of Kentigern, also known as Mungo, has been written in various ways. One version has him coming from Fife and setting up a church on the River Clyde in Glasgow. For around 13 years, he led an austere life in a hermitage and made proselytes by his example. For some reason he had to leave and ended up at St Davids, Wales. Later he founded a church at St Asaph in North Wales before going on pilgrimage to Rome. On his return, he evangelised in the Galloway area and could have visited Finnian at Whithorn. He then moved back to Glasgow and at some point met Columba. Conval was a disciple of Kentigern and helped in the conversion of Glaswegians.

Two miles downriver tradition claims an obscure person called Constantine had set up a small wooden church next to Dumbarton Rock. He was possibly the son of a local king. A church was built at Govan and a date of 565 has been given. It became the ecclesiastical centre for Dumbarton and the Strathclyde area.

The church has been linked with Columbanus, 543 – 615, an Irish monk who was at Bangor at one time before setting off to France. It is said he visited Govan on his journey. Mirin, 565 – 620, was a disciple of Comgall of Bangor in Ireland and set up a church at Paisley which is only 6 miles (10km) west of Govan.

Dumbarton Rock on the Clyde, 73m high.

The Strathclyde area clearly had an early Christian beginning, but the story is unclear in many ways. It would have been on the pilgrimage route from Iona to Northumbria.

There is a story of a Greek monk called Regulus who brought the bones of Andrew, the first disciple, from Constantinople to St Andrews in the 4th century. It is more likely some relics were retrieved by Acca, Bishop of Hexham, and given to a church at St Andrews, c732. Unfortunately, they have been lost. The enduring connection between Andrew and Scotland was, and still is, powerfully symbolic.

Isle of Man

Maughold was tutored by Columba in Ireland and for some reason was expelled. He built a small chapel, known as a keeill, on the north-east side of the Isle of Man at Maughold. His arrival date has been given as 450. Today it is a site where 44 crosses and slabs can be seen and is a good place to see Ogham. There were also 19 keeills in Maughold and 3 can be seen in the churchyard. There have been 175 keeills recorded on the whole island, but only 35 still exist. Most are small rectangular, drystone or earthen buildings with an average size of 5m x 3m. They usually had a bordered enclosure. This simplicity seemed appropriate for an early dating, but recent analysis now supports the notion they were late 9th or early 10th century. Many were thought to have been constructed on sites where a pagan cult was held, so occupying and cleansing old beliefs. It is also the time of Viking settlement, c900, and there must be a linkage. There has also been a re-evaluation of the dates of the crosses at Maughold.

Wales

Describing the lives of the early Welsh missionaries is frustrated by the relative lack of documentary evidence. Most texts were written in the 9th century and afterwards. Romanticising their achievements has also been a problem. There is also a very sparse archaeological record with no known stone church before the 12th century. This has been attributed to poverty, but it might simply be due to a tradition of building in timber and proved to be sufficient for 600 years.

Dubricius was born at Madley, Herefordshire, c465, into a royal family of the kingdom of Ergyng, near Ross-on-Wye. He founded a monastery at Hentland and another at Moccas. He became bishop at Llandaff and later moved his seat to

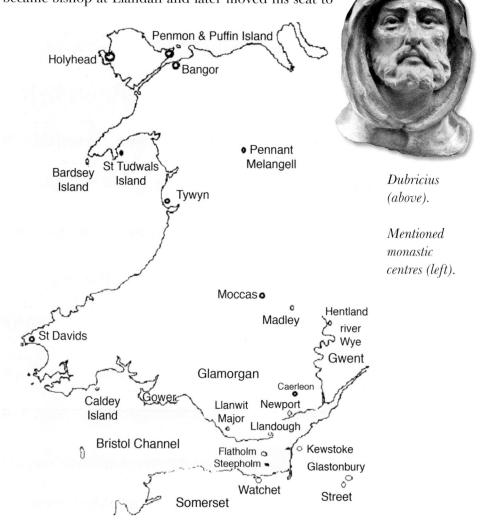

Dubricius (above).

Mentioned monastic centres (left).

Caerleon. He travelled throughout South Wales and there were indications of him praying for people in Glamorgan, Gwent and Herefordshire. Eventually he was made the Archbishop for Wales. There was also a suggestion he crossed the Bristol Channel and helped people in Somerset. He died in 550 and was buried on Bardsey Island. All this is known from a 12th century book and so has to be accepted with caution.

Dubricius taught two important Celtic saints, Samson, c484 – 565, and Teilo, c500 – 560. Samson's life was described in a 7th century account. He was a keen pupil at Llanwit Major and then went on to build churches in Wales, Cornwall, Scilly Isles, Guernsey and Brittany and was clearly a much-travelled wanderer. At one time, he was the abbot at the early monastery on Caldey Island, near Tenby.

View across Tenby to Caldey Island (arrowed) where Samson was the abbot. The current monastery was built in 1910. Today the monks run a dairy farm as well as making cheese, shortbread, chocolate, lavender perfume and various toiletries.

Teilo founded a church at Penally near Tenby, where he was born to an aristocratic family. He also set up the important centres at Llandaff and Llandeilo. In the 540s, he travelled to Brittany where he and Samson are now venerated. Teilo is the patron saint of Cardiff and has many churches dedicated in his name. He followed Dubricius in being Bishop of Llandaff and became a close companion of David.

Dubricius was also friends with a missionary called Illtud, c450 – 535, who set up a monastery at Llanwit Major and then a school, possibly the first centre of teaching in Britain. Many saints, including David, c520 – 589, passed

Teilo's reconstructed church at St Fagans National History museum in Cardiff. It originally stood on the banks of the River Llwchwr near Pontarddulais. This 12th or early 13th century church replaced a very early church.

through this school and went on to evangelise people all across South Wales. Another was the monk scribe Gildas, a native of the Strathclyde area, who wrote an account of Britain early 6th century. Gildas lived as a hermit on the island of Steepholm in the Severn estuary and was said to have later moved to Glastonbury in Somerset, but this could be spurious.

Illtud or Illtyd

There is little verified information on this saint apart from him being the founder and abbot of a monastery and school at Llanwit Major. He was a noble, perhaps of druid descent, who owned the land the monastery was built on. The date of 508 has been given. Illtud's birth and death dates are not

known, but it was reputed he was buried at a chapel near Brecon. There are stories he was a disciple of Germanus at Auxerre and a soldier knight before renouncing militancy, but both appear to be simply good stories.

Church at Llanwit Major showing the entrance into the 13th century Galilee Chapel where early standing stones are displayed. This is a short distance from the north side of the churchyard, where it is thought the early school was built.

Illtud's Great Church was said at one time to have had 1000 pupils and the list included Patrick (not mentioned by him), David at some point, possibly Gildas, Samson, Paul Aurelian, Tudwal and Baglan. It also had 100 labourers and received rent from residents. So clearly a large complex and organisation.

The school had buildings made of wattle and daub, which were rebuilt with timber. These were destroyed by the Normans who then built in stone.

Gwynno and Tyfodwg were two Llanwit monks who established churches to the north of the Vale of Glamorgan.

12th century church at Pennant Melangell. On the right is her elaborate 12th century shrine. Melangell's grave is thought to have been located and the grave slab is in the east apse. There is much decoration in the church connected to stories involving this saint.

Melangell was a 6th or 7th century Irish princess who fled to Powys and set up an isolated community of women. Her shrine is at Pennant Melangell at the head of the Tanat valley. The church is at the end of a long, narrow road, which gives it isolation and a peaceful setting. Truly a church for pilgrimage.

Curig came from Ireland and set up a church at Llangurig, Powys, in the 7th century

Gwynllyw was a warlord who renounced his fighting and turned to being a hermit. He built a church at Newport. He was the brother of Petroc and father of Cadoc c497 – 580.

Cadoc also refused to be a warrior and founded a monastery at

Llancarfan, 7 miles (11km) east of Llantwit Major, around 525. This monastery became an important teaching centre in the Vale of Glamorgan. Cadoc journeyed to Ireland and studied there for 3 years. Later he lived on Flatholm and visited Gildas on Steepholm. There is some evidence he visited both Scotland and Brittany.

Steepholm, the hermitage island for Gildas and Flatholm, the hermitage island for Cadoc. They are 2.7 miles (4km) apart and are seen here from Weston-super-Mare.

Cadoc was supposed to have been taught by Tathan, an Irish missionary who landed with 8 disciples at Caewent near Newport, but this is much doubted. On Anglesey in North Wales Cybi set up a hermitage at Holyhead, whilst Seiriol built a church at Penmon and then retired to a very small hermitage on Priestholm, now Puffin Island on the east side of Anglesey.

The earliest church excavated in Wales was at a little known location called Llanelen on the Gower, Glamorgan. Evidence of a two-chambered stone building considered to be a 12th century church overlay an earlier timber construction, 3m long, dated 6th to 8th century based on finding a glass bead. The foundations of a simple stone building were found nearby along with 31 graves and numerous domestic objects made from stone, pottery and metal. Similarly, a timber building under a 12th century church on the island of Burry Holmes, off the north-west coast of the Gower, could have been early.

David, c500 – c589, is reputed to have been born to a noble woman called Non. He was possibly related to the king of Ceredigion. He founded monastic centres in Cornwall, Brittany and South-West Wales, including at St Davids. There is a mention of him travelling to Jerusalem. His stand against Pelagianism earned him the Archbishopric and he replaced Dubricius. David lived a life of strict austerity and encouraged his monks to work hard, eat simple foods and pray much. He either founded or rededicated the Abbey at Glastonbury and it is said his relics were held there, possibly after Viking raids on St Davids Cathedral. His life and holiness has been important to many pilgrims and is held in high regard by the people of Wales, including his death day of March 1st.

Bardsey Island (above), a refuge and burial centre. It is now a site for pilgrimage.
Cadfan stone (right) with on one face, 'Tengrui beloved legal wife of
Adgan. Grief remains' and on another face 'Cun wife of Celen between
Budd and Marciau' inscribed.

Deiniol possibly studied at Llancarfan under Cadoc, then consecrated by Bishop David and set up a monastery at Bangor in North Wales around 525. He died in c584 and was buried on Bardsey Island alongside many other monks.

The church on Bardsey was set up in 516 by Cadfan who came from Brittany accompanied by a group of at least 9 monks. Cadfan also started a very early religious community at Tywyn, Gwynedd, in the 6th century. In Tywyn Church, there is the Cadfan Stone which has two short inscriptions for two women. It is accepted by many as the earliest incised Old Welsh and is dated to the 8th or 9th century.

Hywyn was a follower of Cadfan and founded a church in the 6th century at Aberdaron on the Llŷn peninsular. It was the centre from where pilgrims crossed to Bardsey Island. The current church contains two gravestones each with a name thought to be a priest in this time.

West Country

Far less is known about Saints who administered to people living in the South-West of England. It is likely missionaries came from France, Ireland and Wales. One of the earliest missionaries was Piran and it is thought he studied at a church in Ireland alongside Finnian. He then sailed to Cornwall and landed on Perran Beach. He built himself a small oratory on Penhale Sands at Perranporth, where he performed many miracles for the local people. He died in 480.

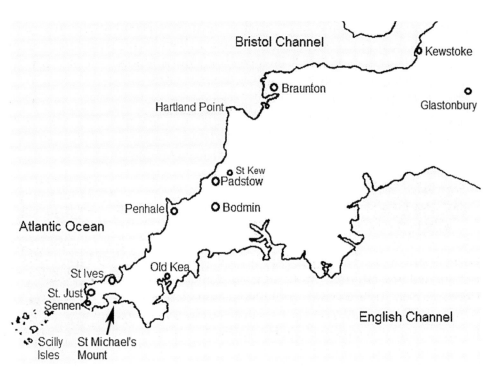

Kingdom of Dumnonia showing the important religious centres.

There is good evidence for an early monastic site at Street in Somerset. Glastonbury just to the north probably had a monastic hermitage on the Tor. Beckery Chapel, next to Glastonbury and situated within the marshes of Somerset, was recently re-excavated. Many male burials were found some time

Left is the cross in Penhale Sands where Piran's oratory is thought to have been located. Right is Glastonbury Tor with the remains of a church tower, 1323, on top.

ago, indicating a monastery, and recently bones have been found and carbon dated to the early 5th to 6th century. This makes it a very early monastic centre and it has been linked with an Irish priestess called Brigid, who is said to have visited in 488.

The life of Kew is unknown, but she was connected with Kewstoke on the Somerset coast. There is another parish called St Kew in North Cornwall and could be the location of a very early monastery.

Decuman was a sixth century monk from South Wales who landed near Watchet and sought the life of a hermit.

The clearest account of a Cornish saint is of Petroc who probably came from Wales and studied in Ireland for about 20 years. He landed in Cornwall near Trebetherick on the River Camel in 6th century and built a monastery at Padstow. There is a story he then visited Rome before building a second monastery at Bodmin with the help of three monks.

Petroc died in 564 and buried at Padstow. His relics, together with his hand bell, were kept at the church. It became a centre of pilgrimage for people in Cornwall, Devon and Somerset. Recently a pilgrim's route has been set out. There is a tale of how Petroc's bones were saved from the Vikings by being moved to a monastery near Bodmin and held in an ivory casket displayed at his shrine. A prior in 1177 stole this casket and took it to an abbey in Brittany. The monks of Bodmin demanded its immediate return. The relics were hidden again during the Reformation and only rediscovered in the 18th century. Yet again in 1994, the relics and casket were stolen by thieves and later recovered

Wheeled cross at Padstow church. The top of this cross is held to have come from Petroc's early church near Padstow. On the right is Petroc's painted ivory casket in St Petroc's church, Bodmin.

The Selus Stone stands in St Just church and bears a Latin inscription which translated is 'here lies Selus'. Selus lived in the 6th century. He was also known as Seleven, Selyf, Levan or Seloman. He is thought to have been the brother of Just.

from a field in Yorkshire. It is a story told of relics forever being returned to Bodmin.

Just is associated with St Just, the most westerly town in England at the tip of Cornwall, but nothing is known of his life.

On the coast at St Just is Cape Cornwall and on this peninsula is the chapel of St Helen. The discovery of two burial cists, one with an urn, and a barrow nearby suggests early ritual. A stone, now lost, marked with a chi-rho indicated a Christian connection. It could be connected with the uninhabited island of St Helen in the Scilly group, which also has an early church associated with a bishop saint called Lide.

There are many other saints associated with Cornwall and Devon, but nothing of certainty is known on their lives. For example, princess Ia founded an oratory in a wood and later buried at St Ives. Nectan, c468 – c510, landed at Hartland Point and lived nearby as a hermit. Brannoc, 6th century, settled in Devon at Braunton after travelling from Wales to Brittany. Kea, late 5th century,

Cape Cornwall with the supposed site of Helen's Chapel arrowed on the isthmus. The story has plausibility because of its isolation and connection with the coastal highway. The chapel is an agricultural building and the cross has been added.

St Michael's Mount which probably has had a monastery since the 8th century. Its equivalence with Mont St Michel in Normandy suggests this. It has been a centre of pilgrimage since the 11th century.

landed at Old Kea on the River Truro. A pillar outside of the church is said to be connected to the event. A Brittany woman called Asenora has been linked to Senora which gave rise to the village of Zennor. It might also be linked with Senan worshipping at Sennen.

An archaeologist claimed in the 1930s, he had found a monastery dated 470 – 500 at Tintagel. Despite much consideration which continues, there was no real evidence. There is a good possibility Tintagel was a major port through which various goods needed by monasteries were brought to Cornwall. Recent excavation suggests it was stronghold of the rulers of Dumnonia.

Brittany (originally part of Armorica)

Brittany had 7 founder saints, Tudwal, Pol, Brieuc, Malo, Padern, Corentin and Samson. Only one was a Breton, Tudwal, and he travelled to Ireland to become a monk, before becoming a hermit on St Tudwal's island off the coast of Wales.

He then founded a large monastery associated with Tréguier in Brittany. Other founder saints came from Ireland, Wales and Cornwall. There were, however, previous saints sent by early popes to preach in this part of Gaul in very early times.

In 461, Bishop Mansuetus represented Britons, presumed to be those in Brittany, at a Council in Tours.

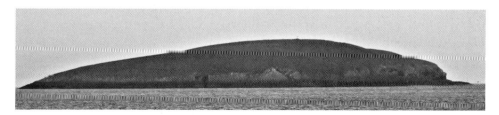

St Tudwal's island from the beach at Abersoch, on the Llŷn Peninsula.

Conclusions

The great difficulty presenting a credible pantheon of Celtic saints is many of them were described, embroidered and even fabricated with a resurgence of interest in Celtism in the 11th century. These stories were further romanticised in Victorian volumes on all the World's saints. Added to this is the problem of churches taking on a dedication to a saint in their particular area and then attempting to validate their presence. Archaeology has sometimes been unhelpful with ascribing a possible saint to the discovery of an enclosure containing perhaps unexplained foundations with hints of burial. Even the topography of small sites showing the appearance of a possible ecclesiastical centre has been given some holy attachment without questioning the history. It is very tempting to ascribe holiness to a secluded well, hillock, caves, or natural harbours. Sainthood, holiness and perfection were decided by the local community and passed on with folklore; there was no pope and sometimes no bishop to recognise and confirm when and where it happened. Consequently, many names are quoted with no supporting evidence.

Despite this historical uncertainty, it is possible to draw some conclusions from the meagre detail. The majority of saints were of noble birth and connected to royalty in their minor kingdoms. Often they were the youngest sons and daughters of the king and presumably, this was because the oldest were destined to continue the royal line. This meant there was no isolation from the warrior elite and the local community if the dynastic ties were maintained. If the kings changed, it often meant the saints had to move elsewhere. Sometimes the kings offered land for building a church and this showed their control over events. Having the king on the side of the church was usually critical to its establishment. In Ireland, there were more than 150 leaders of small kingdoms and it was impossible to organise a church without their support. Indeed, it has been suggested with good reason this is why there were fewer bishops, more saints and many monasteries and nunneries compared with Britain.

The majority of the saints travelled widely and it seemed the Irish Sea was not too difficult to cross. Their voyages were described as a dedicated attempt to reach isolated communities and convince them of the Christian message. It was part of their work for God. However, there is with some journeys a feeling of it being unplanned and fortuitous. Why Columba ends up in Iona, when there were many other small islands, or promontories, where he could have established a centre is a mystery. Why he did not travel farther to establish new churches is also inexplicable. Sometimes this is presented as the Saint sitting in a boat and allowing God to blow them to where he wanted. The facts are the boats were flimsy, many of the waters around the islands were dangerous, the coastline on the Atlantic side is rugged and impossible to access and the journey in poor weather could take days. It is therefore unsurprising many of the minor saints were said in their folklore to travel in fantastical ways, such as floating on leaves, in baskets, or even on stones.

The bishop-saints were usually recorded as visiting Rome, often with detours to the monastic centres in the south of France. Early saints usually associated themselves with Martin, the Hungarian bishop of Tours, 316 or 336 – 397. This clearly showed the pilgrims used the Roman rite of worship. There was also an emphasis on travelling to Brittany, but that might be because there are better records surviving of a saint's travels in Brittany than there are existing in Wales or Cornwall.

There is much travelling between the teaching centres. Which raises the question of which monastic school came first and what was the sequence of centres as they spawned from each other.

Pope Celestine sent Palladius from Poitiers in West Central France to be the first Bishop of Ireland in c431. He landed at Wicklow, and stayed at Clonard Monastery. However, he was quickly banished and fled to Scotland where it is said he looked after a community in North-East Scotland at Fordoun.

Patrick travelled to Ireland in c432, but this date might be a confusion with Palladius. He built his church in Armagh in 445 and it became the earliest ecclesiastical capital for Ireland. Later dates have been posited. Patrick was also associated with the church at Saul near Downpatrick, which makes sense if he crossed from the Solway Firth area. There are many variations in the early life of Patrick in Ireland, but Saul claims to be the cradle of Christianity in Ireland. If this interpretation is accepted then early Christianity, as far as we know, progressed from the Galloway area in Scotland and the Down area in Ireland, and is connected with Patrick. Monasteries were set up by saints who then fanned out across Ireland from Armagh and County Down. Some of these dates are Kildare early 5th century (Brigid – might be fabled), Raholp near Saul (Tassach) mid-5th century, Clonard c530 (Finnian), Monasterboice late 5th century (Buithe), Durrow 553 (Columba and Cormac), Clonmacnoise 544 (Ciaran), Killeedy 546 (Ita), Bangor 558 (Comgall), Clonfert 577 (Brendan) and Devenish 6th century (Molaise).

These dates compare with Maughold on Isle of Man founded in 450, Llanwit and Padstow both founded in 500 and Llancarfan later in 650.

Patrick

Little is known about this early missionary to Ireland and there is clear confusion with Palladius, who was also named in some annals as Patrick. He is now known as the Apostle of Ireland and has become tied with Irish identity. There were many signs and wonders connected with Patrick and his importance has been much discussed.

He lived in the second half of the 5th century, and dates of birth and death can only be guessed. His father was a cavalryman in the Roman army and his grandfather was a priest. Their home was mistranslated and given as *Bannavem Taberniae*, later Bannaventa, and is not locatable. Consequently, many areas from Wales to Cumbria and into Scotland have claimed his homeland. A place along Hadrian's Wall is often given and the Roman fort at Maryport is the most recent suggestion. It could have simply been a farm. When aged 16, he was captured by Irish pirates and taken to Ireland. This might have been a cover for escaping from duty in the Roman army especially if it was returning to the Continent. He was a herdsman and slave for 6 years before returning to his home. Again, this might be a cover story based on Exodus 21.2 and Jeremiah 34.14 describing the release of Hebrew slaves after 6 years.

He became a Christian and it is said visited Germanus in Auxerre to be ordained. On returning to Ireland, a good amount of his missionary work is known, but he clearly had many difficulties. Made to move from his first area, becoming embroiled in conflict with kings, being accused of taking monetary gifts, baptising royal women who then entered nunneries against the wishes of their family, being robbed and sending away some who were working with him were examples of his encounters and difficulties. Despite, all this he was credited with setting up many churches and his reputation went far and wide.

The general view is Patrick was the earliest Christian to apostatise across Ireland. There is some evidence to show this might be true for the northern half of Ireland, but might not be so for the south. Palladius landed at Wicklow, south of Dublin on the east coast, possibly two decades before Patrick arrived. Palladius soon left for Scotland, but left behind monks who began their missionary work of which the names of Auxilius, Secundinus and Iserninus are known and they began the early conversion of the Southern Irish.

Chapel of St Patrick at Heysham, Lancashire, on a headland overlooking Morecambe Bay. It is reputed to be where Patrick landed from Ireland. The chapel is probably 8th century. It was a small 8m x 3m building with the door on the north side and had plastered walls. Excavation found 10 burials in the chapel and 80 outside and it is thought a 10th century monastic site was built alongside. 6 stone pits nearby might have contained relics. A standing cross probably stood behind the east wall.

Many of the monasteries and churches were built in isolated places. It gave the monks and priests a separation from the world and therefore peace and time to worship and reflect. The phrase *monastic islands of asceticism* has been used. They were built by the coast often on promontories or ridges, on river terraces, in valleys usually steep sided, on islands, within bends of a river and invariably at a low altitude. It contrasted with the high-level hill forts and defended positions on rocky crags favoured by the military and royalty. Close by would be a well, stream or river for baptism and supply of water. Settlements would need a ditch, wall or stream along the boundary to keep out animals and this would need much cooperation to build and maintain.

Buildings were simple and mostly square or rectangular. This contrasted with the supposedly church buildings uncovered on Roman sites in which there was an apse. They varied greatly from sod and turf structures such as the early keeills on the Isle of Man, to round houses with timber posts, wattle, daub and a thatched roof, to square timber houses of larger size, to stone beehive huts as seen on the Skellig islands off the west coast of Ireland to large brick built churches often made from purloined bricks taken from nearby Roman sites (but not in Ireland). A Breton monk, who claimed to have been in the monastery at Llanwit, said the buildings were small, with church, school and dwellings separated. He added the monks worked in the fields, toiled as craftsmen, tended the sick, welcomed visitors, compiled manuscripts and carved stones.

Clearly, the larger centres were more than a monastery and school. There is much evidence they were visited by pilgrims, penitents, those who were sick, paupers, mere travellers, those escaping and seeking sanctuary, itinerant craftsmen, and even warriors. Those who stayed awhile would have to follow a quasi-monastic existence. There is much evidence the guesthouses, infirmaries, production centres, hearths and homes were outside and often at a distance from the monastery. Even nunneries in a double monastery were usually some distance from the main complex. Farms could be a considerable distance from the monastery even though they were bound to provide food render and loyalty. It would therefore be too strong to describe these monastic centres as being complete in the sense of a small hamlet. Everything was furnished for the maintenance of the monastery, but in scattered locations. The question of whether any of the craftsmen were resident has been much discussed with little agreement. One known monastery was the centre of bell making, another specialised in stone crosses and those writing gospels must have had a scriptorium and vellum making facilities, but these were a minority. There is documentary evidence of skilled monks and even bishops being involved, but it is meagre. However, there is only a little more evidence for the craftsmen travelling widely and this is often at the behest of kings and noble patrons.

The overall view of Celtic churches is they varied greatly, were positioned strategically, became self-organising, maintained communication with other centres and sometimes with Rome, were not proto-towns and did not aspire to be trading centres, tried to be on close terms with the local royal centre and yet treasured their isolation and asceticism.

The myth of an early Reformation

There is a lingering myth the Celtic churches were separate from the Roman church and the authority of the Pope. A schism readily likened to the 16th century Reformation in England. However, there is no evidence the early church repudiated the Catholic Church or were ever in opposition and gave criticism. Many of the Bishops travelled to Rome, or to other bishops in France, for their consecration and in return welcomed visiting Roman clergy.

Differences were comparatively minor, namely, determining the date of Easter, their appearance and perhaps the kind of tonsure, kinds of penance and the Celtic propensity for going into isolation. This hid the many similarities between the two churches including the general form of worship. There is every reason to believe the Celtic church, like the Roman, believed during the Eucharist the bread and wine were substantially changed and the Mass was a sacrifice. Both churches were Trinitarian. Prayer and teaching were at the centre of devotions. Monastic rules were followed. Pastoral care was a priority. The only conclusion is the churches of the Atlantic Isles were a mixture of Celtic and Roman with all kinds of variations, but all having a common core of belief. Indeed, by 632 or 633, Cumian, an Irish abbot, c591 – 661, felt able to claim there was a flourishing Roman Christian presence.

Pope Gregory believed the church in Britain needed *diversity within unity*. Bede compared those baptised in the Celtic way with those, like him, baptised in the Roman way. Together they emphasised the differences and exaggerated their significance. Underneath this was a quest to make all clergy answerable to the authority of Rome. It was a problem concerning organisation and had little to do with belief. The notion of the Celtic church being different because of a simplicity, oddity and autonomy is completely unsubstantiated.

Theories of Growth

At one time, historians thought the Celtic church grew with the founding of ecclesiastical teaching centres by bishop saints such as Patrick and Illtud. They were then taken over by abbots heading many small monasteries. It was a growth top-down and outwards. Then an alternative study concluded many small churches formed and developed according to the needs of local settlements. Alongside were bishops with their sees. Together they formed the most comprehensive pastoral organisation in Europe. Growth was bottom up. By the 7th century, a hierarchy emerged with certain churches, such as Armagh, Kildare, St Davids, Llandaff and Bangor becoming dominant. These churches could be led by a bishop or an abbot. The smaller churches fed from the larger ones by gaining resources and priests. There was much interdependence and Rome was seen as the ultimate authority.

These generalised views do not correspond with the perceived growth of the Scottish and English church. Here Christianisation was led by redeemed kings with the assistance from missionaries invited from Ireland, Italy and Frankish parts of France. It was a top down growth. The whim or belief of the king was enforced on their kingdom and it lapsed if the king changed. Consequently, at first, its distribution was scattered and there was no national orthodoxy. It was a nucleated evangelism. However, by the end of the 7th century and with many papal missions the church came together and answered to Rome.

Almost certainly, these theories will be tested as more information accrues.

The Other World in the age of saints

Christians in Italy, France, Spain and the Western Isles became attached to their spiritual patrons labelled saints or martyrs and it is the saints who set the theology. They interceded with God and therefore, the view of the world to come was the one given at the saint's shrine. This was an oral tradition and this might be the reason why so few texts survive. Here are how 4 saints saw the other world.

It is generally agreed the Latin hymn *Altus Prosator* has the best chance of being written by Columba. It concerned creation, but ended with its decline into a lurid hell. Even the stars will fall to earth in this cataclysmic judgement. It showed God to be a stern judge and all should be frightened. It also showed the apocalyptic view of Columba, on how everyone will be judged after death. A wise man therefore meditated on the end of his life. It is said the hymn was shown to Pope Gregory and he agreed with its tough tone.

There was a legendary story of Patrick eager to show his converts their options after death by taking them to a deep cave at Lough Derg, County Donegal. By looking into the black chasm his people would know the difference between the torments of hell and the joys of heaven. It was the natural face of Hades. It is now called the *purgatory pit* and has been a site of pilgrimage from at least the 12th century and, perhaps, even earlier since a monastery was nearby from the 5th century. It is likely this teaching device, a hellhole, was repeated at other locations, but such sites are little known in Britain. Gateways to hell are located around the world and clearly appeared in many early cultures.

Ciaran of Clonmacnoise, c516 – c549, was reputed to have said, *terrible is the way of dying. For I do not know what commandment of God I may have transgressed. And even David, son of Jesse, and Paul the Apostle dreaded this day. Also, consider the transitory world and Judgment Day, and what you must do to avoid the pains of hell and to obtain the rewards of heaven.*

An 11th century account of the Life of St David described how on his death his body, was carried in the arms of holy brethren and accompanied by a great throng. He was honourably committed to the earth and buried in his own monastery. His soul without any limit of passing time, so does not go into purgatory, was crowned forever and ever.

Three accounts are apocalyptic and carry a warning. The fourth showed the saint was so holy in life there was no need to be warned. All carry an underlying message of living a Christ-like life.

Chapter 5

THE SAXON CHURCH 577 – 700

All agreed they shall call the Saxons to their aid. This was ordained by the will of God so that evil might fall upon these miscreants.

Bede justifying Saxon immigration to help repel *shameless Irish robbers and Pictish plunderers*.

The Ecclesiastical history of the English People, 731

By 577, it looked as if the Saxons had taken over England. There were very few old British (common Brittonic) words being used. Place names everywhere, except in Cornwall, were virtually all derived Germanic (Old English). Artwork too contained decoration traceable to Germany and France. A total takeover, however, was probably an illusion. Indigenous Britons could have simply taken on the language

By 600, the land east of the dark lines was mostly occupied by Saxons and some Britons. Land to the west was occupied by Britons and Celts. Borders were often changing and kingdoms were sometimes short lived. It was a dynamic geography. Borders were only nominal.

and art of the Saxons because it had advantages of some kind. Doing so did not devalue their wider culture; they were adapting to new circumstances.

Who were the Saxons?

A reference in the 2nd century described a Saxon tribe on the North-West coast of Germany. During the 5th century, they had an allegiance with the neighbouring tribes of Angles and Frisians. This was a pact to stay together and thus resist any advances from their southern enemies the Franks.

Roman soldiers with Germanic names are known and it would be in keeping to expect Saxon mercenaries were recruited into the Roman Legions occupying Britain. Saxon farmers were probably present on the south and east coast of England in late Roman times. The earliest Saxon burials, so far found, date to the early part of the 5th century.

In 463, Saxons attacked the French coast and most likely did the same to Southern England. Some of these invaders might have colonised the south coast after the expansion of the Frankish territory in the 5th century in Northern and Central France. It was known there were Saxon enclaves in the Pa-de-Calais and Bayeux regions of France.

There is another theory centred on the Mongolian Huns entering Eastern Europe in the 4th and 5th centuries and causing a wholescale movement of

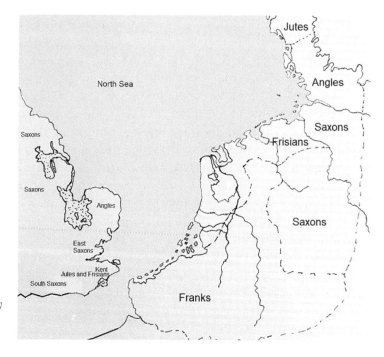

Location of Germanic tribes at the end of the 5th century. Much of this comes from later interpretations and regions are only approximations.

people westwards across Europe. It helps to explain the migration of the Goths (Ostrogoths), but not so much as the northern Saxons. Another reason, often stated, is the Saxons simply took over in Europe where Romans left. This can be restated as they entered a new country in which the neighbours were friendly once the occupying force had gone. They took the opportunity of entering new lands sustainable in food, mineral resources and good locations to make defended settlements. They might also have been escaping from a plague epidemic in Europe. The likelihood is there were multiple reasons for invasion.

By the 7th century, it has been estimated 200,000 Saxons, Angles, Jutes, Frisians and probably other Germanic people had migrated to Britain, but this is only a good guess. They were united by their Old English language, albeit with dialects for each of the kingdoms, fighting with a seax knife (*Saxon* is supposed to come from the word seax), avoiding kingship and instead being ruled by a group of older men who selected which one would lead into a battle, worshipping heathen spirits and venerating successful fighters from the past. Polygyny and concubinage were standard. They cremated their dead, but then gradually changed to inhumation with the graves often containing goods, usually weapons for men and combs and jewellery for woman. They set up tribal kingdoms which gradually coalesced into larger kingdoms. This happened, it is thought, more by pacts, marriage and negotiation during harsh times, than by intimidation and force.

It is stated very often they resisted Christianity, but this is highly speculative. The current understanding is Charlemagne, leader of the Franks, gradually killed or converted pagan Saxons over 32 years, 772 – 804, in the 18 battles of the so-called *Saxon Wars*. Eventually he controlled France, Belgium, Luxembourg, The Netherlands and western Germany and insisted all citizens should be baptised and become Christian. Often it was a conversion from Arian to Nicene Christianity. Charlemagne followed on from Constantine and Clovis. When crowned by the pope in 800 Charlemagne's title was *the most serene Augustus, crowned by God, great and pacific Emperor, governing the Roman Empire*. He clearly saw himself as emulating Constantine and Pope Leo III saw this as a recognition for the religious wars. However, exaggerating paganism in the enemy could have been a pretext to conquering the countries. Furthermore, there were accounts of Charlemagne committing atrocity in his holy quest. Many Moors, Muslims, Lombards and Saxons were killed; the number was probably exaggerated for effect. The wars were full of inconsistencies. Alcuin from the York area became Charlemagne's scribe and rewrote this history by giving it a partisan gloss. From this, it is presumed the Saxons arriving in Britain early in the 5th century to the 7th century were as heathen as their European folk were made out to be by Charlemagne.

So were the Saxons heathenistic when they arrived in Britain in the 5th and 6th centuries? There were tribes in Eastern Germany who believed in an Arian Christianity and how far it extended westwards cannot be determined. It is possible the later migrants in the 6th century to Britain were aware of, or followed this Christianity. Saxons emigrating from south of the River Rhine (Frisians) would have been exposed to Arian Christianity in late Roman times. These Frisians had trading routes to their northern neighbours. Saxons arriving from Gaul in the early 6th century could have been Nicene Christians. Burials along a west-east axis have been found in southern and eastern England and dated to the 5th century and if this is a signature for Christian belief it means these people were converted either immediately before their immigration or soon afterwards. If Sutton Hoo was the burial ground for the Wuffingas dynasty, including King Raedwald, c599 – c625 and they had a Swedish ancestry, then the Christian pieces in the hoard suggest these northern European immigrants at the very least knew about Christianity by the end of the 6th century and into the early 7th. The question, were the Saxons nascent Christians around the time of immigration is still without a definite answer, but if archaeology uncovers more early Saxon Christian graves, a view towards having a Christian awareness will emerge. The change from heathenism to Christian for Saxons might well have been a protracted transitional period.

It is now thought that by the end of the 6th century, monasteries were present over much of Britain and a few bishops were present in the largest settlements. Much had happened in the 5th and 6th centuries and Christianity had a foothold in Britain, but nothing can be said with any certainty as to its extent, or importance or organisation. Except it was not united in the way the papacy wanted. The pope wanted unity and to take control.

The consolidation of Christianity in Saxon Britain in the 7th century can be split into 7 historical events. This is a contrived convenience, but it follows the documentary evidence.

1. The Gregorian Mission

Pope Gregory, 590 – 604, was born into a wealthy Rome family. He became a monk at a monastery on land owned by his family and constructed by converting a villa c580. He even financed much of the work of the monastery. He became the pope in Rome at a low time with much more happening with the pope in Constantinople. After successfully regaining papal control over Spain and France, he turned to do the same for Britain. He would have been aware of the Celtic church spreading eastwards across Britain. He planned for London and York to have bishops who could then control 24 sees. It has correspondence with the *civitas* centres of Roman occupation.

Pope Gregory. The statue at Lichfield has a dove whispering into Gregory's ear and giving wise counsel. He heard whispers about such matters as pagan practices.

He also wanted to increase worship using the orthodox Roman rite and consolidate papal authority. With much upheaval in the world, he genuinely thought the Last Days were not far away. Therefore, he saw it as his responsibility to spread Christianity and prepare people for the imminent end of days. This included the people of the little known North-West Europe. In time, most of these aspirations did not turn out in the way he would have wanted.

In 595, the Gregorian Mission set out for England led by Augustine, who had been the prior in Gregory's Monastery. Before arrival he was consecrated *Bishop of the English* and this might have been at Arles in Southern France. After many setbacks on the journey, Augustine, together with 30 to 40 missionaries, finally arrived in the spring of 597 on the Isle of Thanet,

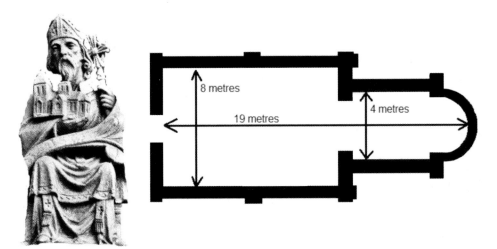

Bishop Augustine (left) holding the church of St Martins, at Canterbury, which is the earliest church still in use. Possible plan of St Martins (right), various layouts have been suggested. It was rebuilt from a dilapidated Roman building, still visible in the chancel brickwork. It is very likely French stoneworkers were used. Augustine was buried, c613, in his nearby monastery.

the most easterly point of Kent. Now thought to be close to where the Romans arrived. The mission was received by the Kent King Aethelberht and his French Christian wife, Bertha. They were welcomed and allowed to move on to Canterbury. A monastery was set up and for a time people in Kent accepted the Romanising mission.

Augustine had at least two conclaves with church leaders. The first was at a location, later called *Augustine's Oak*, placed in the kingdom of Hwicce, south-east of the River Severn (Gloucestershire?). It has also been sited on the border of Kent. The second has been labelled the Synod of Chester, but there is no evidence it occurred in that town. A date of 601 has been derived. It mentioned 7 bishops together with learned men from the monastery at Bangor-on-Dee, Flintshire. If these bishops were Celtic and from Wales, it would have included men from St Asaphs in Denbighshire, St Davids in Pembrokeshire, Bangor in Gwynedd, Llandaff in Cardiff, and someone from the St Teilo group of churches around Carmarthenshire. The meeting ended without agreement and probably was due to the bishops unable to yield in authority to Canterbury, Kent and the king. It is interesting, if these meetings happened, there was an imperative for the Mission to have to talk separately with the clergy of Kent and the Welsh church.

In 601, a second Mission of 4 monks was sent and led by Mellitus. He brought with him books, vestments, sacred vessels and the relics of saints to aid conversion. In 604, he became the first Bishop of London and converted the East Saxon King Saberht who reigned over Essex c604 – 616. It is thought the Christian grave unearthed at Prittlewell and containing gold foil crosses was that of Saberht. After the king's death, Mellitus left for France. He returned in 617 and became the third Archbishop of Canterbury until his death in 624. He is credited with furthering Christianity in Kent despite changes in the royal family bringing opposition and fear.

In 614, members of the Gregorian Mission attended a Council in Paris as part of Aethelberht's attempt at reconciliation with the new French Frank's dynasty. This showed how the Canterbury church was interconnected with the French leaders and churchmen. After the Kentish king died in 616, there was a palace revolt against the church and the new royals renounced their faith. The see of London was abandoned, but Laurence, who succeeded Augustine, stayed as the Bishop in Canterbury.

The story of 597 has been told many times giving the impression this was the start of Christian history in the south of England, which gradually moved northwards. The Roman way of worship had power and meaning and was adopted by the church as it moved to Rochester, London and St Albans, as well as along the south coast. Unfortunately, the Mission did not recognise the already present diverse church in the country, the great reluctance to accept the authority of Rome through Canterbury and its overlords and, perhaps, the small ways the local churches diverged from orthodoxy. The death in 653 of the last of the missionaries arriving with Augustine marked also a crisis of succession at Canterbury and shows how little had been achieved. The National significance of the Mission has been hyped, but it did herald a concerted endeavour to bring the British churches in line with the Roman church and it established Canterbury as the principal mother church.

2. The York baptisms

Paulinus, first Bishop of York.

Aethelberht, King of Kent, had a daughter, Aethelburg, who was a Christian. She married King Edwin of Northumbria and on Easter Day in 626, their daughter was baptised at York. It was conducted by Paulinus who had arrived in the second Gregorian mission and went on to be the first Bishop of Northumbria. Then the pope sent numerous gifts to King Edwin urging him to be also saved from his heathen ways. On Easter Day, 627, Paulinus baptised Edwin and 11 of his nobles in a small timber church built for the occasion, but where it was sited is unknown. York was the obvious location because of its association with Constantine.

Some now doubt Edwin's conversion as being the catalyst for the growth of Christianity in the North because Edwin died in battle 5 years later and Paulinus with the royal family then fled back to Kent. Paulinus died at Rochester in 644. However, James the deacon stayed and continued the evangelising of Northumbria and there is no doubt the church at York grew in importance. A stone church was built, c640, and from then on, numerous members of the Northumbrian kingdom were again being baptised.

Paulinus carried out a mass campaign of baptisms in York in 627, in the River Swale at Catterick and for 36 days in the River Glen near Yeavering, Northumbria. Archaeological excavation at Yeavering has revealed a kind of shallow, tiered auditorium for this mass baptism and preaching. Excavators thought they had also uncovered a timbered pagan temple refurbished as a Christian church, but a pit close by contained many oxen skulls and the thinking now is it was a

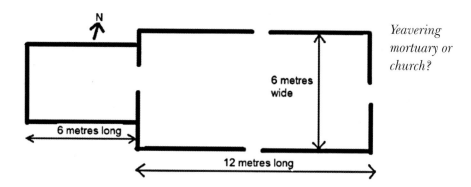

Yeavering mortuary or church?

mortuary for animals. Again, it shows the great difficulty for ascribing Christian use to the foundations of buildings.

There is an account of Paulinus baptising at Littleborough and Southwell, Nottinghamshire, on the River Trent and at Lincoln. If true, it is the first mention of Christian settlements in the Midlands.

In 735, the first Archbishop of York was installed (Paulinus might have been made Archbishop, after he left York) and the monastery became the mother church for the north. The location of this first stone church is unknown, but it has been suggested to have been placed a little distance to the north of the current Minster. A church was burnt down in 741; it is not known whether this was the monastery or another missionary church. In 780, a new large church was built.

3. Dommoc

Bede said the first *bretwalda* (overlord of other Saxon kingdoms) was King Raedwald, ruling c595 – 623. Somehow, he brought Suffolk and Norfolk together and in 617 defeated the Northumbrians. He also held Kent and Lindsey, the name for Lincolnshire. The generally accepted view is it is his burial chamber at Sutton Hoo, containing an eclectic mix of pagan and Christian artefacts found in 1939, held in a 24 metres long ship within a mound. After his death around 625, he was succeeded by his eldest pagan son. His second son, Sigeberht, went to France, became a Christian and then returned in c630. He became the first Saxon king to have been baptised before enthronement as a king. The Archbishop of Canterbury picked out a French bishop called Felix to help him evangelise the people of East Angle.

Felix located his monastery at Dommoc or Dumnoc, but the precise site is unknown and it is even possible it never existed. Some believe it was Dunwich, which has since been submerged by coastal erosion. A better suggestion was the

Roman fort called Walton Castle, now also lost to the sea. This fort lies around half a mile out to sea and on occasions can be seen from Old Felixstowe beach with very low tides. Crucially it lay at the mouth of the River Deben and it was by this river the Sutton Hoo royal burial took place. Whatever, was built for Felix it was close to a school where Bede says they *learnt letters*. This teaching would have been modelled on schools in France. Felix stayed for 17 years and his successor was there for another 5. Some historians downplay the role of Augustine and Paulinus in the conversion of England and instead believe more was achieved by missionaries from France and Ireland, especially in East Anglia. In 637, Sigeberht stepped down after a 5 years reign, and entered a monastery called Cnobheresburg, possibly later changed to Burgh Castle, near Great Yarmouth, Norfolk. This monastery had been founded by the Irish monk, Fursey or Fursa c597 – 650, in 633.

4. Birinus Mission

Pope Honorius I sent Bishop Birinus of Milan to Britain to continue the conversion of the Saxons. He landed at Hamwih, now Southampton, in 634. He persuaded the pagan king of the West Saxons, Cynegils, to allow him to preach in his kingdom, c640. This kingdom extended to the upper Thames area, covering parts of Wiltshire, Somerset, Gloucestershire and Oxfordshire. King Cynegils wanted an alliance with King Oswald of Northumbria who was a Christian. The alliance was agreed on condition Cynegils was baptised and this occurred at Dorchester with Birinus officiating. Cynegils' daughter later on married Oswald. The two kings granted land to Birinus in Dorchester for the establishment of his episcopal see and cathedral church. He became the first Bishop of the West Saxons. He died c650 and buried at Dorchester. His sainted relics were later, c690, moved to Winchester where pilgrimage began.

5. Lindisfarne Priory

King Edwin of Northumbria was killed in a battle with a Welsh army from Gwynedd in c633. His nephew, a young man aged around 13 called Oswald, fled to Iona and became a Christian. He returned to his kingdom 17 years later with an army containing warriors from Scotland and exacted revenge on a Welsh army at Deniseburn, near Hexham. Before the battle, he had a vision of Columba promising to be with him. This resulted in him planting a cross on the battlefield, which then became known as Heavenfield. From this, it is often assumed the kingdom of Northumbria became Christian. However, burials aligned west-east in long cists found in the Lothians, then the northern part of Northumbria, around 600 suggest this region was already following some kind of Christianity. Aberlady

Supposed battle site of Heavenfield with a church amongst the trees. King Oswald, 602 – 642, holding his cross and a bird. The bird occurs in considerable folklore attached to this Christian king.

with its timber hall probably had a Christian community predating Lindisfarne. Stone cross fragments have been found. However, Oswald increased this Christian presence.

Subsequent battle successes gave Oswald supremacy over a large part of England. He made Aidan the first Bishop of Lindisfarne, c634. Aidan was an Irish monk sent to Iona and met Oswald when he was there as a young man. After Aidan died in 651, he was succeeded as Bishop of Lindisfarne by Finan, another Irish monk from Iona. He built an oak timber church with a roof made of reeds.

The great importance of Lindisfarne was it became a centre of learning headed by Aidan and then Finan, protected by Oswald and his brother Oswiu, and from this teaching centre many monks headed south to evangelise other parts of England. This has been called the *Monastic Diaspora.*

Aidan teaching his disciples with the young King Oswald (top left) interpreting and joining in.

An early church

An 8th century source suggested Lindisfarne had two churches, guesthouse, dormitory and watchtower. In 2016, very large sandstone blocks giving a 2.5m wide wall enclosing closely packed cobbles in a square 8m wide were discovered that appeared to be the foundation of a watchtower. It might have held a ceremonial cross. It was on a narrow, rocky ridge known as The Heugh and overlooking the bay towards Bamburgh Castle. In 2017, around 50 metres east of this site and still on The Heugh, the foundations of two joined buildings were excavated. Their size, location and orientation suggested an early church. The white sandstone was crudely shaped with a pick and had no mortar which points to an early date. It would have needed a large group of labourers to carry the sandstone blocks from across the island. Much stone had been robbed for probable use in a later church. The larger room could be a nave and the smaller one a chancel. Perhaps, the upper structure was timber and reeds. Some stone appeared to have been crudely fashioned to give slit windows suggesting this was a stone church, thus it could be Cuthbert's church. Whether it was once the smaller timber church of St Mary and later the second stone church of St Peter is uncertain, but it is a remarkable discovery and more awaits to be found on this site.

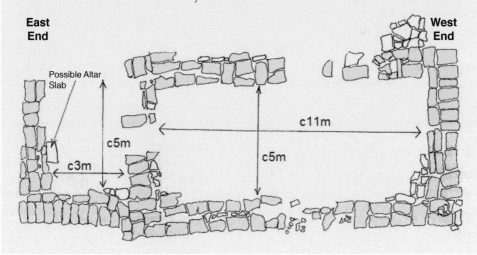

6. Oswiu's Mission, c642 – 671

In 653 Cyneburh, the daughter of Penda, the pagan king of Mercia, married the son of the Northumbrian Christian King Oswiu. Perhaps, at the same time, Peada, the son of Penda agreed to marry Oswiu's Christian daughter. It was all

King Oswiu, Peada holding his cross showing conversion. Bishop Finan and the Irish monk Diuma after being made a bishop.

part of a dynastic contract to meld the two large kingdoms of Northumbria and Mercia. Maybe part of this contract was Peada should first be baptised. It seemed the pagan Penda saw the advantages of linking with his northern enemy as being more important than offspring nominally becoming Christian. The marriage took place at a location called *Ad murum* which is thought to be at Walbottle in Newcastle upon Tyne and not far from Hadrian's Wall. It was conducted by Bishop Finan of Lindisfarne and four monks attended; Diuma, Adda, Betti and Cedd all trained at Lindisfarne.

Afterwards Peada became the vassal king of Middle Anglia, that is, south-east of Mercia and including Leicestershire, Buckinghamshire and Bedfordshire. His residence could have been at Repton in Staffordshire, or possibly at Castor or Medeshamstede in Cambridgeshire. Castor had a high status Roman building in 250 and local finds with chi-rho symbols indicate it had Christians in the 4th century. In 664, Cyneburh, Penda's daughter, with the help of her younger brother, Wulfhere, set up a monastery at Castor and this might have become the main religious house for Middle Angle. Alternatively, Castor could have been a nunnery and 4 miles east was its prime monastery at Medeshamstede, Peterborough.

Of the 4 bishops attending the (double?) wedding, Diuma in 656, became the first Bishop of the people of Mercia, (Midlands and more). Nothing is known about Adda's location, though his brother was in a monastery near Durham. Betti is thought to have founded the church at Wirksworth, Derbyshire; so presumably not in Mercia.

Cedd, c620 – 664, was soon recalled by King Oswiu and sent to support the mission in the kingdom of East Angle. He does not appear to have a defined see, but travelled widely throughout East Anglia. It is thought he built churches at Tilbury, Prittlewell and possible Mersea. One chapel he founded was on the Roman shore site at Bradwell-on-Sea, Essex. To begin with, this first church was possibly wooden. Later a monastery was built from stone taken from the adjacent Roman site and this has been dated c654, though a later date is far more likely. No further record exists and it was not until the 15th century when it was rediscovered. Today the nave remains, though its apse and side chambers have gone.

Betti at Wirksworth.

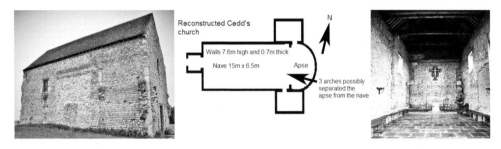

Cedd's Chapel of St Peter on the Wall, Essex. It was built on the edge of a Roman shore site south of the River Blackwater, probably by workers from the Continent. It is on a Roman road and this strong foundation together with unique buttresses might be the reason it has lasted. The roof might have been shingles purloined from the Roman site. Interior shows a simplicity. The cross with crutches at the end of each arm resembles crosses in the Lindisfarne and St Chad's Gospel. It is claimed to be the oldest church in England still providing very occasional services.

Cedd, aided by his brother Cynebil, was also given land at Lastingham, Yorkshire, to build a monastery and its original crypt could be the one under the current church.

There were many other monastic centres set up with Oswiu's patronage. For example, Heiu was a nun at Lindisfarne with Aidan and later founded Heretu Abbey, Hartlepool around 640. Excavation shows a remarkable concentric layout reminiscent of many Irish and some Pictish monasteries. The Abbey was at the centre and around in bounded circles were the dwellings, workhouses, mortuary area, cemeteries for the clergy with the nuns separated and a burial area for those with lower status. The nuns and monks dwellings were small, being on average a

Crypt below Lastingham church. The Horse Stone at Lastingham is thought to be part of a seat used by a bishop. Horse motifs also appear elsewhere in Northumbrian iconography. If this was the original site then Cedd was buried to the right of the altar in 664, though it would have been a wooden church.

mere 4.1m x 2.3m. They were strongly built with timbers and some had interior plastering and decorative stonework. Heiu trained Hilda, 614 – 680, who then took over in 649. King Oswiu sent his one years old daughter to stay with Hilda who was a princess in the royal family. In c658, Hilda founded Streoneshalh, later called Whitby Abbey. It became a large nunnery with a community of men attached. Unfortunately, its complex layout has not been properly determined, but many stray finds show the inhabitants lived in comparatively fine style.

Escomb Saxon church, Durham, was built c670 – 690 (some date it 8th century) and therefore was after Oswiu, but it showed his legacy with the

Escomb, probably the best Saxon church surviving. Built from stone taken from the nearby Roman Fort at Binchester. The south porch was added on and the original door was probably at the west end. The nave to chancel screen is an arch. It is notable for having a long nave that is narrow and tall. The cornerstones are large and might be a reason it has lasted for so long.

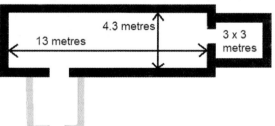

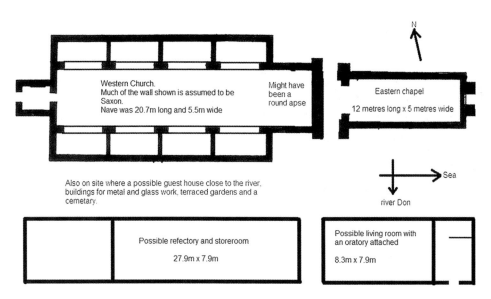

Layout of Jarrow Monastery interpreted from an archaeological excavation.

expansion of the churches in the north of England. Being small suggested it could have been a private church built by a local landowner.

Benedict Biscop, c628 – 690, was a thegn with Oswiu's army, but stopped when aged 25. He then made pilgrimages for almost 20 years, including 5 visits to Rome. He accompanied Oswiu's son on his second pilgrimage. Between 665 and 667, he stayed at a French island monastery and became a monk. He accompanied Theodore of Canterbury on his returning third trip. In 674, the Northumbrian king gave him land at Monkwearmouth and he built a church called St Peter. There is no above ground stonework surviving and the below ground stone is very fragmentary. Seven years later he was given more land at Jarrow, 40 miles (64km) from Lindisfarne, and he with monks from Monkwearmouth started to build a sister church in 682 and had it finished within 3 years. This church survived and its associated buildings have been thoroughly excavated.

The Monkwearmouth and Jarrow monasteries were built to be one church centre, yet are 7 miles (11km) apart and had marshy ground in-between with a long distance path connecting. By 710, there were 600 monks and was very much a large foundation. They became a centre for priestly instruction and a scriptorium for writing illuminated Bibles. It was the monastery where Bede wrote his historical accounts. The monasteries at Tynemouth and South Shields were earlier, but much less is known about the work undertaken at these sites.

Eastern Chapel at Jarrow, probably named St Mary. Its original length was the length of the current modern roof. The chapel is now attached to the western church with a tower in-between. The large window is 14th century, but the small windows (one is left of the drainpipe) are original. It is not buttressed because the original corner stones on the right end were laid in a way to give strength. On the right is a dedication stone above the entrance to Jarrow church. It reads the church was dedicated on 23 April AD 685. It is the oldest church dedication stone in England.

Cuthbert's, c634 – 687, early life is little known and many stories have been woven. It is possible he met King Oswiu at Lindisfarne and there has even been a suggestion he fought for him. However, he became a monk at Melrose Monastery, Roxburghshire, in 651, but shortly after moved with its abbot Eata to help found a monastery at Ripon, Yorkshire. He then moved back to Melrose in 661 to become its prior. In c663 he became the prior at Lindisfarne given the task of persuading the monks to change from their Celtic rite of worship to one used by the Roman church. Cuthbert had changed his form of devotion and he was now persuading others to do the same. Indeed, he followed the Roman rite with the strong conviction this was the way to bring unity to the church.

For reasons not very clear, though it is often romanticised, he withdrew to live a hermitical life for over 10 years on Inner Farne Island. This seems to be more a feature of Celtic priests

Cuthbert with Oswald's head.

View from Holy Island or Lindisfarne from the Heugh Ridge where Cuthbert's church probably stood. It was written that on Inner Farne, Cuthbert's mind might be wholly on heavenly things.

than Roman ones, so perhaps his predilection had not altered. Somehow, his standing grew and he was chosen by Archbishop Theodore and the Northumbrian king to be the Bishop of Hexham. For reasons unrecorded, he quickly exchanged his see with Eata for that of Lindisfarne in 685. Sensing his life was coming to an end he withdrew again to his beloved Inner Farne Island, where he died on 20 March 687. Today his relics are kept at Durham Cathedral, alongside the severed head of King Oswald and not too far from the shrine of Bede. It is a long established site for pilgrimage.

Wilfred 633 – 709 was very different. Coming from a noble Northumbrian family, he must have been known to King Oswiu. Aged 14 he enjoyed being trained as a priest at Lindisfarne. In 653, he travelled to Rome, the first of three visits, and then spent time at Lyons in France. In 664, he became bishop of Northumbria, probably at York, but then again went on a pilgrimage to Rome. So Oswiu gave the see to Chad from Lindisfarne around 666. Wilfrid meanwhile obtained strong Papal support and on his return organised the building of many churches and monasteries. They were based on the Roman basilica. His grand church at Hexham

The noble Wilfred with his papal privilege confirming his possession of Hexham and Ripon. One foot is on someone's head; his career was turbulent and on 3 occasions, he was deprived of his see. If it is Oswald's head, it is a cult that Wilfred encouraged.

had three levels and became a model to copy. He insisted on worship following a Catholic rite. He is thought to be the first English bishop to reject Celtic ways of worship and replace it entirely with a Roman liturgy.

During his ministry, Wilfrid raised much funding, acquired much land and obtained support from several kings, including King Wulfhere of Mercia. He also gained riches from various queens for his churches; he encouraged women to enter the church. He often travelled with as many as 100 followers and critics charged him with dressing his household in clothing fit for royalty. It is thought he spent 26 years away from his northern homeland. His church at Hexham was embellished with many sculptures and paintings; visitors considered it equal to any church in Rome. He commissioned altar cloths made with gold thread, obtained books with the expensive purple dye and consecrated churches with feasting that lasted days. It is known he commissioned *a casing of purest gold set with most precious gems* for a Gospel book which he then presented to Ripon.

Wilfrid, probably based at Ripon, spent much time helping Mercia and being close to Wulfhere's court and later Aethelred's. It is thought he later became bishop of Leicester and was clearly associated with many Mercian monasteries, 6 have been identified between 692 and 703, and this association continued right up to his death. He was buried at Ripon.

Wilfrid was outstandingly ostentatious, the antithesis of Cuthbert. Aged 74 and close to death he ordered his treasurer to open the church treasury, spread out the gold, silver and precious jewels and distribute them to his abbeys and monasteries so that they might purchase friendship from kings and other bishops. He gave to the rich. Bede wrote much about Wilfrid knowing he could not be ignored, but he did not enthuse.

Left is Wilfrid's Hexham crypt built using purloined Roman stone. Middle is Wilfrid's stone chair at Hexham. Right is Wilfrid's crypt at Ripon.

Stephen of Ripon wrote Wilfrid's biography and gave him the highest praise. Wilfrid was very important in 7th century church and state history and many events were orchestrated by him. He was a fixer and often in the centre of disagreements.

Whitby Synod

King Oswiu wanted some uniformity between the Celtic rite and Roman rite of worship and called a Synod at Whitby in 663 or 664. There is some uncertainty of both this date and whether it was held at Whitby. The Celtic side was led by Colman, the third bishop-abbot of Lindisfarne. Supporting him was Cedd, bishop of the East Angles and Abbess Hilda of Whitby. The Roman side was represented by the visiting French Bishop of the West

Tonsures; Roman on the left, Celtic to the right.

Saxons, Agilbert. He asked Wilfrid, then abbot at Ripon, to speak on his behalf since he could not speak in the vernacular. In support was Romanus, chaplain to the queen, James the deacon from York, and Agatho, a priest present with Agilbert. Oswiu's son was also a supporter of Roman customs and he might have been the instigator of the Synod.

The outcome was a victory for the royal party and it meant the Roman way for calculating Easter Day was to be followed, monks and especially their tonsure were to Romanise, kinds of penance were fixed and ideas for going into eremitical isolation were established.

The Northumbrian's bishop's seat moved from Lindisfarne to York and Wilfrid took Colman's position. Some monks, said to be more than 30 (Bede states *all the Irish*), unhappy with the result retired to Iona and Ireland. Oswiu replaced them with Rome supporting priests.

Too frequently, the Synod, confirmed three years later, is presented as a passionate conflict. In reality, the conflict only paralysed the Northumbrian church and royal family. Also, it is often given as the time the Rome church became ascendant. The reality is the Celtic and Roman churches were rarely in opposition. Also the Roman Christian presence was already flourishing. Alternatively, to diminish its significance as a mere harmonising of the Easter date is also a distortion. In the background was an argument being pursued by Oswiu with his son, plus a standoff between priests at Lindisfarne with those at

York. The real outcome was it caused an improvement in communication and trade with Rome and the Continent, so for these reasons it was significant.

7. Diuma and Mercia

Diuma was an Irish monk who resided at Iona and then Lindisfarne. Finan, c655, made him the first Bishop of Mercians and Middle Angles, which meant a bishop for people without a fixed diocese. He could also have had responsibility for Lindsey, Lincolnshire. It is often assumed this could only occur after *pagan* (?) Penda died in 654, but since his first son was at this time, a baptised Christian the date might have been a little earlier. Bede does accede Penda did not *forbid the preaching of the Word*.

If Diuma's responsibility was not geographically defined, then neither was his ecclesiastical centre fixed. Some place him in Repton, but it is without evidence. Diuma died in c658 and so had a very short time in office. He was buried amongst the Middle Angles and this has been sited at Charlbury, Oxfordshire. Clearly, there is much ambiguity with this first middle-England bishop given an exceptionally large community. Perhaps, he was simply the Northumbrian king's placeman. Curiously, Bede does not emphasise Diuma's conversion of Mercia in the same way he did with the 6 previous events and kingdoms. This has led some to speculate there was an already nascent Christianity in the region and Diuma, quickly followed by others, was simply reorganising the church. There does appear to be a rapid build of religious centres at Repton, Leicester, Lichfield, Wirksworth, Peterborough, Castor, Worcester and elsewhere suggesting, but certainly not proving, Christianity was nascent before the next Northumbrian monks arrived.

Diuma was followed by an Irish or Scottish monk called Ceollach or Kellach as Bishop of Mercia, but probably when Wulfhere regained the Mercian crown, he returned to Iona within a year. Wulfhere then arranged for an Englishman, trained in Ireland before becoming abbot at Ingethling Monastery, near Richmond, Yorkshire, called Trumhere or Trumheri to be bishop, c659 – 662. Finally, another monk from Lindisfarne, possibly with an Irish biography, called Jaruman, or Jurumannus, became bishop, c662 – 667.

This succession of bishops from the north began with the first two bishops having some allegiance to Oswiu of Northumbria. They were accepted by the kings of Mercia and always had direct connection with Lindisfarne. Lindisfarne was the mother church of Lichfield. It reached a climax with the arrival of Chad.

After a vacancy of two years, in 669, Chad (Old English – Caedda) became the fifth bishop of Mercia and Lindsey (Lincolnshire) and the first to be recorded to have a seat at Lichfield. It is assumed he was the younger brother of Cedd mentioned earlier in connection with the baptism of Paeda. His date of birth, somewhere between late 620s and 634, and his early life are unknown. He was

Diuma, Ceollach without his mitre and not holding a staff and so might not have been formally installed, Trumhere and Jaruman. Jaruman holds the first church of St Mary, almost certainly a timber church, with a date of 666 derived. However, it was much more likely Trumhere built the first church, around 659. Was it similar to the early church recently uncovered at Lindisfarne?

trained in the priesthood by Aidan at Lindisfarne. If this was when Aidan arrived in 634, Chad would then be at least 12 years old making his birth around 622. This would agree with him becoming a monk when 30 and then a missionary in Ireland, c650 to 660s. Thus, he was possibly in his late 40s when he returned to Northumbria.

In 664 Chad became abbot at Lastingham Monastery in Yorkshire after the death of his oldest brother. In the same year, King Oswiu of Northumbria invited Chad, according to Bede, to be *bishop of the church of York*. For this Chad travelled to Canterbury and then Wessex where he was ordained a bishop, by three bishops

Left shows Chad and his three older brothers, Cedd, Cynebil and Caelin being taught by Aidan. Bede placed Chad fourth in line when naming the brothers and from this, it is presumed he was the youngest. Right shows Archbishop Theodore consecrating Chad for a second time and on this occasion in York.

not recognised by Rome. It is uncertain whether Chad ever became the bishop of York because this had also been given to Wilfred by Oswiu's son; there was a father-son clash. His title was more likely to have been Bishop of Northumbria. In 669, the Christian Mercian King Wulfhere, under some obligation to the Christian Northumbrian King Oswiu and perhaps receiving advice from Wilfred, arranged for Chad to be sent to Lichfield as a way to further good relations as well as removing him from York.

The new Archbishop, a Greek called Theodore, agreed for Chad to be moved out of Northumbria and away from Wilfred. It was almost certainly managed by the kings, approved by Canterbury and Rome, and apparently accepted by Chad.

There is another side to this consecration of Chad. Chad had been elevated to a bishop in the Celtic manner in Wessex and Theodore at Canterbury opposed this. Furthermore, it was by a bishop suspected of attaining the office by buying it. So he removed Chad from Northumbria, completed his consecration in the Roman tradition in York and moved him to Lichfield. Chad agreed to all this, but at heart he must have remained a Celtic monk, and conscious of being taught by Aidan, and from the school founded by Columba.

In the short time Chad presided at Lichfield he was, according to Bede, greatly loved for his humility and asceticism. He had 7 or 8 brothers at his communal hermitage, must have quickly developed the site and its church of St Marys, and founded a monastery at Barrow, Lincolnshire on land given by King Wulfhere. He impressed Bede and Theodore. One of his pupils called Trumberht (Trumbert) went on to train Bede, which must be a good reason why Bede's account of Chad was so fulsome. It was in stark contrast to Bede's lesser treatment of Mercia and its Christian development, knowing it could potentially rival and threaten Northumbria.

Why Lichfield?

Why would a major church for Mercia be centred in a relatively insignificant village? Indeed, in 1070, the Normans moved the bishoprics of 3 cathedrals, including Lichfield, from villages to walled towns with new bishops residing near castles and garrisons. It was not until 1128, Lichfield regained its bishop and then followed the building of a town and walled cathedral. Antiquarians of the 16th to 19th century explained the minor location by storytelling. They said Augustine had visited the site, a massacre of Christians in Roman times necessitated a spiritual cleansing, and Chad conversed with local forest animals. These vivid, fictitious tales are still repeated in general accounts.

Later historians chose to justify the site with power-play events by kings. Oswiu of Northumbria was commonly seen as selecting the centre, but it could have been the choice of Wulfhere of Mercia. The management by kings is still the preferred way to introduce Lichfield, but it still begs the question why there? In the same way, the statement Chad chose the site is both incorrect and explains little. Recent analyses of other church centres suggest the topography with seclusion, but not complete isolation, and support from an existing settlement underlies the reason for their location and Lichfield complied with this favoured layout. For the pioneering priests the site might have been a *sacred landscape* based on a biblical interpretation. They felt its geography greatly assisted their devotion. Its connection with Lindisfarne and Iona raises this distinct possibility.

The Cult of Chad

Chad was in Lichfield for 2½ years before he died in 672, possibly in his early fifties, probably from a variant of plague, but smallpox and yellow fever have also been implicated. Bede described it as a progressive bodily weakness which grew worse over 7 days. Chad had foreseen he was soon to die. He told his fellow monks he had been visited by *the beloved guest who has been in the habit of visiting our brothers*. All this indicated the plague bacterium, but he was surrounded by 7 or 8 other monks and there is no record of them succumbing to the disease. He was buried near to his church of St Mary and it became known miracle cures occurred close to his tomb leading to him being quickly besainted. From then it became a site of exceptional pilgrimage. Pilgrims would visit the shrine for a desire to be healed, for penance, to fulfil a vow, as a personal act of devotion, in proxy for a loved one or simply as part of a journey.

It has been said in this *age of saints* (7th and 8th centuries) that every monastery had to have a saint and over 100 Saxon sites with a cult have been identified. Chad at Lichfield was one of the earliest, proved to be one of the most enduring and in terms of numbers of pilgrims was exceptional. Chad died on March 2nd and this day might well have been kept for a special service from 672 and could be one of the oldest acts of patronal remembrance in England.

By the middle 9th century, Lichfield was claiming to have Cedd's relics (Chad's oldest brother) and thus adding much to the significance of the pilgrimage site.

Chad at Lichfield.

Chad at St Chad's church, Hanmer, near Wrexham, Wales, and close to the route for Irish pilgrims journeying down the Wirral, across Cheshire to Lichfield.

Pilgrimage

It is difficult with modern eyes to see the power and attraction of a saint and their relics. It had Roman origins and was a central determinant of belief until the 9th century. It regained a new vigour in the 11th and 12th centuries, continued throughout the Reformation after relics were removed and it is still significant for some. Pilgrims believed the relics and the saint's tomb still held the living personality or spirit of the saint. They were an intercessor to communing in prayer with God. They were also an undying leader championing the mores of the pilgrim. Therefore getting close to the *person soul* was very important. Walking long distances was nothing when it was possible to receive direction and wellbeing through the holiness of the saint with his or her link with God. The sheer number of saints, the many sites with their presence and the very long time in which they have changed people testified to their work and religious importance. In our world today, this spirit cannot be undervalued; it was powerful.

The Mercian Mission

With the death of Oswiu in 670, the whole of Southern England came under the lordship of the Mercians. With the rise of Mercia as a major kingdom came an increasing participation in the organisation of a larger church. It started with the Council of Hertford, or possibly Hartford in Cambridgeshire, in c672. It was led by Archbishop Theodore of Canterbury, but sponsored by King Wulfhere of Mercia. Four bishops from the sees of West Saxon, Rochester, East Angle and Mercia were present together with a representative from Wilfrid of Northumbria. The area under the control of Canterbury was defined and the very large see of Lichfield was split up; Bishop Wynfrith of Lichfield was removed so, perhaps, he could not agree the change. Hereford began in c676, Lincolnshire 678, Leicestershire 679, but not established until 737, and

Wulfhere shown holding the first church at Peterborough, known as Medeshampstede. He reigned from 658 to 675.

116

Worcester 680. The Easter dating was confirmed, the behaviour of bishops, monks and clergy was defined, it was agreed how often Councils were to be called, wedlock was encouraged and divorce allowed, but remarriage was made difficult. The united church was now being systematically organised. The church was showing confidence and being obedient to Rome in a way not seen anywhere in Europe. So confident were some bishops, they now began to organise missionary work into Europe.

Councils were to be called on the 1st August each year and to meet at a location called Clovesho, Clofesho, Clofeshoch, or Clofeshoas, whose exact location is sadly unknown and has teased historians ever since. There is a long list of suggestions where the Councils took place and the most recent suggestion is Brixworth, Northamptonshire, but another has the nearby Medeshampstede Monastery at the centre. It might have simply been a hill, mound or field and the assembly was in a tent. It is ironic the first councils to decide matters of common Christian importance and which continued for over 150 years cannot even be located. Logic would suggest it was in Mercia and yet accessible for all the southern bishops, and a place which was neutral, yet valued by the king. If Wulfhere was establishing his credentials as a great Christian King and following on from Oswiu, then a location in his ancestral homeland would be an egotistical choice.

If Aethelberht of Kent was the first king to support a bishop (Augustine), and Oswald of Northumbria the first king to strongly support priests (Aidan and Finan), then Wulfhere of Mercia was the first king to enthusiastically support an archbishop (Theodore). When Wulfhere died in 675, he was succeeded by Aethelred.

He consolidated the Mercian hold and stabilised the sub-kingdoms. A Mercian bishopric was established at Dorchester for Oxfordshire and land was given to the abbot at Malmesbury Abbey. This showed he ruled over much of Wessex. Aethelred befriended Bishop Wilfrid, after he had been marginalised or expelled from Northumbria, and for a time he administered the whole of Mercia. Wilfrid brought many riches to Mercia and Middle Angle and greatly extended the area covered by the church, including the large see of Lindsey, Lincolnshire. When Aethelred retired in 704, he became the abbot at Bardney Abbey in North Lindsey.

Aethelred pointing to his rules agreed at Clofesho.

There is a mystery concerning a lack of communication between Mercia and the Celtic church in Wales in the 7th century. It has been summarised as Mercia having full participation in the Christian Latin Culture and this culture spreads in all directions, but strangely not west to Wales. Considering King Penda c605 – 655 had Welsh allies (Cadwallon, Cynddylan and others) in every one of his battles there is no documentary evidence to show any correspondence between the Christian Welsh and the warriors of Mercia. It has been written Repton was founded c600 by David of Wales, but this has to be folklore. Equally, it seemed the evangelism of the Welsh missionaries extended to all points of the compass except eastwards and into Mercia. This missionary work was even absent when Christian kings took the Mercian throne. Perhaps, it happened, but was on a small scale and there was no one to record it for posterity. It is a Mercian Enigma.

The underlying drivers of change

Generally, the first half of the 7th century was much about kings increasing their kingdoms and achieving domination. Firstly, the East Angles and Kentish kings, followed by the Northumbrian kings and finishing with the supremacy of the Mercians. Other kings took part in the growing of kingdoms, but by 650, many of the enduring alliances had been established. Then came an intensive growth of the church and its origins have been much debated. Circumstances which promoted the rise in power of the bishops has been partially explained by the following developments; the list is almost certainly incomplete.

- Papal authority came to be recognised and with the Synod of Whitby enshrined in rules governing churches by 667. There was now a unity.
- Bishop Theodore of Tarsus arrived at Canterbury in 668, the 8th Archbishop, and determinately set about reorganising dioceses. He was not the first choice of the pope; that was Hadrian, a Berber from North Africa and a monk from Naples. In the end he sent both, with Hadrian ensuring Theodore stayed on message with Rome.
- On his arrival, there might have only been 3 bishops, Wine of London, Chad of Northumbria and later Mercia, and Wilfred

Theodore and a map showing his country of origin, Greece.

returning from Rome. By the end of his Archbishopric, 690, there could have been 12 bishops at Rochester, London, Winchester, North Elmham, Dunwich, Lichfield, Leicester, Worcester, Lindisfarne, Hexham, Lincoln and York. It was still only half the number suggested by Pope Gregory at the start of the century. By 737, the number had risen to 17.

- 670 and subsequent years saw a plague passing through the country and killing many priests. It caused some monasteries to close and others to increase as monks moved to avoid the disease. There was a reorganisation and a concerted effort to train new young priests. Large centres of teaching arose to meet this demand.

- The French model of double monasteries which became common by 640 began to be copied in Britain. Abbesses were often drawn from noble families including royalty. Indeed, by 670 it became common for kings to remove their daughters, unwanted queens or royal widows, to monasteries for safekeeping and, perhaps, out of the way from military adventures. Double houses became part of the dynastic strategies. Over 30 double monasteries have now been recognised, including Whitby, probably the largest, Barking, Repton and it is now thought Lichfield.

- Werburgh, daughter of Wulfhere, became the fourth abbess of Ely succeeding three women from her family. She much reformed the organisation of nunneries. She was buried at Hanbury Church in Staffordshire.

- A list of royal nunneries for 735 has 33 sites, with another 4 possibilities. Nazeingbury nunnery, Essex, is typical of this arrangement. Land was given c700 to someone called Ffymme (the name was probably corrupted when the charter was copied), who is now thought to be a close relative of the East Angle king. She set up a church and excavation showed a high status burial in this church. The cemetery had 150 to 200 skeletons of which 86 were women. They showed little sign of wear and tear and it was concluded they were the nuns. 32 male skeletons were found with many showing a life of hard work and they were thought to be the keepers and labourers of the church.

- Kings began to use the land gained in battle to give to monasteries which would in turn look after the king's interests. Much endowment of land occurred and this saw the writing of charters, which thankfully are now a source of much information. Bookkeeping turned into a church profession. Churches became the safe boxes for the kings and their treasure, if the king had need, could be withdrawn anytime.

- Monastic sites formed communities in which a wide range of crafts developed. Great books were written and were often used as royal gifts. Monks engaged in all kinds of menial work, helped by labourers and itinerant tradesmen. Farming expanded and returns would have been high. The monastery stayed physically separate from this ecclesia, but enjoyed rent and tithe.

- The greatest unknown in Saxon church history is the place of the pocket church. Documentary evidence does not record the very small timber building with a cross and occasionally receiving a visiting priest. Their abundance, usage and significance within the community was not mentioned. They were the equivalent of the local Celtic church and there is no reason for assuming such a church was found only on the West side of Britain. Location on top of a heathen site was recommended by popes and appeared as necessities in some bishops teaching, but how often this was followed was never stated. Assuming they were common meant most people would now be reminded of their Christian obligations. Christianity was breaking out of the confines of the dedicated mother church.

The Other World taught by understanding an Apocalypse

Recent analysis has shown the apocalyptic end game set out in story form with strong imagery in the Book of Revelation coloured and explained much that happened in the 6th and 7th centuries. When Pope Gregory sent his Augustinian Mission, he exhorted them to convert the British by *terrifying them, by flattering them, by correcting them*. Gregory took the view that no one knew when the world would end, but it was imperative the lessons of the apocalyptic story should be known to everyone and with some urgency. Worship, behaviour and attitude had to be moulded with the revelation the world might end at any time.

During prolonged thunderstorms Chad would go into his church at Lichfield and both pray and sing psalms until calm returned. His monks regarded this as an extreme reaction even to the weather and asked him to explain. Chad said storms were sent by God to remind humans of the Day of Judgement, *we ought to respond to his heavenly warning with due fear and love*.

Bede wrote a poem entitled *On Judgement Day* to remind people to reflect on their sins and correct their behaviour. His first venture into interpreting the Bible was *Commentary on Revelation*, c703, and this vigorously opposed the temptation to calculate the time for the end of the world. Yet many believed the age was getting close to being 6000 years after the calculated start of Creation and therefore the end time was imminent. This was based on 6 ages each 1000 years long and supported by II Peter 3.8 and interpretation of the Book of Revelation. The birth of Jesus started the 6th age and after the year 1000, it would be the World to Come. Two previous calculations had been the years 202 and 500. Another forecast was the end year would be 800. Bede dismissed all this heresy and argued Revelation was not a literal prophecy by which the end date could be predicted, but instead was a symbolic struggle between the church and heretics. It was a vision leading up to the end of the world as directed by God and was therefore a hopeful vision. It offered hope and salvation and the timing was of little consequence. Unfortunately, today the word *apocalypse* invokes a catastrophic *end of the world* caused by man or nature and is a doom-laden expectation, but that was not its original biblical intention.

There is another wider aspect of apocalyptic history. The eastern Roman Empire collapsed between 610 and 620 with the Persians capturing Jerusalem in 614. The extent of brutality of the invasion has been questioned, but Jews and Christians saw this as the first stage of the apocalypse with the appearance of barbarians in the Holy City. In 629, a Roman emperor took Jerusalem back, but then the disparate Arabian tribes, known as Saracens, united with the teachings of the Islamic prophet Muhammad. Muslim forces began to conquer the Middle East. Damascus fell in 634. In 636, they won a major battle said to be near the Yarmouk River in Syria and in the following year, Jerusalem surrendered to the Caliphate. They built a large and impressive mosque on the highest site in the city, where the Jewish temple once stood, and is now known as *The Dome of the Rock*. Alexandria was taken in 639. Constantinople was besieged in 674 and surrounded for 4 years before the blockade was suspended. It was besieged for a second time, 717 – 718, and if the Arab army had not been defeated, the Christian world would have been very different. Islands in the Mediterranean were captured and Carthage fell in 698. North Africa was conquered by 710. Eventually Islam was to spread around the Southern Mediterranean into most of Spain, 711, and penetrating for a while as far as the Loire River in France. After entering France around 717, the invaders were removed with two battles in 732 and 759.

On the eastern front, Muslim forces advanced through Persia to Pakistan and India. By the middle of the 8th century, more than half of the Christian world was now speaking Arabic and seeing coins and displays with the words, *there is no God but one God alone. He has no companion.* Trinity was gone, Christ was demoted, his resurrection doubted and God's foremost prophet was Muhammad. First Damascus and then Baghdad became the new world centres. All this fighting brought an apocalyptic *End of the World* tension which pervaded Christian, Jewish and even Islamic thinking and the Roman church particularly wanted everyone to heed the warning. No event had greater significance for Christianity in the first millennium as the rise and rapid spread of Islam. It should not be given any significance for the world today and it is sad to see when the far past is used politically to justify current situations.

Muslims, the followers of Islam, believe that on a day decided by Allah (God), life on earth will end and all will be destroyed. At this moment, all souls will be raised from the dead and face the judgement of Allah. Allah will judge each person by his or her good and bad deeds, as well as intentions. If good outweighs bad, the person will go to paradise (Jannah meaning a garden) and have both joy and bliss. There are 8 doors into paradise and there are 7 levels to be placed. Otherwise, they will go to hell (Jahannam) for punishment from heat and torture. Since Allah has given free will, it is the responsibility for everyone to prepare for this eternal world (Akhirah).

Chapter 6

THE ILLUMINATED CHURCH

Then I saw a new heaven and a new earth, for the first heaven and the first earth had passed away.

A Heavenly Jerusalem, Revelation 21.1 and Ezekiel 40-48

Sometime after 630, a change in furnishing the church occurred in the Atlantic Isles. A rough timber oratory changed into a rectangular stone church, with either a square or a round apse. Stonework might have been intricately sculpted and the floor was tiled. On the walls were paintings. Windows were glazed. Wooden and stone crosses were replaced with detailed icons made from precious metals and jewels. They were now on an altar covered in embroidered cloth. Standing crosses with biblical scenes were erected at meeting places. Books were illustrated and pages painted artistically with colourful pigments. Libraries were commissioned. Bishops wore elaborate garments and used superior liturgical objects of value. Singing and playing music were encouraged. It was not ennoblement, but a way of showing awe to God. For the craftsmen it was a devotion and working to produce the best for a perfect God. Manufacture showed the power of the Spirit and a new heaven. If God was the light of the world, then the church would reflect his illumination.

Emperor Severus Alexander, 222 – 235, took an open view of religion and encouraged both art and science. One dubious biography claimed he commissioned statues of Christ and Abraham to add to other deities for his private shrine. These could have been the first graven idols. He allowed the building of a synagogue in Rome and received an education from a Christian. It all presaged Constantine. From Constantine onwards the new Christian church was going to be an Imperial Church and reflect the splendour and glory of Rome. It would emulate pagan temples. Emperor Justinian I in Constantinople, ruling 527 – 565, took this to a higher level and it was estimated 300,000 pounds of gold were used to decorate palaces and the churches along the banks of the Bosphorus.

Therefore, churches on the continent from the 4th century onwards began to collect great amounts of artwork. Whereas in complete and total contrast, the British and Irish churches shunned this until after the year 630. The few Christian pieces found in the 5th and 6th century in Britain were from either graves or settlements, and were not liturgical objects used in church service. It could be argued this was a result of little wealth in the early church, but, in fact, there were goldsmiths around furnishing armies with prized ceremonial weapons and they could easily have made elaborate items for the church. The obvious explanation is the early Celtic and Roman church in Britain avoided any kind of symbol of wealth and luxury. They were standing by the 1st to 3rd century church view of avoiding images of Christ since it reduced his divination. Attention was given to the word of God and it could not be dressed up. Instead, its treasure was books without any fancy illumination. An early stock list of liturgical items used by Patrick in the 5th century included bells, chalices, patens, altar stones, books of canonical law and the gospels, but none were described as being decorated. Art was minimal like monastic life.

All this began to change, slowly at first, after 630 (some authors give a later date of c650). By 670, the *Golden Age* for Saxon artwork was advanced and furnished churches were accepted. The asceticism of the early church had become the aestheticism of the Continental Roman Church. It is difficult to pick out an event that began this change, but the 597 Gregorian Mission brought a good list of valued objects to England. In 601 came sacred vessels, bishops vestments, relics and books. Perhaps, this was a papal permission.

Reproduction of Patrick's bell.

St Augustine Gospels or the Canterbury Gospels

A Gospel book was brought to England in either 597 or more likely in 601, which is thought to be the Gospel kept at Corpus Christi College, Cambridge. It is the oldest surviving Latin, illuminated Gospel Book. Written in Italy, near Naples, in the 6th century, it was kept on an altar at St Augustine's Monastery, Canterbury before being moved to Cambridge in the 16th century. It could have been Augustine's Gospel and after his death, it was treated as his relic. It is now used again for the swearing of oaths by a new Archbishop of Canterbury in their enthronement. There are 265 leaves, 25.2cm x 19.6cm, of parchment, and most likely goatskin. It includes two full pages of tinted drawings with many being miniature scenes from the Passion; there is much emphasis on the suffering of Christ. Figures resemble Roman statues and the uncial lettering is like a Roman manuscript. An illuminated book is one that is decorated with initials, borders and illustrations, but for some art historians this must be in gold or silver, which came later. There were some corrections or additions when it was at Canterbury.

Scenes from the Passion.

In 625, Pope Boniface sent to King Edwin of Northumbria a letter imploring him to accept the Christian faith and accompanied it with a gold robe. To his queen he gave a silver mirror and an ivory comb adorned with gold. Later he sent gold crosses and chalices for York which were retrieved after the king's death and taken to Kent. Again, the pope was sanctioning the use of decoration.

A list can be made of sumptuous Christian artwork in the 7th century. A Gospel book at Ripon was written in gold letters on purple parchment and kept in a cover made of gold inlaid with gems. The Ripon jewel was found near the cathedral and the gold medallion, inlaid with amber and garnets hints at ecclesiastical use. A scallop shaped pendant signifying baptism was found in a late 7th century grave of a high status woman at Street House Farm Cemetery in Redcar and Cleveland. Ripon had an altar with a purple cloth woven with gold thread. Bishop Wilfrid bought objects from his 3 trips to Rome and they were described as invaluable. He also had several reliquaries with one containing a lock of Cuthbert's hair. Perhaps he sat on a chair, 674, made of Roman stone, appearing like an emperor on a throne. It can still be seen at Hexham Abbey and is known as the Frith Stool. We know Hexham Abbey was ornate and described as equal to any church in Rome. In 664, the year of the Synod, the Kings of Northumbria and Kent sent *no small number* of gold and silver vessels to Rome. Benedict Biscop had arranged for French stonemasons and glassmakers to work at Jarrow. Stained glass windows, possibly the oldest in the world, were installed. Glass making at Whitby has been seen in excavations. On his 5 visits to Rome, Biscop brought back many sacred books, relics and icons showing Mary, the Apostles and scenes from the Apocalypse. On his last visit, he returned with silks for kings and Cuthbert.

The windows of the first church in York were re-glazed between 669 and 671. Queen Etheldreda wore jewels and then renounced them to become a nun and built a monastery which turned into the first Ely Cathedral in 673. The church at Kildare, Ireland, was described in c650 as having shrines surrounded by silver, gold, gems and precious stones. It had a Gospel so intricate it was described as *the work of angels*. The building was spacious, high, with many windows and was adorned with painted panels. In the 8th century, the Minster at York had 30 altars decorated in many ways, which was probably an understatement for gold embellishment. At Canterbury, there was a large gold crucifix or cross. Bede described St Alban's shrine as a beautiful church. A church, possibly Malmesbury, was described, c680s, as having an altar cloth which shone with twisted thread. King Oswald gave his Northumbrian churches wall hangings made of silk with gold thread. He also had a gold enriched banner. After his martyrdom, his right arm was kept in a silver reliquary at Aidan's church, Bamburgh. The fragments of stone at the base of the tower to Monkwearmouth church, built 674, show it was constructed to impress.

Bugga's Church of St Mary

Aldhelm wrote a poem, 689 – 709, and described a church built by Bugga, possibly his sister. It was described as rectangular, lofty and with 12 altars. It glowed within with gentle light, presumably from oil lamps or bees wax candles. It had glass windows. The altar cloth glistened with gold twisted threads. A gold chalice had jewels attached and the platen was silver. A main cross was burnished gold and silver and had jewels attached. A metal censer embossed on all sides hung down by chains and through openings, it let out the smell of frankincense. There were many decorations and ornaments.

This poem gives an insight into a late 7th century church. It is offered as a place of light, luxury and peace. There is a good chance the walls were plastered or lime washed and even had some painting. If there was a painted image, the likeliest would be Mary, since the apse was dedicated to the Virgin. 12 altars suggested some reference to the 12 disciples. The floor might have been covered in tiles. If a baptismal receptacle was present it could have been wooden, but equally possible would be a stone bowl with incised figures. The altar table would most likely be made from stone and positioned so that worshippers could stand close to it. On it might have been a small calling bell. It stated there were twin choirs of monks and nuns singing antiphons and psalms, so presumably they were separated in some way and the church was a double-cell. The abbot could be carrying a cross-staff.

Guesses for this church's location are Barking, London, Wareham and Wimborne in Dorset. All three had monks and nuns.

Aethelwulf's imaginary churches

A poem known as the *Song of the Abbots* written between 803 and 821 by an unknown monk, gave some detail of three imagined churches which might have been based on Bywell Monastery, Northumberland, or Crayke Monastery, Yorkshire. It described a cruciform church with lofty walls and lead on the roof. Three large altars with substantial jewelled crosses were placed with one in the nave and one in each side porticus. The altars with golden offerings, perhaps a reference to a chalice, had garlands of gold flowers which could have been on the altar cloth. There was also a tomb with relics and across the top was a sparkling vestment of fine linen.

Cuthbert's coffin

In 1827, his grave at Durham was opened and the middle of three coffins had biblical figures incised naively into the wood. The lid had Jesus surrounded by symbols for the 4 evangelists of the gospels, one long side had the 12 disciples and the other long side had 5 archangels, the one end had two archangels, presumed to be Gabriel and Michael, and the other end had the Virgin and Child. It represented the bringing together of all in heaven with Cuthbert's remains in the centre. The figures had drapery in a Byzantine style and this showed a liking by Northumbrian monks for 5th or 6th century Christian imagery. In the coffin were his pectoral cross on his breast, an ivory comb, a wooden travelling altar enclosed in silver plate, fragments of rich textiles and a small Gospel of John, sometimes known as the Stonyhurst Gospel. The coffin had previously been opened in 1104 and a paten, scissors and chalice made of gold with onyx stone were listed, but now lost. It has also been opened many times in the intervening years. The coffin, contents and veneration were without equal; even plundering commissioners of Henry VIII backed away from sequestering the treasure.

All this evidence is fragmentary, but the conclusion can only be a profusion of rich artwork began to adorn the 7th century churches. They joined a gold standard in art and especially in religious art. Plastered walls with paintings gave enlightenment. Shaped woodwork and sculpted stone brought comfort and pleasure. At the same time, bishops became wealthy patrons. Simple devotions were replaced with elaborate ritual worship. Saints were venerated. Clergy were given offices. Pilgrimage was expected. The church became extravagant and beautiful to see.

The Crondall Hoard

A hoard of coins found in Crondall, Hampshire, in 1828 and dated c640 is thought to be some of the earliest coins in circulation in Saxon Britain. 73 of the 98 gold coins were English and the rest were French. Their designs show a royal and church ownership and that was most likely centred on London or Kent. Some show a cross. The hoard, with its good artwork, is strong evidence for increasing wealth and a new metalworking.

Christians knew from reading Revelation, chapter 21.18, the foundations of the New Heavenly Jerusalem were decorated with every kind of precious stone. The twelve gates were each made of a single pearl. The great street of the city was of pure gold, like transparent glass. Similarly, Christians would be in awe with the description of the temple of Solomon. Built of cedar wood it was said to have its interior walls and altar overlaid with pure gold, gold chains closed the inner sanctuary, candlesticks and censers were gold, and cherub decorations were also gilded.

Saxon poetry had many words to describe the reflection of light from gold with great emphasis on the precious, lustrous, golden, brightness and radiant aspects of whatever was being described. Subsequently, in the epic poem *Beowulf* the hall had to be gold plated. The light effects from gold would be how the Saxons could brighten their dark places of worship. All of this was an antithesis of heathen temples situated amongst trees, in shaded river valleys, open to the elements and dreary on grey days. Gold, glistening garnets and spectacular jewellery brought reflected light into their dark world and gave a sense of awe in God's house. It would turn the heads of unbelievers.

Everyone wanted glint except certain monks who stuck to their asceticism and returned to Iona where they held out until 716; some historians think it was later. Northern Ireland Romanised by 697, Southern Ireland had already changed around 630, most of Wales took longer, 768, and Cornwall even longer, 940. In certain parts of Wales and Ireland, Celtic monasticism continued until the 12th century. In isolated parts of Scotland, it could have been the 14th century. There were churches that did not accept the Roman way and there were monks who did not like the new art. It was idolatrous.

A Christian Hoard

The largest Saxon gold hoard was found at Hammerwich, Staffordshire, in July 2009. Around 10% by mass has a Christian connection and many pieces show clearly the new artwork being produced. Dating the fabrication of the Christian pieces is

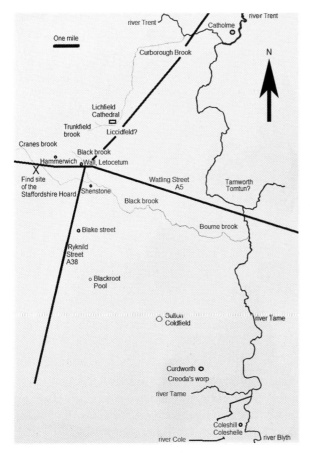

The Mercian homeland around the rivers Trent and Tame. Curdworth is the best place name to be linked with the name of Creoda, possibly the first Mercian king who reigned c585 – 593, but the evidence is very weak. Roman sites include Coleshill Roman Temple and Wall (Letocetum) mansio. Some artefacts have been found in Lichfield. A large Saxon settlement was found at Catholme, at the confluence of the Trent and Tame rivers. This might be the Tomtun, or royal village by the Tame, of Aethelred. Many of the villages have a Late Saxon beginning. A Saxon pathway called Black or Bleak Street, from Chester to London, passed across this area from the north-west to the south-east. The word 'black' is also seen in Blake, Cole and Col; Tame could mean 'dark-river'.

not possible, but conflating them with the military pieces whose date can be fixed to before 700 is almost certainly an error. This hoard was found in the centre of the kingdom of Mercia. The geography of the area gives some clue to its provenance.

Three Christian pieces stand out as being exceptional.

1. Pectoral cross

The pectoral cross is almost the same size and shape as the cross of St Cuthbert found in his coffin and now at Durham Cathedral. The only difference between the two is the decoration on the front face. The hoard cross has a pattern of twisted wire filigree in linked coils in a 'C' shape like an eyeglass.

The Cuthbert cross has garnets instead, 4 around the centre ⊚⊚ symbolising the apostles and 12 along each arm denoting the disciples. The date of Cuthbert's cross has been estimated to be 650 – 670 and there is no reason to think the hoard pectoral cross is dissimilar.

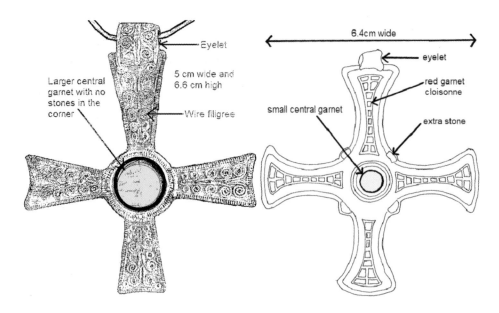

Drawing of an intact pectoral cross, contrasted with the Cuthbert cross.

In 1776, a small gold Saxon cross, also with eyeglass filigree, was found in a barrow on Winster Moor, Derbyshire. It was missing the middle stone, but the shape and design is very similar to the pectoral cross. The Winster cross is smaller being 3.5cm long and just under 3cm wide. Winster is by the River Derwent which flows into the Trent south of Derby. It is 43 miles (70km) from Hammerwich.

There is also a similarity in shape and size between the hoard cross and the 7th century Holderness cross, which is 5.3cm high and 5cm wide and has an infill of garnets like the Cuthbert cross. Holderness is north of the Humber, but not too far from the mouth of the River Trent. Crosses are also known from Ixworth, Suffolk (4.5cm high), Wilton, Norfolk (5.6cm high), Thurnham, Kent (3.5cm diameter) and Milton Regis, Kent, (3.1cm diameter). Smaller crosses attached to necklets have also been found.

Drawing of the Winster Moor Cross which can be seen in Weston Park Museum, Sheffield. When found it had its central garnet missing, as shown here. A date of 650–700 has been given. If this is a bishop's cross, who would have been buried in a barrow on a moor? Bishop Betti was at Wirksworth, which is close by.

The hoard pectoral cross has an eyelet at the top and because of little wear inside the eyelet; it is thought a leather thong or silk thread passed through to hang the cross around the neck and over the chest. Cuthbert's cross was found with a twisted gold silk cord. This means it is really upside-down as you see it in the image, so the wearer would turn it the right way up to their face and perhaps kiss it. Its size and design is meant to label very clearly the man who wore it as a Christian with high status.

In 2012, the centre of the hoard cross was found to be a box structure with a space below the central garnet which stands out and is set on a gold shelf. In the space could be, or has been, a relic which makes it an *encolpion*. Seeing and proving the cross contains or contained a relic is difficult since the garnet is very opaque and gold cannot be X-rayed. It has long been speculated Cuthbert's cross was also an encolpion.

A pectoral cross was mentioned in connection with Pope Hilarius in 461, so wearing such a pendant has a long history. Almost certainly, it would need the status of a bishop or abbot to wear such an important piece. So could any of the early Mercian bishops have possessed the pectoral cross? Did Chad bring it to Lichfield? The great similarity with Cuthbert's cross and the closeness of the two saints having been to school together at Lindisfarne adds to this plausible supposition.

2. 'Crumpled' cross

An incomplete and folded cross, made from 140g of almost pure gold, was found as well as five roundel attachments, two garnets and a D shaped stone. One garnet

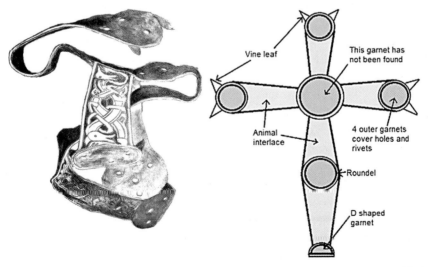

Left is a drawing of the folded cross. Right is the unfolded cross with garnets added.

was broken and wired in to a roundel. Folded it measures 11.4cm long by 7cm wide and is 1.3mm thick. Using computer technology it has been unfolded, missing bits added and a replica made. The central roundel filling has not been found and might have had a rock crystal, or image of Christ, or most likely a garnet. If it was a garnet, it could well have been a dark, almost purple, stone. The bottom D stone was found sometime after conservation began and fitted perfectly into the base of the cross. A replica was given to Pope Benedict XVI when visiting Birmingham in September 2010. He said, *the cross is the true tree of life*, and that is why it is spectacular.

The ends of the arms have ears which are vine leaves. Jewelled crosses are known where the face decoration is the *Tree of Life* which is a vine winding up the cross and ending in leaves at the ends of the arms. Instead of showing Christ on the cross, they substituted a vine basing it on the metaphor from John 15.5: *I am the vine you are the branches*. God is the vine grower, Jesus is the vine, and you are the branches of which some are pruned and lost and others will bear fruit. Vines were commonly sculpted on Saxon stone crosses such as at Hexham, Bewcastle and Ruthwell. The Ruthwell cross has two faces with vines, birds and animals feeding on the grapes which referred also to the Eucharist. It is also a cross or column showing the tree of life.

The 'Tree of Life'

A *tree of life* is an ancient and globally used motif depicting an evolution of some sort. Almost every religion had a tree of life symbol. From a single trunk, many branches grow out in ever-greater profusion. So moving from the roots, up through the trunk and into the wider canopy is a journey that represents life. The evolution can be passing from simple to complicated, ignorance to having wisdom, early beginnings to final-outcomes, a passage from the underworld to the high heavens, or the first life to advanced forms. Charles Darwin's 1837 iconic notebook drawing of a branching tree of life showing species evolution was similar. Precisely how the Saxons used this motif is lost to us, but attaching it to a cross must mean they saw the cross as a tree with the base buried in the earth where life begins. The apex looks to heaven where perpetual life begins and this rising upwards was through Christ. The cross was spiritual growth and the Saxons embraced its imagery.

Behind the outer garnets, the roundels have large holes with rivets and suggest the cross was once attached to a wooden base. The back is plain and supports this idea. The best idea is it was attached to the wooden cover of a Gospel. Size wise it would fit perfectly on the front of a Gospel like St Chads or Lindisfarne and possibly other unknown Gospels because they were probably all similar in size.

Left: Outline of a squared penitential cross from the carpet page of St Chad's Gospel. It resembles a carpet page in the Lindisfarne Gospel. Right: Drawing of the cross ornamentation.

The four outer red stones represent the four apostles. The bottom D stone represents the rock of Golgotha on which the original cross might have been fixed at Calvary. This arrangement of 6 stones is similar to the cross in the carpet page of St Chad's Gospel and in the Lindisfarne Gospel.

The decoration on the front of the arms is not a climbing vine, but instead consists of various interlaced animals. This animal ornamentation resembles decoration on the rim mount of a Maplewood bottle found in the Sutton Hoo hoard. This adds to the idea of a particular motif having a definite meaning.

Sutton Hoo
A ship burial at Sutton Hoo, near Woodbridge, Suffolk, was excavated in 1939. Sutton Hoo today is over 8 miles (13km) up the Deben River from the North Sea. A long Saxon ship, capable of having 40 oarsmen, was dragged from the river shore, up a small hill of 30m (100 feet) height, laid in a trench, filled with a body of a high-ranking warrior (only phosphate traces were found) and surrounded by a large trove of 263 weapons, personal goods and ceremonial pieces. Today it is known as mound 1. The supposed body was laid in the wooden centre of the ship. It was thought to have been under a pitched decking

which had collapsed. On the floor was placed a flax rug and objects were carefully positioned around the chamber in an arrangement that appeared to have symbolic meaning. Some could have been hanging from some kind of superstructure. About 2kg of gold was recovered.

This hoard contained mostly pagan objects, but there were some with Christian symbolism. Coins have been dated to c610 – 635 and many believe burial was between c620 and 635, with a preference for 625. It is right at the beginning of elite rulers owning and valuing decorative Christian artefacts.

So what does the animal interlace mean? The cross is a weird mixture of Christian iconography (5 wound garnets, vine leaves, a half-stone representing Golgotha) and pagan or abstract art (quadruped heads joined to worm-like ribbon bodies). It is ambiguous and even contradictory. Could this iconography have a biblical foundation? The obvious explanation is it must represent the *Tree of life* considering the vine leaves at the ends of the arms. Also, the entangled birds and dog/quadruped in the angular Latin cross in St Chad's Gospel carpet page has been interpreted as representing the tree of life. Similarly, the highly abstract Latin cross in the carpet page introducing the Lindisfarne Gospel of Matthew has been seen as symbolising the tree of life. The Gospel artists must have noticed what the goldsmiths were symbolising. Therefore, it would be logical for this animal interlace to be a tree of life. However, to understand the ornamentation it is necessary to find the relevant theology and the following verses provides its description.

On either side of the river is the tree of life with its twelve kinds of fruit producing its fruit each month, and the leaves of the tree are for the healing of the nations.
Revelation chapter 22.2

The same idea of a tree of life being a band of running water and having permanent leaves and fruit in due season is found again in Psalm 1. This vision is represented in interlace. The ribbon is not an elongated animal body, but instead the river of the water of life. Wrapped around the river ribbon, but positioned to one side are fruits on the ends of stalks; there should be 12 on the cross according to the Revelation reference and the total on the cross was 12. Bede interpreted this passage as both 12 fruits and 12 months which for him was *blessed immortality*. He also saw *the cross of Christ bears fruit through the doctrine of 12 apostles*. At the end of the rivers are the permanent leaves that cannot fall off. The first and the last. Bede saw this as everlasting life and redemption. Therefore, this stunning cross depicted the believer living with God forever.

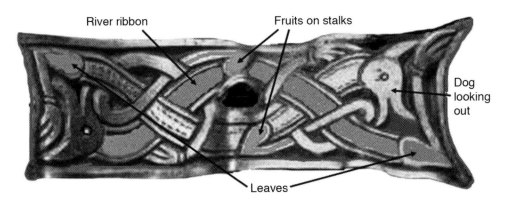

One river ribbon has been marked in grey and is a bell shaped curve. Two leaves are shown at the top left and bottom right of each ribbon. Two fruits on stalks, tick shaped, appear at the top and bottom of the middle part of the plate. The fruits are on either side of the river of life. The dogs' heads and legs are at the outside ends looking away. It fits the Revelation verses.

The animal heads do not look like lambs, yet are definitely quadrupeds. The feet have 4 toes which are not cloven. They could be dogs. These dogs can be explained again by Revelation 22, but a little further in the text at verse 15.

> *Outside are the dogs and sorcerers and fornicators and murderers and idolaters, and everyone who loves and practices falsehood.*
>
> Revelation chapter 22.15

The dogs are at the ends of the river ribbon; they are on the outside. The dogs are looking outwards on the outside keeping the sinners away. They are guarding against evil and falsehood. In a similar way, the dogs drawn on the posts of the chair Luke sits on in the St Chad's Gospel are looking away.

Therefore, the message on this cross is uncompromising. Let anyone who wished to take the baptismal river water of life as a gift, simply reach out to the cross. Come away from the outside and its sin. Surely, this cross with its Saxon message is unique. It is

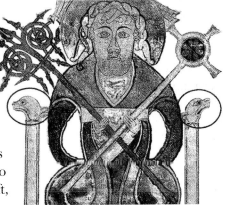

Centre piece of Luke's Gospel page with dogs, encircled, looking outwards.

Christian artwork at its very best. It is biblical scripture in superlative gold work. Surely, it ought to be a top national icon and displayed in the British Museum next to the Sutton Hoo helmet.

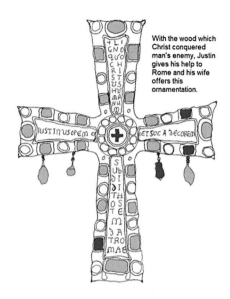

With the wood which Christ conquered man's enemy, Justin gives his help to Rome and his wife offers this ornamentation.

It is also a rare jewelled cross or *crux gemmata*. After the mother of Constantine, Helena, journeyed in 326 on a pilgrimage to Palestine and claimed she had found Calvary, every Christian Emperor following Constantine thought it necessary to go on the same pilgrimage. In 417, the Roman Emperor Theodosius II on the now expected pilgrimage to Jerusalem planted at Calvary a large silver cross, other accounts say gilded bronze, into the supposed rock of Golgotha. This cross, had jewels, presumably garnets, vine leaves, pearls and the shape of the unfolded cross. From 417, for

Drawing of Cross of Justin II showing the inscription.

at least the next three hundred years the design of the cross was in this form. There are very few early *crux gemmata* known. The earliest are two mosaics in Italian churches (basilica of Pudentiana in Rome, c384 and the basilica of Apollinaris in

Three kinds of crux gemmata. Left: Semi-dome apse mosaic at the basilica of Apollinaris, first bishop of Ravenna, Italy. This mid-6th century mosaic shows the cosmos as a dome with the hand of God above the cross. It is a scene of transfiguration. The central roundel has a jewelled cross. Middle: The coin is of Emperor Marcian, 450 – 457, and is a gold victory solidus. Right: The Rupertus Cross replica is gilt copper sheeting attached to a wooden base and has glass inlays. Thought to be Northumbrian and made somewhere between the late 7th century and the mid-8th century. It was taken to Salzburg, Austria, where it became associated with Rupert, c660 – 710, a missionary from France.

Classe a province of Ravenna, 549) and the most decorated is the recently restored Cross of Justin II in the Vatican Museum, 565 – 578.

The crumpled cross in pure gold with wonderful animal interlace is therefore exceptional. Lichfield Cathedral and Birmingham Museum and Art Gallery are fortunate to possess this icon in replica form and enable visitors to see the earliest design for a cross, in gold and with wonderful animal interlace expressing *life everlasting*.

3. Hand bell

Three separate items have been connected to give an object whose purpose has still to be agreed and so has been called *the mystery object*. It consists of a top button which has a black and white squared glass pattern, and underneath are holes which match the top of a cylinder. The bottom of the cylinder matches to a base plate which is circular and domed, but a little flattened. The bottom plate has rivet holes all around the edge. The rivet holes around the base could have attached it to a bell which would be either bronze or iron, perhaps iron clad in brass. If it makes the handle of a bishop's hand bell, then it would have been used to call people to prayer, baptism or for a funeral. The flattened shape enabled the bell to be rung in either a north-south direction or an east-west direction so giving two different sounds. Alternatively, it was hit with a small hammer.

The history of bells used for religious purposes is unclear. Romans signalled the time of bathing by ringing a small bell and it has been suggested Christians followed this by using one to call for worship. A small bell has been found at Vinolanda near Hadrian's Wall. They were used in the catacombs of Rome and this made sense if you imagine a procession trying to keep together in the dark tunnels. Another view is they were not used for worship until adopted by monasteries in France in 6th century. Pope Sabinian, c605, encouraged their use instead of wooden clackers. Columba, c597, heard a midnight bell at Iona before dying at the altar. In his biography, it stated bells were used to summon the monks at Iona to prayer. It is said Teilo received a bell when on a pilgrimage to Jerusalem in the 6th century and used it when healing the sick in his church at Llandaff. There is another story of Gildas making a bell for David. Bede described a bell at Whitby, 680, which called nuns to prayer as well as being used to mark a death.

Many hand bells have survived, and one of the best is the bell of Cuileáin, reputed to come from a monastery in County Tipperary and is 7th or 8th century.

It can be seen in a splendid gallery at the British Museum. Ireland has a good collection, Scotland has 19, and England has a few. There is a small bell in the Sutton Hoo hoard, and there are some in Wales that could well have belonged to early Celtic saints, such as the bell of Gwynhoedl on display in Cardiff. Most of the Welsh bells are roughly rectangular shaped and vary from 10cm to 30cm in height. Almost all of these early bells belonged to the Celtic churches. The Celtic word for a bell is *cloc* and so was linked with timing the day. It was also linked with the office of abbot or bishop in the same way as a staff or crozier.

The hand bell in the 7th century was consecrated or blessed and kept in a shrine reliquary. Since the hoard bell is finely decorated with gold and garnets, it would not have a crude metal loop. The high quality of decoration sets this hand bell apart from all other known hand bells. Some surviving bells have Christian symbols incised on the bell or its reliquary and it would be expected small crosses would have been attached to the bell or wooden container.

These three examples show the high quality of Christian pieces in the hoard. You will go wow to the excellence and sophistication of the pieces and this is an introduction to going wow to the power of God. To state again, it is not about storing treasure on earth, but about seeing the creativity in God's world.

Drawing of a small cross, 2cm x 1.5cm, found in the hoard that could have decorated a bell case.

Gospels

Worshipping God with metal artwork was equalled, if not bettered, by the devotion of scribes in laying out God's word in illuminated books called a Gospel. The word is Saxon for *God-spell* meaning good news.

An early Gospel

Tatian c120 – 180 was an Assyrian ascetic who travelled to Rome and Alexandria and c170 – 175 took on the difficult task of bringing together the 4 Gospels. Up to this time, the Gospels were written and circulated separately. By writing the Gospels as one tract, called a harmony, he gave a full story of the mission of Christ. No original book has survived, but there are commentaries which give a nearly complete collection of his writing. It was called the *Diatessaron* meaning made of four. There could have been versions in Syriac and in Greek. It has been suggested the structure of this book inspired scribes of Gospels in the 7th century.

The best 7th and 8th century Gospels are the Book of Durrow c680 (could be later) and possibly written in East Angle or Iona, St Chad's Gospel (St Teilo or Lichfield Gospel) c700 (could be later) and Mercian, and the Lindisfarne Gospel from Northumbria c721. All are altar display books and show the diligence and skill of the scribes.

St Chad's Gospel is 236 pages of calf vellum containing the Gospels of Matthew, Mark and the beginning of Luke. The rest of Luke, the whole Gospel of John, its wooden cover and the jewels that undoubtedly would be fixed to the cover have been lost. The strong suspicion is they were removed sometime in the troubles when the Vikings arrived in Lichfield at the beginning of 875.

The Celtic Insular script has the diminuendo feature of each line tapering down in height from left to right. Also red dots decorating particular capital letters.

St Chad's Gospel is the oldest book still being used in worship in the UK. New Bishops of Lichfield swear their oaths of allegiance to the Crown and of obedience and fidelity with this book and the tradition could go back to c700. The first cathedral started at the very end of the year 700 and it would have had a new shrine to Chad for the many pilgrims arriving. Logic suggests an altar display book like this would either have been commissioned, or already have been written for this occasion. It parallels the way the Lindisfarne Gospel was commissioned for Cuthbert's shrine when set up in 698. Indeed, the chi rho page shown has similarities to the same page in the Lindisfarne Gospel. This suggested some kind of correspondence continued between the two centres and both were following the same kind of project.

Examination of the handwriting using new technology has concluded there were at least 4 different ways certain letters were written. This suggested it was written in sections by at least 4 different scribes. The latest conclusion is the script was the product of a well-orchestrated effort by multiple scribes directed by a master scribe. Indeed, with powerful lighting and lens, names have been found dry scratched into the vellum and they could be associated with the writing and, or making of the Gospel. Three of the names (Berhtfled, Elfled and Wulfild) were women. This adds to believing a mixed-sex scriptorium existed on the site at Lichfield around 700, an arrangement seen elsewhere.

The eight pages of artwork are stunning. The Lindisfarne Gospel artwork shows around 90 different hues made by mixing around 40 infusions from lichens, plants and minerals. St Chad's Gospel was less colourful and very pastel in colouring, but would have had a similar chemistry of colours. It is known the hues, mainly yellow, pink and pale blue, were made by layering the pigment on the vellum and even the pH was being changed to obtain the right tint. The ink was candle soot colloidal suspension, possibly dispersed in a medium such as fish oil or egg white. All this would have required men and women working in one or several buildings dedicated to producing vellum, ink, feather pens, cover-boards and metal embellishments and fastenings. The complete book was thought to have needed the skins of around 50 calves, but a herd of around 200 would be needed since many skins, scratched and holed by parasites, would be discarded. The type of cow is unknown and would have been very different from modern breeds. It would have resembled the ancestral cow or auroch without its hump, but having a slender build and forward pointing horns. Auroch horns were found in the Sutton Hoo hoard. These cattle were used by the Romans and still wild in parts of Eastern Europe until 1627. There is a Dutch project using crossbreeding to bring it back. It must have required an extensive farm with many oblates working it and having to be careful with these very wild cows.

Overtime the Gospel has gained marginalia, as people have wanted to add something personal to the holy book. The earliest written Old Welsh (Brythonic) appeared in two places at the end of St Matthew's Gospel. It concerned a land transaction and was written after the Gospel words, *And remember, I am with you always, to the end of the age.* Matthew 28.20. It is referred to again in Chapter 8.

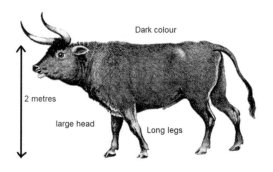

Reconstructed image of an Auroch.

Another at the bottom of Luke's page concerned the freedom, or manumission, granted to *Bleiddudd ap Sulien and his progeny forever* from slavery; thought to be the earliest British reference for a liberation gained.

Perhaps, the most significant feature of this and other early Gospels is how it brings together cultural influences. The artwork in St Chad's Gospel has much Celtic, some Mercian Saxon and a little Pictish element. Produced in Mercia, but having correspondence with scribes in Northumbria and possibly East Anglia. Used to wow pilgrims arriving from a wide area and many travelling a long distance. They were books deliberately intended to bind people together. The writers believed salvation came through God's grace, but all and especially sinners should be exposed to his Word. Illumination had to shine on all people.

Codex Amiatinus

Three bibles in the Jerome Latin form were commissioned in 692 from the Jarrow and Monkwearmouth monasteries. A grant of land was given to farm the 2000 cows needed for the vellum. Bede was probably involved in the editing. One bible was gifted to the pope, but somehow it ended up at an Italian monastery. In 1888, its Northumbrian origin was identified and it is now in a library at Florence with a copy at Jarrow. The other two copies were lost, though one might have come into the possession of Offa who then passed it to the monks at Worcester. There are some fragments held in the British Library.

It is a very large bible with 2060 pages and weighing 34kg. It needed 1550 calf-skins. Holding together so many large folios was innovative. It has the distinction of being the earliest surviving Bible in the Latin Vulgate translation. Plus the most accurate copy of Jerome's text.

In the 8th to early 9th century, many illuminated books and manuscripts were written providing a testament to the devoted scribes. The books were gifted around Europe providing evidence of the growing network of churches as well as interconnected kings. Tropes were borrowed and made ever more elaborate. Greater use of gold and purple dye was evident. Scriptoria included Canterbury, centres in Mercia (Lichfield, Worcester), Winchester, Barking, Flixborough, Whitby and Jarrow. Between the years 500 to 900, 76 known Saxon illuminated manuscripts were made. Between 900 and 1066, there were 134 manuscripts written. 210 can only be a fraction of all that was produced.

Stonework

It is likely the Atlantic Isles had very many standing stones from the 6th century onwards. There is a good number still surviving, but many would have been the target for invaders wanting to eliminate the local identity and later on the iconoclasts preferring minimal decoration. In addition, standing alone at isolated sites makes them easy prey for the vandal. Much has been written on a landscape of crosses, pillars and various stones in locations with *sacredness*, marking pilgrimage routes, pointing the way to a religious house and yet there is the thinnest of evidence. Since most currently known stonework is close or within the boundary of a church, it might instead have been a landscape of monasteries with their own cherished stonework standing in their grounds. Some might have marked an altar from a closed and destroyed church. Conflating Christian pillars and crosses with countryside signposts could be a big mistake. Those situated on isolated roads are late editions.

6 types of stonework, not to scale. A. Ruthwell monument from Ruthwell church, Dumfriesshire with biblical scenes. B. Grave marker at Margam stones museum. C. Wheel or Houelt cross at Llanwit Major marking Kingship. D. Wayside cross from Eyam Parish churchyard. E. Sundial stone at Tywyn church. The hole at the top had a peg to cast the sun's shadow. F. Pictish cross at Aberlemno churchyard, Angus, Scotland. Reverse side celebrates a battle victory.

Stonework varied from cross-incised stones, with some having an inscription in either Latin or Irish, but rarely in Welsh, to elaborate crosses with ornate sculpture. Crosses, pillars, markers and monuments therefore varied enormously and often showed a local identity.

The early 8th century Ruthwell cross, Dumfries and Galloway, is considered by many to be the best Saxon example. It has the oldest English poetry, *The Dream of the Rood,* in the form of a runic alphabet down the sides. It was broken in pieces by Scottish iconoclasts in 1642 and then restored in 1823 with a cross being added to the top. Its height is 5.5 metres (18 feet). The Margam stone was found near a pool on Margam Mountain, Glamorgan, in 1695. It is a 6th century grave marker in Latin to someone called *Bodvoc.* A Maltese cross is inscribed on the top suggesting a Christian connection. The Wheel cross is a marker for a king of Glamorgan. At the base is an inscription that reads, *In the name of God the Father and of the Holy Spirit. Houelt prepared this cross for the soul of Res his father.* This date is c886. The Eyam cross, Derbyshire, was guessed to be a wayside marker. A section is missing, but when intact must have exceeded 2 metres in height. Best guess for its date is 8th century. The Tywyn, Gwynedd, sundial stone is 7th to the 10th century and at one time was at a monastery. The Aberlemno cross of late 7th or early 8th century has decoration resembling Gospel interlace. The large slab is possibly the finest outside stonework.

High crosses served a variety of functions. Some were associated with churches and monasteries and had scenes from the Bible, often associated with a warning to remain faithful. They were a device for teaching and a reminder for those who might lapse in belief. They were the forerunner of the stained glass window. There is a mention in an early text of people praying daily by the cross. Some acted as cenotaphs and marked a burial, often of an elite individual. These funerary inscriptions have a similarity with those on Roman grave markers and it has been suggested this shows a continuity. Other stones might have simply marked a boundary or a path across a difficult terrain, but this is speculation. Some of the tallest were marking wayside pulpits or places to settle disputes, make proclamations and agree on administrative change. A small number had a sundial and therefore assisted the passer-by to know the time. Some of the very earliest monuments reused prehistoric standing stones. For example, across Dartmoor, the Welsh hills and Peak District are marker stones and travellers, perhaps pilgrims, have incised a cross to show their Christianity. The earliest standing crosses, around the 8th century, were planted by the local inhabitants and later ones were arranged by the church. Some were paid for by the wealthy elite and to reflect their influence they were positioned on their estate. The Vikings added their markers to celebrate their own culture, but used Christian sites.

Such stones, known as hogbacks, are associated with churchyards, yet lack explicit Christian symbols and do not appear to cover a grave. They date from 920 and could be the result of Viking migration of people still holding on to their Scandinavian beliefs, but looking to a churchyard and a Christian setting. Similar transitional imagery can be seen on the Gosforth Cross.

Dating many stones is problematic. Several attempts have been made to classify stones and place each class in a chronological order, but each

Bakewell, Derbyshire, (right) church has possibly the best collection of Saxon stonework. The left standing cross has been given a date of early 9th century. One side has obvious biblical images. The side shown has swirling vines, a rider on a horse and a dog eating the fruit of the vine which could be Christian, possibly a hunting scene or even a Germanic folk depiction. The cross pillar on the right has been dated to 1000. It has interlace which could be Christian, but also Viking. All this shows ambiguity and therefore are awkward to interpret.

Decorative stone (below) found in the churchyard of St Peters, Heysham, Lancashire, c1812. It might have the Christian symbols of priests holding hands in an oran posture and a possible tree-of-life (circled). It has also been interpreted as Norse mythology concerning Sigmund and Sigurd. With 6 dogs, stag and bears it could also have been a hunting scene.

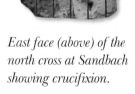

time objections have been raised. Perhaps, the only safe conclusion is the earliest stones were unworked and crudely shaped.

Almost 50 high crosses are known in England compared with fewer than 8 standing crosses in Wales. Wales instead has over 600 carved stones. There are 7 high crosses known in Scotland, but over 300 Pictish stones. Ireland has around 70 high crosses, many still in their original locations, and very many incised stones. Most Welsh stonework appears in the South-West and North-East Wales with very little in central Wales and along the English border.

Two of the best Saxon crosses occur in the market centre of Sandbach, Cheshire. Their original location is unknown, but considering the many Biblical depictions, it must have been a great help to any preacher standing close. They were painted and colourful. The patterned sculpture would have given it a precious appearance. The many figures indicate the church as a community and so infer unity. Two winged beasts at the foot of the cross assist dating to the early 9th century. They have gaping jaws, prominent eyelids and interlaced tongues. This motif has been identified as broadly Mercian and corresponded with parallels in St Chad's Gospel, Book of Cerne, the Tiberius Bede and the Royal Bible, all of which might have been written in Mercia, in which case Lichfield is a good possibility. Six gold snakes with gaping jaws have been uncovered in the Hoard found at Hammerwich and could have a linkage.

The Sandbach crosses, like most high crosses, remind the onlooker to think about being saved. Frequent Salvation depictions included, David saving the sheep from the lion, Jonah surviving after 3 days inside the whale, David slaying

East face (above) of the north cross at Sandbach showing crucifixion.

Refined image (right) of Mark's lion symbol in St Chad's Gospel having a protruding tongue. The creatures each side of his head also have elaborate protruding tongues.

A stone at Bakewell church (left) showing a beast trampling a serpent. A stone from Southwell Minster (right), perhaps 10th century, showing Archangel Michael with a sword attacking a dragon-like beast. Mercian Beasts, especially gaping serpents, need further explanation.

Panel (below) from the west face of the north cross at Sandbach showing two beasts with long tongues. Being placed at the base of the cross, shows they were primordial creatures at the beginning of time. (This assumes fragments were reassembled in the right order in

1816). It is a Tree of Life with beasts placed at the foot showing our original nature. If it is a winged lion, it is the symbol for Mark. Having wings implies spiritual elevation so it is saying start here and follow the story depicted upwards on the cross. Go from beastliness to elevated salvation.

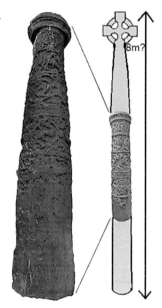

Goliath, Isaac the son of Abraham being saved from sacrifice, and the crucifixion of Christ often showed on the west side with his resurrection on the east side. They would have been powerful teaching aids.

Wolverhampton was at the centre of several important Saxon trackways and there was an early mention of a stone called Byrngyd or Beorgip on one road, presumably as a wayside marker. This might possibly be the pillar still standing in the City's central church graveyard. It is thought to be the middle section that has survived, so either it was a pillar, or it had a cross of some sort. It is said to be now on the site of a monastery built c994. The charter describing

Wolverhampton Pillar, or was it a cross? Its date is unknown.

this new build refers to an ancient Minster of Hamtun, but this charter and early history is now in doubt. If there ever was an early Saxon presence, some writers have placed this in Wulfhere's time in the mid-7th century.

The stonework is now much eroded, but an attempt to retrieve the faded images suggested carvings of a lion, ox and eagle, images of the evangelists Mark, Luke and John. The fourth is of a deer. Its size and general shape are similar to the trackway markers seen in the Peak District.

Irminsul

The Saxons north of the Rhine and on the west side of Germany kept a pagan totem known as an Irminsul. It was a large wooden pillar, or possibly a tree, with good height, girth and strength and believed to be the central pillar of the world supporting the sky. It had connections with the god Woden. In c772, Charlemagne demolished the pillar to demoralise the Saxons. Perhaps, tall pillars associated with Woden became tall pillars praising God. They appear to be analogous.

They also correspond with the tree of life concept. The new church of Sagrada Familia, Barcelona, has a central portal on the front topped with a Tree of Life. It is a sculpted tree complete with white doves and crowned with a cross.

A small amount of decorative stonework has somehow survived weathering and destruction by iconoclasts. Most pieces fall into categories of beasts, angels and archangels, apostles and Mary with a young Jesus. A short list of examples includes: winged angels at the church of St Lawrence, Bradford on Avon, Wiltshire, dated 8th to 12th century; the draped figure of Christ on a cross at St Matthews church, Langford, Oxfordshire, believed to be pre-Conquest; the Virgin and Child in York Minster which could be 12th century; the various carved stones at Breedon-on-the-Hill church, Leicestershire including the 8th or 9th century angel and the early stones at St Mary the Virgin, Wirksworth, Derbyshire. There are many pieces of indeterminate date and many so badly eroded it is difficult to categorise them, but the Lichfield Angel stands out as being exceptional. It has been dated to c770 and located in Offa's cathedral. It was buried under the cathedral floor, possibly from the time of Viking destruction, until its discovery in 2003. It has had very little weathering and could easily be the best-kept Saxon sculpture. There is a good similarity to an archangel carved on an ivory panel in the British Museum (ref.OA9999). This panel is part of a diptych from Byzantine Constantinople, 525 – 550. There is some similarity to the Breedon Angel, Leicestershire and the worn figure of the Deerhurst Angel, Gloucestershire, and both 9th century. It has some resemblance to the archangel by the side of Christ in the Codex Amiatinus, drawn approximately 70 years earlier.

Lichfield Angel, image refined. Gabriel was on the left end of a shrine chest with a coped lid that could have held the relics of Chad. The background was white, the angel was red, yellow, white and ochre and the halo possibly gilded. It still has specks of pigment on the costume and carbon black on the wings for shadow. It stands 60cm tall. From early on, it was realised the appearance and position is similar to the head end of Cuthbert's wooden coffin with the figures of Gabriel and Michael incised. Again, it shows an affinity between Lichfield and Lindisfarne.

There are ambiguities in the way the right hand blessing is given. Two fingers extended represent the twofold nature, human and divine, of Jesus. The three curved fingers show the Trinity. However, touching between thumb and small finger might be symbolising the 'Eye of the Lord', Psalm 33, 18, especially within the arch of the wing. Another ambiguity is the right foot. Is it trampling a vine or two-headed snake, and what is Gabriel holding, a vine or lily cross-staff? A lily could be the earliest reference to Annunciation, but is more likely to symbolise Christ and resurrection. The bobbled hair, round ears, large chin and round, drilled eyes are much like the drawings of Mark and Luke in the St Chad's Gospels. Pigments are also chemically similar. Rich red, bright yellow and probably gold on a white background epitomizes illumination.

148

Iconoclasm in the East

In 726, another immense volcanic eruption on the island of Santorini in the Aegean Sea, 120 miles (200km) south-east of Greece, blackened the skies over Constantinople and the Emperor took it to be a sign from God. It was used to support the growing opposition to the use of exalted artwork. Over the next fifty years, icons used for veneration were removed in the Greek speaking Eastern Church. In 843, at a Church Council this iconoclasm was revoked. It led to a resurgence in the portrayal of many scenes from the Bible being shown in church artwork. Highly coloured images now became mandatory for decoration. In the Latin speaking Western Church the stance taken was icons should remain, but not used for veneration or as a distraction from worship. Yet another distinction between East and West churches resulted.

The Other World in stone

Scene from the Wirksworth Stone in St Mary the Virgin, Wirksworth, Derbyshire, showing Mary (5) being borne on a stretcher for burial. Presumably, the apostles (1 and 2) are pulling the bier and (4) could be a High Priest who has been dragged underneath. Figure (3) is John leading the procession and carrying a palm. Figure (6) is a cloud with six angels singing praises. There are over 50 early texts describing the fate of Mary, but all are part of the Apocrypha and so not in the Bible. Nevertheless, this was a favourite image and Mary dying or sleeping and her ascension into heaven was for many centuries seen in church iconography. It is thought this is the earliest surviving depiction of this scene in the western Latin Church. Elsewhere on this stone is a simple cross with a lamb at the centre and since this depiction was banned at the Council in Trullo, Constantinople in 692 it is claimed this wonderful stone is earlier than this date. That makes it remarkable.

Chapter 7

THE KING'S CHURCH 700 – 821

King Alfred prefaced his translation of Pope Gregory's *Pastoral Care* with, *Kings who fail to obey their divine duty to promote learning can expect earthly punishments to befall their people.* It is the oldest known book written in English, c890s, and shows how kings believed their duty was divinely given. King Alfred's bronze statue in Winchester depicts him holding his sword up like a cross.

Early Saxon English kings are often separated into one of two stereotypes. The favoured type is they were pagan, bloodthirsty plunderers and brutal killers of rivals, including family, and they led their kingdoms in a perpetual state of hostility. A contrary view is they were *priestly kings*, calling Councils, making laws, forging liaisons and ruling ostensibly by mediation with God. Much time had passed since they were heathens, now they were behaving spiritually. The king, not the bishop, put matters right through God, and this was seen with their ceremony. The coronation feast had similarities to the Eucharist with the king's cup being passed around loyal thegns. Regalia was worn on Christian festivals of Easter, Pentecost and Christmas. In council the king would sit centrally with the bishop on his right and the chancellor on his left. When making laws and offering treaties the king invoked divine vengeance if anyone ever transgressed. Their baptism was special with oil anointing. So priestly were they, a relatively high number ended their days in or near a church or monastery. At least four kings made their own pilgrimage to Rome. Several gained close papal support. From the mid-9th century onwards, wandering saints lost their importance and royal saints increased, often given sainthood by a family member, especially if they happen to die in exceptional ways. Relics of kings were venerated. In 8 sub-kingdoms, the family line was traced back to the Gods Woden or Saxnot and made out to be divine. If the bloodline could not directly be traced, then obscure and distant origins were cited or fabricated. With a bishop alongside, the kings appeared to all as if possessing extraordinary holy attributes. A canon from the 786 Council, organised by Offa of Mercia, stated, *let no one conspire to kill a king, for he is the Lord's Anointed.*

The reality, of course, was some were ruthless, a few were saintly and most were a mixture, changing when it suited them. Some would have little to do with churches; some borrowed church customs and most became closely involved with the church. They did not always share the values of the early Christian missionaries, though they still welcomed, protected and used them. Some accepted baptism, but only a few early kings appeared to be convincing catechumens. A few even imposed baptism on others as a way of obtaining trust and loyalty. They had rituals to enhance their own position and would not willingly give them up and allow bishops to enforce a spiritual overlordship, so they took on this quasi-priestly role. Their problem connecting with the church was they were not able to discourse in Latin, the language of the church; King Aldfrith of Northumbria, reigning c685 – 705, was an exception. Therefore, most of them relied on bishop advisors. It was a kingship relying on a very close church state relationship. King Aethelberht of Kent welcomed Augustine, 597, Edwin of Northumbria worked with Paulinus, 626, Oswald of Northumbria promoted Aidan, c634, Cynegils of the West Saxons helped Birinus, c640, Sigeberht of the East Angles accepted Felix, 630s, Fursa, 633, and Cedd, c654. Ecgberht of Kent assisted Bassa in 669 and finally Wulfhere of Mercia introduced Chad, 699, and then made church laws with Theodore of Canterbury, c672. To begin with, Bede approved of this model of hallowed kings with spiritual direction from a bishop. It did not last.

Within this symbiotic holy kingship came a tension which affected the church for more than a century. The problem came when the kings endowed land for building new monasteries and later gave established monasteries to loyal followers who only took a passing interest in their gifted church. Nobility began to furnish their acquired church as a way of expressing wealth and power. Spiritual greed set in. Some patronised their church to such an extent it gained precedence over leaving wealth to their own kin folk. Royalty and nobility placed their abbots in charge who could be trusted to look after their holy assets. Often these placemen had little theological understanding with some not even being able to converse in Latin. Bede described the appointments of abbots, prefects, ministers and servants of the king with little experience of monastic life. It led to a deterioration and a very long letter from Bede to his Bishop in York in 734 lamenting this decline in spiritual standards. The letter said in some cases laymen were taking over monasteries after they had given a money bribe to the king. A monastery could be owned and privatised. Some occupied the monastery with their wives and children. They in time bought more land to erect a convent for their wives who became superior to the nuns who then had to obey their proxy abbess. Bede opined, *Wasps, though they can make combs, yet store them with poison instead of honey.*

Bede's great complaint of personal churches might be evident in burial practice. In many Continental churches of the 7th and 8th century, the building was over high-status burials and rulers were buried near the altar. This was not so evident in Britain, and kings instead were buried alongside the outer wall of churches and close to the doorway. By the 8th and 9th century, rulers were placed in exceptional side-chapels or crypts of churches customised for royalty.

Bede c673 – 735

Bede was possibly born at Monkton, not far from his future home at Jarrow, Northumbria. Aged 7, he entered the new monastery at Monkwearmouth and was entrusted into the care of the abbot Benedict Biscop, c628 – 690. In 686, he survived a plague epidemic which decimated the Monkwearmouth-Jarrow complex. He became a young deacon at 19 and a priest when 30. Around 7 years later he had begun to write commentaries on the Bible. Almost his entire life was spent at the two monasteries and he said his chief delight was studying, teaching and writing. His best known work, *The Ecclesiastical history of the English People,* was finished in 731. This was the first detailed history of Britain. The achievement was helped by the great library at the monasteries, by the network of monks who gave information from far and wide and the diligence he paid to detail and its context. He easily wrote in Latin and the vernacular Saxon and was able to distil historical data and give it meaning. This capability was seen at the end of his life when he continued to sing praises to God, translate a Gospel of John and comment on a book from Northern France. He died in May 735. Within a few decades of his death, his relics were venerated and are now held at Durham Cathedral.

In 733, Bede travelled to York to visit Ecgbert, the newly installed Bishop of York. In 734, he wrote his letter to Ecgbert pointing out the difficulties of the church. He described the calamity which the country was suffering and in polite language urged Ecgbert to rectify the misfortune. Perhaps, he could see York being elevated to an archbishopric in 735 and demoting Lindisfarne. Maybe Bede was not in good health, which explained why the letter contained many groans and complaints. Woes included the altar was being profaned by vulgar priests who gave little service. Bishops were indulging in laughter and jest, were revelling in drunkenness and being tempted by an idle life. Houses and hamlets in inaccessible places were being denied holy ministry. Priests were accepting money and not preaching the Gospel, or confirming the baptised and were reciting the Apostle's Creed and Lord's Prayer in the vernacular tongue instead of Latin. Bede must have died a disheartened monk.

Bede's letter has often been cited as a downturn in the administration of the church. It might just be he was a very meticulous writer and disciplined monk who could not cope with seeing lesser individuals struggling to follow his beloved monastic tradition. He wanted perfection. Indeed, the perfection of Christ is an aspect he loved to repeat to others. However, he was not the only one to think this way.

Aethelbald reigned the longest of any Saxon king, 716 – 757. He was the first to take the title *King of Britain*. In a land grant to a monastery at Ismere, near Kidderminster, Worcestershire, in 736 he signed it *king of all the provinces called the South English*. In 744, he signed a land grant to Glastonbury Abbey, Somerset, and gave himself the title *Monarch of Britain*. These self-imposed titles were taken not long after Bede's book which has the phrase *People of the Angli*, so the idea of a united country was now a common weal. The people could now be called Anglo-Saxons. Paradoxically, *Angli* meant a hook or barb. Its origin is unknown and could be the result of a misunderstanding. Bede called Aethelbald the king of all that is south of the River Humber, a little exaggerated.

Aethelbald's charters were probably written at Worcester by his servant bishop; the Mercian centre had moved southwards. For much of his reign Aethelbald controlled Wessex and so gained London and Middlesex. Kent was subdued, but not entirely controlled. Parts of Wales were controlled, but not entirely subdued. Good terms with East Angle were arranged and parts of Northumbria devastated. He had overlordship of the South-West Midlands. So far, it was the largest Saxon hegemony.

It is no surprise those under his domination described him as haughty, arrogant and hostile. One historian went as far as calling him a barbarian master of a military stronghold. Worse is a letter from the Archbishop of Germany, known as Boniface, which was edited by Archbishop Ecgbert at York and delivered to Aethelbald. The letter began with much praise acknowledging Aethelbald's generosity to the poor and widows as well as keeping the peace. It then slighted the king by claiming, we have heard almost all your nobles desert their wives and live with women, including nuns, who live in adultery, and they follow your example. This is hard to understand since Aethelbald appeared never to have married. His and his armies' adultery was said to occur inside the monasteries and if it continued, it would lead to degeneration of the whole country. The letter does not stop there because it added the sin of taking revenue from the churches and monasteries, of thegns causing violence to priests and monks and of undoing the apostolic mission of Pope Gregory. Clearly, a top priest from Germany, who hailed from the now subdued Wessex, could remonstrate via York, which had seen some devastation, to a supreme ruler of the Southern English and describe hearsay as being factual. The power of the church was now felt across Europe and being expressed in stilted and jaundiced language. Even so, it had to be heeded.

Boniface c675 – 754
Born Winfrid, or Winfrith, to wealthy parents possibly living in Devon. It is claimed he began his schooling at a monastery at Exeter. Later he entered the Benedictine monastery of Nursling near Winchester, Hampshire, followed by teaching in the abbey school. When 30 he became a priest. Around 716, his abbot died and he was expected to take over, but instead chose to evangelise abroad. It is said he much admired a previous mission by a Yorkshire-man called Willibrord, c658 – 739, to Christianise part of The Netherlands and he wanted to do the same. In 719, he led a mission to central Germany eventually becoming the first archbishop of Mainz and primate of all Germany.

Boniface at Brugge, Belgium.

He greatly shaped and unified the German and European church. By strongly supporting Pope Gregory II, he gave him the name of Boniface, it increased the power of the papacy and some see this as the beginning of the domination in Europe of the Catholic Church. During Boniface's evangelism, he requested books, relics, investments and priests from Winchester to help in his mission. This helped to form a strong attachment between the new German and established British churches. Many of Boniface's sermons and letters have survived and give an insight into the 8th century church across Europe.

It is sometimes written there was an irony in pagan German Saxons invading Britain only to receive back missionaries who then introduced their religion, but this is not entirely true. Boniface said he found the Germans did not accept Christ *in their entirety* and from this, it is deduced they were pagan. In fact, most of the people were Christians, but of the Arian persuasion and had been for at least two centuries. Boniface's accomplishment was to convert them to Nicene Christianity.

Boniface retired to The Netherlands, and there was killed when waiting for the arrival of some newly baptised Christians who wanted confirmation. He was set upon by a wandering group of thieves and martyred. His relics became a point for pilgrimage and he is still venerated in many parts of Europe.

Aethelbald's response to Boniface's trenchant letter was to head a Council of Clofesho in 747 and address the problem of laypeople in control of monasteries and the excesses in dress, drinking and immorality of the clergy. The bishops too came in for criticism. They were told to stop neglecting their diocese and assemble all people in convenient places to teach the word of God, and especially to those people who rarely hear a priest. In return for this reordering of the church, in 759 at Gumley, Leicestershire, Aethelbald in a new deal accepted all

Crypt at Repton Monastery church, 7th century. It had previously been a baptistry. Four side recesses made it cruciform shaped. In each recess could have been an ossuary with bones. It is reminiscent of Jewish practice, early Christian catacombs and a reliquary holding the relics of saints. A stone cross fragment showed a warrior on a horse and perhaps it depicted Aethelbald. If so, it is the earliest image of a Saxon king and the stone is displayed in Derby Museum.

churches in Mercia, but not elsewhere, should be free of royal food rents and financial burdens caused by building local bridges and fortresses. Not exactly a complete concession, but at least Aethelbald was listening to the church.

In a charter of the 740s he styled himself *gens Anglorum* from which the word *Aenglisc* is derived and much of the country now referred to themselves as English.

Aethelbald ruled over more land than any of the other Mercian kings, was probably the first Mercian to mint coins, developed London into a prime market and port, made fundamental reforms to the running of the church and ruled for 41 years with few battles. Inexplicably he was murdered in 757 in what could have only been revenge. He was buried in the crypt at Repton Monastery, so his murder might not have concerned a grudge from the church as has been implied. Aethelbald's ancestors were probably in direct line from Creoda, the first Mercian king, and a burial at the early Mercian church seems appropriate. Two other Mercian royals were buried there and a third is sometimes speculated.

A third chronicler was Aldhelm and his relationship with the king of Dumnonia and the Celtic church gave another insight into the church state tensions.

Aldhelm c640 – 709

Possibly Aldhelm descended from the royal family of Wessex, but nothing is known of his early life. It is thought he received his education from an Irish monk at Malmesbury and corresponded with a number of Irish teachers. He was trained by Hadrian at Canterbury and so must have known about Gregory. In c673 he was made abbot of Malmesbury Monastery, Wiltshire. In c705 he became bishop of Sherborne, Dorset and in this time founded two monasteries at Frome, Somerset and Bradford on Avon, Wiltshire. He died at the church of Doulting, near Shepton Mallet, Somerset in 709 and his body was taken to Malmesbury where pilgrimage to his relics began. Thus, for much of his life, Aldhelm was in a location where he would have taken a leading role in relating with the king and clergy of Dumnonia, a kingdom that included Cornwall, Devon and much of Somerset.

Aldhelm wrote, and later visited, Geraint, king of the Britons/Celts in the West Country who reigned 670 – 710. He quoted the rulings from the Council of

Hertford, 672 or 673, and exhorted Geraint to instruct his bishops to follow the Roman practice of worship, to calculate Easter in the now accepted way, and for monks to wear the tonsure of St Peter. He then referred to the heretics and schismatics in the kingdom and concluded they must change or there would be a cruel scandal in the church. As an example of clergy taking the wrong course, he referred to the bishops on the other side of the strait of the River Severn in Dyfed and described them in very lurid ways. He also castigated those eremitic monks who lived a life of contemplative retirement in some squalid wilderness. Aldhelm was sorting out the West Country clergy and doing so by imploring the king. He made it Geraint's responsibility to put right the Dumnonia house of God. Geraint's reply is unknown, but subsequently Geraint gave a grant of land to Sherborne Abbey and from this it is assumed he had agreed to Aldhelm's remonstration. Unfortunately, after Aldhelm's death Wessex and Dumnonia went to war with Geraint being killed and the Wessex king gaining Somerset and Devon. Another battle in 722 reversed this with a victory for Cornwall, which meant they did not Romanise until much later, around 940.

There is no written account in Wales from a churchman detailing the uneasy relationship between church and state, but it must have occurred judging from the circumstantial evidence. There are a few charters which show the elite gave land to monasteries and there are monuments recording the burial of kings in church cemeteries, such as the Houelt stone at Llanwit, that point to royal privilege. The wealth of the mother churches must have been a tempting resource to control by rulers who often were not so rich, particularly in land. Dynasties could disappear without heirs, but religious houses were easily able to develop, consolidate and pass on their assets. It is not easy to ascertain how dominating the kings were. Many of the Llandaff charters recorded the provision of land from nobility as expiation for some kind of misdemeanour or violence against a religious house. Marginalia in St Chad's Gospel record atonements for wrongdoing with a land dispute at the centre, and this was seen also in the Hereford Gospel. Perhaps, in Wales and unlike England, many more of the priests came from the nobility and their spiritual control of their church compensated for any one ruler having patronage and possession.

The new churches in England

One of Aldhelm's legacies was the building of a wooden church at Bradford on Avon around 700. It is thought to have been on the site of the current Norman church standing close to the river. A very recent archaeological dig has found Saxon graves under the church. At some time, the wooden church was replaced

Left shows the south front side with the chancel is on the right. The front door could have had a porticus seen on the right image. The blind arcading and small window is original. The right shows the rear north side with the chancel now on the left. The off-centre door suggests the porticus might have been a side chapel with its own altar.

with a stone church, a little to the north, which still exists. However, St Laurence was only realised as being a Saxon church in the 19th century.

Four early churches have now been described: The Chapel of St Peter on the Wall at Bradwell, Essex 654; Escomb church, County Durham 670 – 675; St Paul's Monastery, Jarrow, Tyne and Wear 685 and now St Laurence, Bradford on Avon, early 8th century. There are no more early Saxon churches standing as a complete building and therefore it is more theoretical than actual to describe the church at this time. There is a

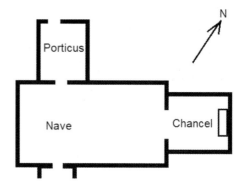

Floor plan. The side porticus might have been added to hold the relics of a king. The position of the altar table is guessed.

church, with many additions, which also has good Saxon credentials. It is the priory church of St Mary at Deerhurst, Gloucestershire. It has a font, mid to late 9th century, considered one of the finest for a Saxon church.

Certain features strongly suggest there was an early 8th century church at Deerhurst. However, the earliest mention of the priory was a land endowment in 804. The discovery of Roman remains in the vicinity and the possible site of a 7th century church at nearby Tewkesbury suggest the centre of the sub-kingdom called the *Hwicce* was not far away. This sub-kingdom supported

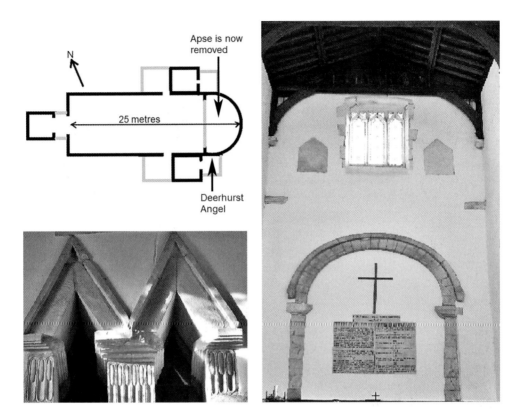

Top left: Plan of Deerhurst Priory church showing Saxon walls, though of different ages. Its size indicates a royal connection, which in the 9th century would be under the lordship of Mercia. Indeed, it is similar but smaller than the derived Offa's cathedral at Lichfield. Left: The two pointed windows with fine detail are thought to be 9th or 10th century. Right: The east end of the nave of Deerhurst Priory shows the arch to the apse, which is now blocked and removed. The two upper plaques, each side of the window, had painted images.

Mercia for most of its supremacy, probably through to the 10th century. It was therefore powerful.

Even though few complete Saxon churches still exist, certain aspects and features can be listed with some confidence.

- There was a progression in the developmental complexity of churches. It is easy to see this as an evolution, but there are insufficient churches to state unequivocally the sequence from simple to complex being linear with time. Nevertheless, a generalised order from simple functionality to elaborate ritual can be discerned in the architecture.

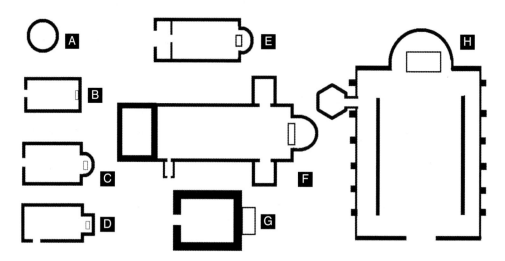

'A' is a roundhouse, oratory or beehive and could be made from earth, timber and wattle or stone. 'B' is the simple longhouse made from timber and brush. Altar was against the wall.'C' and 'D' are stone rectangular buildings with an apse or a square chancel. An apse the same width as the nave could be as early as 8th century. Many see the square chancel as being later in time. Square chancels are seen more in early northern churches and apses are commoner in early southern churches. It has been suggested the altar table had a space behind for the clergy when it Romanised. 'E' has the feature of a separate anteroom or narthex for those who were not confirmed, or it was possibly dividing women from the men. The altar table is on the diameter of the apse circle. At the early churches of Reculver and Winchester the altar could have been at the end of the nave. 'F' is cruciform in shape with side chapels or porches (porticus). Also, it had a tower either at the west end or over the chancel. 'G' is a tower church with perhaps a baptistery. 'H' is the very late Saxon church with aisles, side Chapter house, buttresses and sometimes a crypt. There could be three towers, presumably showing the trinity. Side chapels might contain the remains of high status individuals so they were buried close to the altar, but not part of the nave.

- Early churches were short rectangular shapes with high ceilings. From the outside they looked double storey. It would be easy to conclude they, like later cathedrals, were making worshippers look up to God. Alternatively, it might have improved acoustics. Benedict Biscop c680 brought back from Rome a singing master called John to teach the monks of Jarrow and Monkwearmouth how to chant for the liturgical year. This cycle was written down and copied in other monasteries. Later on John became an abbot of his own monastery.

All Saints, Brixworth, Northamptonshire. The first impression on seeing the church is its height, especially on a small hill. The round tower and staircase on the left is post 870. The small chapel on the right was added in 1300, but there were side chapels of some sort along the length of the nave. The spire and upper tower are late Saxon. After a comprehensive investigation ending 2011, the early church is now dated to late 8th century. Three quarters along the nave was a triple arch dividing the nave into two sections with a favoured group being positioned closer to its altar. Some bricks were reused from a nearby Roman site, but most came from across the County. This alone points to a high status Saxon church.

Building upwards was clearly connected with prestige, with the highest churches having royal connections. From the 9th century, smaller churches were built on hilltops achieving this reach in an easier way.

- Early windows were small and either one, two or rarely three arched. Benedict Biscop brought French glaziers to Jarrow and similarly glass windows were added to the church in York.

Right is a single arch window at St Pauls, Jarrow and far right is a double arch window at St Peters church, Barton-upon-Humber, Lincolnshire.

- Towers were added. There can only be one reason for building an upper room and that was to store valuables. If it was over the altar, it added protection since thieves would have hesitated to break into the most sacred part of the church. Valuables would have included the holy liturgical vessels, but also could have been the king's treasury. Various charters show endowments from the king to churches and monasteries and in return would expect loyalty to the crown and that might include holding and protecting the king's treasure. Little is

St Peter's tower, Barton-upon-Humber with buildings added on in later times. Note the blocked base door. There are no windows in the first floor room. A baptistry was attached and opposite a chancel added. Its date is uncertain, but c900 is mentioned with the current nave added on in the 11th century. The earliest dated graves were early 10th century.

In 669 Chad founded a monastery not far away and this does indicate an early Saxon settlement, perhaps, with a wooden church.

Earls Barton church, Northamptonshire from the north-west. The Saxon tower shown has been separated from the Norman nave and the 15th century battlements removed in the image. The most quoted date is c970. Notice the long and short stones on the corners called quoins and a feature of Saxon buildings. Also the stone decoration or pilaster, which is said to mimic timberwork. The 5-arched window and pilaster are also seen in churches in the Rhineland. The floor nave has a ladder, possibly original, used to access the first floor room which suggests a way to keep safe either valuables or a priest. The top floor holds 8 bells. It is likely there was a previous timber tower, but there is no evidence.

known on the shape of towers in the early churches and guesswork is necessary in any reconstruction.

By the late Saxon period, turriform or tower churches appeared. The base of the tower was the nave with an altar, the upper floor was the priest's room and a belfry might be at the top. Sometimes a small chancel was built from the base on the east side. Only three such churches are now known, St Peter's at Barton-upon-Humber, and St Mary's church at Broughton, both in North Lincolnshire and All Saints church at Earls Barton, Northamptonshire. Some have gone as far as suggesting these churches were the earliest type of church built in Saxon England, especially if made using tall timbers. Undoubtedly, there were many more. By adding naves and chancels, the tower shape disappeared.

- Naves became long for procession in those churches endowed by kings. Archaeological excavation at Lichfield Cathedral revealed a Saxon building under the present nave. So far, there has been no recognition of a church which could have been built by Offa to reflect his acquired status.

A church at Lichfield for the late 8th century could have been similar to Brixworth, Northamptonshire, the mid-Saxon church at Canterbury, the early church at Rochester or a larger version of the church at Deerhurst. All would have been known to Offa. Therefore, it would have had an apse the full width of the church, a long nave of at least 30 metres for procession, an ambulatory for the burial of revered family, perhaps a tower and possibly internal piers to partition a section restricted for royalty. It would be basilica in shape and size. Clearly, there is still much needing a new understanding.

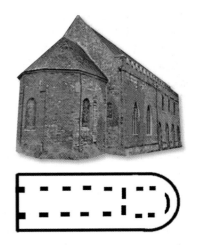

Offa was the first king to call himself *King of the English*. His kingdom extended from the Midlands to the south-east coast. There were no sub-kings; it was now all Mercia. One of his daughters married the Northumbrian king. Offa's Dyke was more likely a deterrent for rustlers and raiders, than a defensive earthwork against armies. It placed him equal to Roman wall builders and the rulers on the Continent who had constructed similar obstacles. So, perhaps, its prime purpose was to impress and deter. Charlemagne called him *his dearest brother*. He was the first king to hold a Council with papal legates attending and

Thirteen dioceses in Offa's kingdom.

approving. This gained the pope's support for Offa's request for a third archbishop, 787, to be installed at Lichfield. Consequently, the new archbishop, probably a Mercian, led a coronation of his son and heir c788. It was the first coronation in England with anointing using oil and probably the first ceremony with a religious element in the making of a king. Offa and his archbishop would have wanted a magnificent cathedral for this display of power and a long nave built for procession must have been essential.

The archbishopric at Lichfield lapsed after Offa's death in 796 and the archbishop retired in 801. Apparently, the

Offa, 757 – 796, looking resplendent in an opulent robe.
He is on the west front of Lichfield Cathedral and is looking
southwards to Rome whilst holding his Archbishop's mitre.

bishops decided Canterbury should regain its primacy because of where Augustine started. Offa also built a monastery at Bath, Bedford, possibly Cambridge, St Albans, and Winchcombe. He altered Peterborough Abbey and Repton church making them cruciform in shape. He would have furbished his ancestral monastery at Bredon, Worcestershire, built in 780. He gave generously, usually land, to Worcester and Hereford and many other monasteries, particularly if they were on his borders where he wanted loyalty. For example, Glastonbury, Winchester, Cookham, and churches near Bath, in Middlesex, and West Sussex. Many Mercian charters showing Offa's patronage have been lost, and an unusually large number of charters are spurious, but it is most likely much land was given to monasteries and during his 39-year reign, many religious houses would have been built and extended.

He is supposed to have resided at a defended royal complex at Tamworth in 781, but the charter showing this is dubious. There is very little evidence of Tamworth being a town until the late 9th century and any royal complex has still to be found. Offa probably stayed at the large 7th century timber Hall excavated at Northampton, equal to that at Yeavering. On other occasions, he was at Kingston upon Thames and Hereford. It has been speculated All Saints church, Brixworth, Northamptonshire was a royal church and Offa probably made many changes to the church. It included holding relics, perhaps a larynx bone, of Boniface, which would have pleased Charlemagne. A 12th century writer claimed Offa was buried at his monastery at Bedford, but Lichfield or Brixworth ought to be considered. Despite this detail, Offa is the most obscure of the 8th century kings since no contemporary history or copy of his laws survived. Therefore, his record can only be an understatement, subverted by opinions from unsympathetic early writers outside of Mercia. His achievements were the minting of coins which then enabled taxation, the development of ports for exports and the building of many churches. Perhaps, his greatest achievement was the reaching out to kings on the Continent and to his understanding with several popes; he was the first cosmopolitan king of the English. That aspect was documented. He also greatly promoted and extended the church; and surprisingly is still discernible in surviving churches.

- The location of a Saxon church was carefully selected and there was a distinct conformity in chosen sites. Early churches were often positioned at secluded places with islands, promontories, peninsulas, deep wooded valleys, confluences and middle of forests being favoured. Yet they were also not far from main trackways, Roman roads or navigable rivers. Many were at low altitude, but on rising ground and almost all had a river, stream or well close by and often on the south side of the church. Curiously, many had higher ground to the north-west. The earliest churches were often surrounded by an enclosure with a ditch, or palisade or by trees. Later on monasteries were being sited on hills, often old hillforts with Breedon-on-the-Hill Monastery, Leicestershire, founded in 676 as a good example. Some were built in wetland areas on slightly raised land, as seen at Ely Abbey, 672, and Glastonbury Monastery, 688 – 726. When Saxon kingdoms were divided into administrative areas known as Hundreds there were churches sited near the epicentre, Lichfield is an example. All this suggested the clergy wanted to be disengaged from the secular leaders and warriors and not be placed close to the palaces and courts, but still be close to rivers and pathways and so accessible for the local community. It is also reasonable to suggest, as many writers have done, the locations had a kind of topographical aura or spiritual presence. Whether or not this landscape emanation was based on a biblical foundation is unsure.

A research study has shown a good proximity between the sites of early churches with the location of settlements. Such by the year 800 most people in England, and it probably also applied to Wales and Southern Scotland, were within a good walking distance of a religious house. Of course, upland settlements without trackways were isolated and exceptional. It meant the majority of people would be familiar with, and possibly obliged to a church of some sort, even if it is only to pay a tithe. In 850, there were at least 30 monasteries in the diocese of Worcester.

By the 10th century, many churches were connected to manorial estates and the lord was managing most aspects of the religious observances. Indeed, in some places the church was an annexe to the Hall. This trend started in the 8th century and the rate lords took control of church and estate is difficult to gauge; there was much variation. A good example of this is the wonderful Earls Barton church near Northampton. It stands on a hill above the River Nene where Roman and post-Roman settlements have been found along the river valley. It was a site perfect for the movement of people along the valley, had fresh water nearby and fertile soils for growing crops – the Barton name is derived from barley. On the higher ground behind the church is a mound that was for either burial or defence. The prefix *Earls* was added later with the settlements homage to the Earl of Huntington. Location, derivation and development were typical for a Saxon church at this time.

Naming a monastery also showed a pattern. In Wales and Cornwall, the name was derived from a saint. In England, it was often a word derived from the environment, such as grey wood, beaver stream, seal island, place of eels.

- Groups of churches and chapels were known and often they were built linearly west-east. The prime example was at Canterbury where the three churches of Peter and Paul, Mary and Pancras lie more or less in a line. It was also seen at Hexham, Jarrow, Repton, Glastonbury, Gloucester, Wells, Winchcombe and possibly Whithorn. In contrast, groups of churches occur in Wales, Scotland and Ireland. 8 churches survived at Clonmacnoise, County Offaly. Sometimes the second building was a burial chapel and is practical to think it might have been a new church for a growing congregation. At Lichfield, the shrine for Chad would not have been too far from the first church of St Mary. When St Peter's was built in 700, it appeared to be more-or-less in line with Chad's funerary church and so repeating the arrangement at Lindisfarne and Jarrow. This schematic layout was not the tradition on the Continent and it raises the question why it happened. A clue might be seen in the recent excavations on Iona. The discovery of a vallum, bank and ditch, dated to as early as the 7th century, the realisation of a small hut being the cell of Columba and the very recent finding of a curved wall that might be part of an early stone church suggest the entire 9 hectares site was laid out in a particular way. Adomnán became the ninth abbot of Iona in 679 and wrote 3 books on the layout of Jerusalem and other holy cities. It has been suggested the layout at Iona in the 8th century was made to resemble the layout of the church, true cross, chapel and Holy Sepulchre in Jerusalem. Pilgrimage was to a copied Holy City. If this proves correct, it then raises the question of whether Lindisfarne and other Columban inspired centres had a Jerusalem-like arrangement.

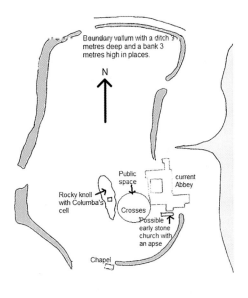

The churches and chapels in Wales have a very different developmental path. Stone churches were not evident in Wales until the 12th century at the earliest. Religious houses were constructed in timber, a tradition that must have worked well. Stonemasons were available to decorate stone for burial or wayside markers, but there was no call for building in stone. The consequence was their buildings were never tall and elaborate until stone began to be used.

If Aethelbald built an extensive kingdom and Offa developed it financially, then Coenwulf, possibly a distant cousin of Offa, tried to sustain its integrity. During his reign, 796 – 821, he had to resist the advances of kings in Kent, East Angle, on several occasions in Wales and once in Northumbria. In Kent, a pretender to the throne arrived from abroad and seized the throne, 796 – 798. This might have been the reason for Christ Church, Canterbury losing all its charters, books and records and for at least 4 bishops giving up, with some going abroad. After consulting the pope, Coenwulf removed the usurper king from Kent and settled the region. He then made a peace treaty with Wessex, followed by Northumbria and took control of East Angle. He engaged in several battles with the Welsh kings, gaining much territory. He is now thought to be associated with the building of Wat's Dyke, a 40 mile (64km) earthwork through the northern Welsh marshes, clearly indicating a barrier for the Welsh to see.

Coenwulf called himself the king of Mercia, the English and once referred to himself as *Emperor*.

One documented event during his rule was his disagreement with Wulfred, the Archbishop of Canterbury. Wulfred asserted Coenwulf did not have the right to appoint his loyal family and friends to look after nunneries and monasteries. His daughter was the abbess at Minster-in-Thanet and Reculver, both in Kent. Yet two popes had allowed Offa to do just this and a pope allowed Offa to have his archbishop placed at Lichfield. Furthermore, Offa had asked Pope Hadrian if he could permanently possess for him and his heirs all his churches and monasteries he had built or acquired that had been consecrated in the name of St Peter. This included Lichfield Cathedral. When Coenwulf protested to the pope, he received support and Wulfred appeared to be suspended for 6 years. One historian believed Wulfred forged a Charter to support his argument. This showed very clearly the way religious houses were being managed and Archbishops could be overruled. It also showed how popes saw powerful leaders as being protectors of the church and benefactors for family monasteries. Equally, it shows how Wulfred thought in the same way as Bede.

In Northampton on a small hill near to the confluence of two tributary streams of the River Nene, a 7th century large timber Hall was replaced in the early 8th century by an ever larger stone Hall. Its proportions, 37m x 12m with walls 1.2m thick, suggest a very large palace complex with two possible church sites nearby. It would have suited Coenwulf's magnificence. Coenwulf was buried at

Winchcombe Abbey, now run by his daughter. His son Cynehelm, sometimes called Kenhelm, was supposedly martyred early in his life, though there is no evidence for this folklore. His relics were held at Winchcombe, which then became a place for pilgrimage. All this raises the question of why the kings favoured and developed religious houses. The charitable view is they saw themselves as protectors of God's property and so had a spiritual duty to fulfil. They were being priestly. A conventional view is they were acquiring assets and wealth which increased their status and reputation. They were being bankers. A third alternative is they were using the religious houses to maintain peace and order. Many of the grants were to monasteries located on boundaries where it was necessary to anticipate an uprising. The kings were using priests as informants to raise alarm whenever the neighbouring king might strike out. That is a reason why the king used his placemen and women to run the religious house. They were keeping abreast of events. The religious houses were a very important component for ruling a kingdom. State and church were communicating intensively. They were entangled. A new power was now set to disrupt this cosy arrangement.

After Coenwulf's death, 821, a letter claimed there was much discord and innumerable disagreements within the kingdom. Between 825 and 827 former Mercian sub-kingdoms covering Essex, Kent, Sussex and Surrey fell to the West Saxon king. In subsequent decades the Mercian and Wessex kings found accommodation and made alliances against a new and very powerful threat. The whole fabric of secular and religious organisation became fearful of an impending disaster and staying united was increasingly being imperative. The Vikings began to sail farther from their homelands.

Priestly Emperors

The entwining of church and king in Britain in the 8th and 9th centuries was also played out on a grander scale across Northern Europe. It began with the *prince of the Franks*, Charles Martel, beating the invading Muslims at Poitiers in 732. When he died, 741, his son, known as *Pippin* (sometimes *Pepin*) *the Short*, became king of the Franks and started the Carolingian dynasty. He made a far-reaching pact with the pope, promising to defend Rome and lands in Italy, and in return was oil anointed at his coronation by Boniface. Between 755 and 774, the Germanic Lombards were removed from Northern Italy and Rome was freed of their control. His son, Charles, became king of the Franks in 768 and extended his empire to include France, Belgium, Holland, Germany as far as the Elbe River, Austria, Switzerland, northern regions of Italy, parts of Bohemia, Hungary and Spain. This was almost all of the Latin speaking Christians except those in the Atlantic Isles and parts of Spain. He was known as *Charles the Great* or *Charlemagne*. Another title was *Father of Europe* and this was the first appearance of the word *Europe*, which means *broad face*.

This expansion also became a Christian crusade. He entreated his subjects to attend church on Sundays and feast days, he enforced baptism for all infants in their first year, he expected tithes to be given and time spent helping the church, burial was only to be in a church cemetery and heavy fines were set for a range of indiscretions against the church. It is said he converted his people by the sword, bribery and coercion. Alongside this enforcement was a reform of education. It included the production of books for study, worship and administration. A new way of writing was introduced with capital letters, commas, question marks and full stops at the end of sentences. Liturgical music was reformed and the way it was used in services was regulated. He encouraged classical art in a sumptuous form which prepared for the later Romanesque and Gothic styles.

Charlemagne was crowned Emperor in 800 by the pope in Rome. He established his capital at Aachen on the border of Germany with Holland and built a large stately palace. It was embellished with gold. In the State Room, a large mosaic of Christ in the dome looked down on an elevated Charlemagne's throne. He was now Christ's priest-mediator for the Christian west. For this he was canonised in 1165.

All of this was noticed by the Saxon kings and admired. The extent of Charlemagne's influence on British kings cannot be emphasised enough.

He died aged 72 having reigned for 47 years.

The Other World and time needed to forgive sin

In the 8th century the idea of purgatory, a time between death and heaven, or hell, in which there was a cleansing of sin and preparation for the world to come became prominent. It developed as a potent belief from the 11th century until Martin Luther, 1517, and John Calvin, 1534, argued against the idea by saying it is without reason or scriptural support. Calvin used the phrase *soul sleep* to describe this intermediate state.

Fursey, c597 – 650, was an Irish monk who travelled to many areas, including to the kingdom of the East Angles where he set up an early church. He experienced several visions and might have been the first to visualise purgatory and record it. During an apparent mortal illness he fell into a trance and saw angels singing. Three nights later the angels took him to heaven where they argued with demons for his soul. At this place he saw the fires of hell and sinners being burned. One year later he had another vision in which angels taught him how to be a good monk.

In 672 Chad at Lichfield was dying of the plague and according to Bede had a vision in which angels had told him of his place in heaven and it would happen 7 days later.

Bede also recorded that someone in Ireland had seen the heavenly company coming to collect Chad's soul. Clearly, his soul was in the Celtic world and it would not stay long in an intermediate world.

According to Bede, a monk called Dryhthelm at Melrose Abbey, Roxburghshire, had a life threatening illness, c700, which caused a vivid dream. In this hallucination he was taken to the world to come. The place where souls were kept in purgatory was hot and cold, whereas hell was a place where they burned. Heaven was full of light and paradise was lit up even more.

Bishop Boniface in 716 wrote to an abbess and described to her a vision had by a person he knew. The man had been carried high into the air by angels and saw the whole earth was on fire. He was then reminded of all his sins and virtues and shown a pit with black birds perched on its rim groaning in human voice. From the pit came greater groans. The angels explained the birds would eventually fly to heaven, but those in the pit were lost and all this would occur on the Day of Judgement.

The man was also shown another place that had shining walls and gleaming splendour and it was called the Heavenly Jerusalem. Here the light was so dazzling he was unable to see who was living there in joy forever. In purgatory, he could easily see an abbot, a girl thief and King Ceolred of Mercia who died in 716. According to Boniface, this king had broken the laws of God, it is alleged he was profligate, and there was some suggestion he was murdered by poisoning because of it. He was buried at Lichfield; but is missing from the many statues on the west front of the Plantagenet cathedral. It seems obvious this vision by an unknown man was being used by Boniface to further his projects.

All this looking at the face of hell presaged what the church was about to encounter.

Chapter 8

THE RAIDED CHURCH 789 – 1016

A grant of food to St Augustine's Monastery, Canterbury, was given c850. In return, the donor wanted the monks to remember her and her husband by singing Psalm 20 every day. There was a caveat. *If it should come to pass, as we hope it will not, that any panic should arise through a heathen invasion or any other calamity, so this cannot be provided that year, then twice the amount must be given in the following year.*

How the Saxons fought is often described and yet little is certain. Around 616, Aethelfrith, ruler of Northumbria, at the battle of Chester defeated a combined army of men from Powys and Mercia, and, according to Bede, 1,150 priests mostly from the monastery at Bangor perished. The monastery is thought to have existed on the terraces of the River Dee at Bangor-on-Dee, south of Wrexham in Flintshire, but no site has been confirmed.

Killing around half a monastic community, if numbers are believed, appears ferocious. A later chronicle listed 200 priests killed; it was more likely to be a tenth of this. Bede made out this was an act of treachery and butchery done by a pagan army. Most likely, the ferocity of Saxon battle was always exaggerated.

Francis Pryor (2005) described Saxon conflict this way.

Possible site of the monastery at Bangor-on-Dee.

I do not suppose for one moment that life in the 7th century was calm and peaceful, but it would seem that aggression, by and large, was managed. Societies could not afford to lose harvests or have their flocks dispersed by large-scale warfare. So raiding would have predominated over actual pitched battle – which is not to say

*that these raids would not have involved death and injury to dozens of people.
Much of the fighting, too, would have been to do with social status within, rather
than outside, a particular group.*

Battles often occurred in August and September when rivers were at their lowest
levels so enabling fording. Most were not
far from roadways and occurred on fields
without settlement. Some were close to
rivers and this could have been strategic.
Long distances were travelled before
armies met and it is likely many of the
warriors were on horses, though
they most likely dismounted for
fighting. Estimates of between
50 to 100 warriors for an army
have been given, with 200 being
the greatest suggested. All of which
indicated battles were arranged, they followed predictable ways and lasted hours
not days. Harrying the lost enemy after the battle was rarely mentioned. Taking
the king as hostage occasionally occurred. Gaining territory was not always the
priority. Claiming a new kingship seemed to be the prize, and with that came
plunder. Losers often went into exile and either returned later or entered a
monastery. Battles were personal and tribal.

The Mercians waged 43 battles over 250 years; 18 against the East Angles, 14
against Wessex, and 11 against the Welsh and Northumbrians. 22 battles were
recorded for the 7th century and every sub-kingdom at some point lost their
king. These are the battles known and recorded, so how many more skirmishes
and battles occurred can only be imagined. Saxons are too frequently portrayed
as hostile and forever seeking strife, but compared with people in other centuries
this clichéd portrayal is wrong. With the meagre evidence available, it seems there
was rarely bloodlust in the way recorded with the Romans and Scandinavians.

Therefore, an encounter with an enemy that fought in different ways and
amassed great numbers of warriors would have frightened the Saxons. The Dani
and Northmen came to be greatly feared. Battles in the 9th century were totally
different in style, extent and frequency. For England and Wales, the *Viking Age*
extended over 2 centuries, for West Scotland it was 4 centuries and Orkney and
Shetland remained part of Norway for over 6 centuries. The end-point was
sometimes given to be the moment when the invaders with the invaded turned

Prow and middle of Skuldelev 3 at the Viking Ship Museum, Roskilde, Denmark. Built of oak from as many as 12 trees with the prow being a single piece of timber. It was 13.8m long and 3.4m broad with the height from the keel to the gunwale being a mere 1.6m in the middle and having a draught of only 0.9 metres. Clinker built with 8 rows of overlapping planks, around 1.5cm thick, fastened with bog iron rivets that did not rust. It was caulked with wool or fur and tar. The sail area was about 45m² and could achieve 10 knots. It had a crew of 5 to 8 men and carried 4 to 5 tons of cargo. This ship was built c1040.

Christian, 1030 is quoted, but this is a convenience. For England, the end-point was recognised to be 1016 with complete conquest and 1066 with a new invasion.

Norwegian and Danish Vikings tended to raid the Atlantic Isles and Western Europe including Holland, France and Spain. Swedish Vikings turned eastwards and crossed the Baltic Sea and penetrated Eastern Europe and Russia reaching the Black and Caspian Seas. Why Scandinavian warriors broke away from their homeland and conquered has invited intense speculation. Reasons suggested have been: overpopulation due to excessive sex (mentioned c1020), poverty (late 11th century explanation), tyranny of kings (a 13th century rationale), retaliation from Christian missionaries (a self-justifying Christian response), and Charlemagne taking over the sea-going Frisians in the Netherlands, which then let the Danes rule the North Sea (blaming another). A recent suggestion has been a population increase that could not be supported by the amount of farmland, in today's parlance they were economic migrants. Another is a grievance from being shut out of trading between Christian merchants. Perhaps, it was no more than a simple quest for adventure and looting, as mentioned in several poems. In 854 Horik, King of the Danes, who had allowed Christian missionaries into his kingdom, was slain in a family feud with his nephew, Guthrum, taking over. The kingdom disintegrated allowing the elite to organise piracy and adventure. It was a breakdown in internal control. It does not explain any excursions before 854, but it does imply blatant conquest of new territory was the underlying force. Probably, there were several triggers for the widespread marauding, which might be summed as *loot, land and later liquidation.* One certainty is the Vikings had a new weapon, a battle carrier, a longship.

Longships were longer and narrower than the cargo ships. They were built to flex and ride the ocean's waves and have a low draught capable of sailing along shallow rivers and easily beaching on shores. There was a constant need to bail out water. A sail made of wool or linen and sealed with fat enabled speeds of 10 knots. Most longships had 13 benches accommodating 26 oars, but later ships had 35 benches with 70 oars. A replica of a 16.3m long ship averaged 6 to 8 knots. This meant with optimum conditions, sailing from Denmark to Tyneside would take one and a half days only. In 1893, a replica ship, 24m long and 5m wide, sailed across the Atlantic in 28 days. Navigation instruments were probably unknown and reliance on knowledge of coasts, islands and tides, wind direction, position of the sun at noon and the passage of birds would be all that was needed. There is a log detailing a sailing to Greenland and navigation was mostly by spotting distant remote islands. Most journeys were short and involved island hopping. There has been much speculation on a possible use of navigational aids, but since none have been found in graves, it has still to be verified.

After 850, fleets of 150 to 250 ships were recorded and in 890, a fleet of 200 was reliably noted. It is calculated some ships were each carrying up to 80 warriors.

More is known on how the Vikings fought because they often buried their warriors with their weapons. They fought with well-made swords, axes, short spears, long javelins, bows with iron-tipped arrows and stones. Swords were 75-80cm long and used for one handed slashing. Axes, small for throwing and large, with a haft of more than a metre, for hacking, became the standard weapon. Spears were much used. They defended themselves with large, brightly coloured, round shields, round helmets and perhaps armour including chain mail, though little has been found. Skulls have been unearthed with teeth filed in a way to look fierce. Sagas mention warriors with tattoos and blackened faces. For sieges, they carried battering rams and catapults. Like the Saxons, most fighting was on foot, but occasionally battles on horseback and in boats roped together occurred. Speeches before battle were made and war cries used to frighten the enemy. Wind instruments gave signalling and standards were used to show dominance. Most of the early battles were undertaken with speed, fury and surprise. It is thought fighters were all male volunteers paid from plunder.

Beowulf

This long poem, over 3000 lines, described events in Denmark and Sweden in the 5th century, was probably written between the 9th and 10th century and the only existing copy is dated late 10th century or 11th century. To claim it shows how the Saxons fought is nonsense, even though characters names bear a resemblance to Mercian Kings. Equally, it has to be handled with caution if used to show how the Vikings thought and fought. It is chronologically incoherent, at times violent, dwells on fame and heroism, has a central character dying when trying to gain treasure, holds to only one God and could thus have been written by a Christian. It is most likely a story handed down, exaggerated and embroidered to give a good read. Nevertheless, it tells how kings maintained loyalty by giving treasure and good weapons, especially prized swords, to retainers. How wearing gold, feasting with the king, sleeping in the hall with the nobility and being ready to die were the highest aspirations. This meant the king had to be forever plundering in order to gain treasure so that his followers were perpetually in fealty by being rewarded. Power was measured by the size of the treasury.

Saxons recorded Viking encounters whereas Vikings left a poor written record. They had a rudimentary writing in the form of runic symbols incised on stones and wood, but they were only brief descriptions. Therefore, carnage could be told in a one-sided way. Victories were claimed when no gain actually occurred. The Vikings attacked where weakness was evident, but it would not be admitted. In time, both sides adjusted their tactics and made better preparation. It was a conflict of attrition and ultimately the Scandinavians proved they had endurance and were persistent. They also had much to gain.

The earliest raids were opportunistic. It started somewhere near Portland on the Dorset coast in 789 with a small raid. The queen for this kingdom was Offa's daughter. In 792, Offa referred to defensive structures being built and roaming ships being sent around the Kent coast for the protection against pagan seamen. They expected more to come. The anticipated happened the following year, 793, but surprisingly it came to the north-east coast. This was the most mentioned invasion at Lindisfarne by Norwegian adventurers, who were most likely to have sailed from a base on the Shetlands and Orkneys. Again, they raided in 794, but this time attacked Monkwearmouth and Jarrow. It was repeated in 833, and by 866, the two monasteries were destroyed. In 875, the relics of Cuthbert were taken to Norham-on-Tweed, then Chester-le-Street for 91 years and eventually Durham Cathedral in the 10th century. Hartlepool (Hartness) and Tynemouth (Tinmouth) monasteries, on the north-east coast, were destroyed around 800.

Lindisfarne

In this year, 793, the harrying of the heathen miserably destroyed God's church in Lindisfarne by rapine and slaughter.
The Peterborough Chronicle written in the 12th century

The ruins seen today at Lindisfarne are those of a priory built c1122, so any devastation in 793 has still to be verified. The Christian outrage could be hyperbole and the Viking assault might have been no more than a party intent on pilfering. Real archaeological evidence for the sacking of Lindisfarne has still to be found. The possible site of an early church has been located and perhaps the extent of destruction can now be measured. It is known the assault in 793 was followed by another greater sacking in 875. Yet some members of the community seemed to have continued their occupation. Therefore, some believe Lindisfarne was plundered but not ransacked. It stands out as a site where pre-and post-Viking sculpture was known and there appeared to be a continuation of its saints cults. Perhaps it was a functioning monastery into the second millennium, albeit with a small number of priests. Alternatively, there might have been a few lingering residents still preserving its traditions. Lindisfarne has become a litmus for measuring the destruction rendered by the Vikings, but there is little chance of knowing precisely what really happened.

There is much uncertainty of the date when the Norse settled on the Shetlands and Orkneys, but c800 is often quoted. Securing a base was crucial. These buccaneers having raided the east coast now moved down the west coast of Scotland. The monastery on Iona, off the west coast of Scotland, was pillaged in 795, 802, and 806 when 68 monks were killed. Many left the monastery, though some stayed. It was attacked again in 825 and the monastery was virtually abandoned. By 849 the relics of Columba, which had been hidden, were taken to Dunkeld, Perth and Kinross, and some went to Kells in Ireland.

These early Viking raids were mostly hit-and-run attacks with pillaging. However, there must have been some destruction since most monasteries in the north were closed for decades. No major illuminated manuscript was written between c835 and 930. Book production ceased between c835 and 885 when Alfred started to make up for the loss. Legal documents and charters continued, but were often inferior in their Latin and therefore appeared increasingly with a vernacular script.

Tarbat and Auldhame contrasted

Tarbat is a small peninsular on the east coast of Scotland in the region of Easter Ross. In 1984 at Portmahomack, a D-shaped ditch was discovered and seen to be reminiscent of the vallum wall at Iona. This little fishing village is at the north-east end of the Great Glen and so has a direct travel route to Iona at the south-west end. Excavation revealed Pictish stone carving, tools for making vellum and working with leather, hearths with crucibles for metal and glass making, and burials, mostly elderly males, with stones incised with crosses. It was concluded to be a Pictish monastery started in the mid-6th century. Columba has been mentioned as a visitor in 563. One abbot was suggested to be Egbert, an English exile who died at Iona in 729. It is the decorative carving in stone, which sets this site as being special. The archaeology showed a major fire consumed the vellum workshops and over 200 stone monuments were deliberately smashed and tipped into the fire. Two burials showed brutal sword wounds. After this tragedy in the late 8th or early 9th century the site continued as a workshop, but Christian pieces were now absent. So the survivors continued craftwork, but the monastic side had gone. Vikings, probably Norse, were implicated, but it cannot be securely established. So the conclusion is it might have been a case of great Viking devastation.

On a headland at Auldhame, near North Berwick, East Lothian, excavation has shown the likely location of a monastery which suffered some kind of cessation of use around 850–900. 5 burials appear to have occurred at the same time with one skeleton showing fatal injury from a sharp weapon. Later skeletons in a cemetery indicated Viking settlement. So it might have been a case of a small-scale attack.

In 839 a large Viking fleet, believed to have been Norwegian, entered the River Tay and then the River Earn and engaged with the Picts, wiping out most of the royal family and nobility. It led to the uniting of Picts and Scots under one king in 843 in a kingdom called Alba.

Ireland ravaged
At least 50 sites suffered Viking raids in Ireland. Remote islands off the west coast, such as Inishbofin and Inishmurray suffered damage early on in 795. Also Rathlin Island on the north coast in the same year. A small church on the island of St Patrick, on the east coast, was burned in 798.

By 820s, Vikings had visited the entire Irish coastline with numerous small raids reported and slaves taken. This early raiding was greater than reported around the British coast. The destruction of Bangor Monastery, County Down, in 824 and Armagh in 832 with the loss of much treasure would have sent shock waves through the monastic world. Monastic pieces, thought to be from Armagh, have been found in the nearby Blackwater River and with this collection was a Viking ring. The inference is the raiders' boat sank and some of the plundered treasure was lost until found in the 1990s. Armagh was raided again in 839 and 869. Vikings camped at Cork in 846 and Waterford in 850. They were removed from Cork in 848 and Waterford in 864.

Dublin was hit in 837, 840 and again a year later. By 853, Dublin was ruled by a Viking chieftain and held until 902. After a defeat, they retreated to the Isle of Man. They returned in 917 and held it again until 980.

Clonmacnoise was hit on at least 10 occasions and in 884 completely burned down. Kildare was struck 15 times between 836 and 1000. At a number of sites, Clonmacnoise in Offaly, Glendalough in Wicklow, Devenish Island in Fermanagh and St Brigid's cathedral in Kildare there were tall towers holding valuables and the Vikings simply burned some of them down.

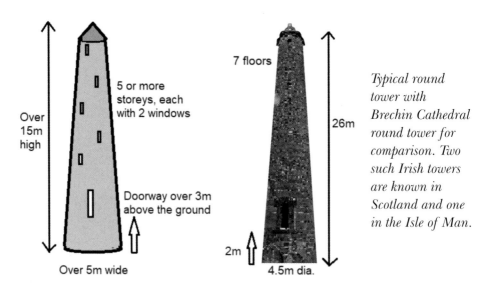

7 floors

5 or more storeys, each with 2 windows

Over 15m high

26m

Doorway over 3m above the ground

Over 5m wide

2m

4.5m dia.

Typical round tower with Brechin Cathedral round tower for comparison. Two such Irish towers are known in Scotland and one in the Isle of Man.

There were at least 60 monasteries with round towers, around 12 are still complete, so this experience must have happened at many other sites. The answer was to build underground tunnels and chambers called souterrains which from above would not be seen. Over 3,500 have been listed.

In 914, a large fleet appeared in Waterford harbour and an invasion left many monasteries destroyed. By 950 Vikings occupied the larger towns and turned to trading. It also has to be said there was much infighting amongst the small kingdoms and a good amount of desecration was extra to the Viking incursions. However, in all cases the prime target was the monastery with its wealth and king's treasure.

Be thou my vision

The modern version is a well-loved hymn, but it originates from an early Irish prayer. Tradition holds it was written c600, but there is no evidence for this. The earliest text is 14th century, but some think it refers to events around 1200 years ago. It is a prayer asking for protection and is assumed to have been written by a monk. A small part refers to protection needed from those with shields and swords and places the prayer in the time of struggles between kingdoms and with Viking attacks.

> *Be Thou my vision, O Lord of my heart;*
> *Naught be all else to me save that Thou art.*
> *Thou my best thought, by day or by night;*
> *Waking or sleeping, Thy presence my light.*

Fear of larger assaults on England came when the Danish Vikings raided Sheppey, North Kent, in 835. In almost every one of the next 45 years some kind of raid occurred. Within a span of 30 years, there were at least 12 Danish invasions, each making a longer reach along the main rivers into the interior of England. Raiders gained combat experience and became invaders.

In 836, a fleet of up to 35 ships landed in Devon. An incursion along the River Severn left Offa's monastery at Bredon, Worcestershire, destroyed in 841. What happened when they reached Worcester has not been recorded. Hamwih, now Southampton, was raided in 840 and again a year later. London too was raided in 842 and again in 851. Invasions at Wembury, near Plymouth and another on the Thames in 851 were defeated, though Canterbury was damaged. This defeat of the Vikings in 851, said to be an assault from 350 ships, surely exaggerated, must have been a slaughter. Whatever the truth, it shows the battles were not one sided. By 855, the *heathen* were around the Wrekin in Shropshire, so yet another incursion along the River Severn. Winchester was assaulted in 860.

Reports of Northmen invading many towns on the continent added to the expectation and fear. For example, 841 Rouen was plundered, 843 Nantes was sacked and Tours in 853. In 865, the Danish stripped the entire contents of the monastery north of Paris at St Denis and it has been stated took 20 days to remove the booty.

State of England by the mid-9th century
There is detail to show the East Angles were independent, continuing to trade, minting coins and making pottery. The Northumbrians had a stable kingship which then splintered with dynastic disputes. Control fragmented and caused the minting of numerous debased coins. Under Burgred, 852 – 874, in Mercia, the kingdom of Powys was taken, coinage was prolific but gradually became debased, numerous charters were given but most were grants of privilege not land, and the church was slowly being robbed. The church-state relationship was disintegrating and Mercia began to shrink. The West Saxon royalty sorted their disputes over succession, lost and then gained ground from the Mercians and unified kingdoms along the south coast. Measuring the 9th century by its coins and precious artwork found and recovered shows prosperity, but that might also have been a result of the increased turmoil and loss. It is thought the nation had a rich aristocracy continuing to profit, a church losing buildings, land and wealth and people labouring under strict laws and suffering poverty. The fault was the kingdoms were still pursuing old tribal conflicts. In 865, conflict went into overdrive; there came a need for *common unity* against an increased external threat. The Vikings were now amassing.

The Danish Vikings realised how vulnerable many monastic centres were and knowing there was plunder in the small towns turned their attention to the inner parts of England, especially where access via rivers was possible. Autumn of 865 was the pivotal time when a seriously attempted Conquest began. A Great Danish army with 2 to 3 thousand warriors, its size has been much argued, led by the brothers Ingwaer (possibly Ivarr the Boneless) and Healfdene arrived in East Anglia. They made peace with the East Angles and in return received a large number of horses. They were now mobile and dangerous. In 866, on November 1st, All Saints Day, when the townspeople might have been occupied by the festival, they captured and secured York. They held it for most of the next 9 decades, changing its Saxon name from Eoforwic to Jorvik. In this time, York prospered as the capital and base of Anglo-Scandinavia. A new network of streets and a strengthened city wall were added. Churches were built. Walls to avoid flooding of the Ouse and Foss were constructed. Craft shops increased considerably and merchants traded across Europe. Coins were minted. Even new artwork appeared. York made great economic progress with Scandinavian occupation becoming second in size to London.

In 868, Vikings occupied Nottingham in Mercia and by 869 controlled most of East Anglia having horrifically killed Edmund the Martyr king. For the next 3 centuries, Edmund was raised to hero status becoming the patron saint of England. The Danes took over Lincoln around this time, but overwintered at Thetford. In 869, they destroyed the abbey at Bardney, Lincolnshire. In 870, the monastery at Icanhoh (Iken), Suffolk, was destroyed. In the same year, several battles were fought in the Thames valley area with the West Saxons led by Alfred and his brother. It is said Medeshamstede Monastery, Peterborough, was destroyed in 870 and 84 monks, including Hedda its abbot, killed. Some think the destruction was overstated.

Hedda or Monk's stone purported to show 12 monks, 6 each side, killed by the Vikings. It has been dated to late 8th or early 9th century. If these are 12 disciples, it has a small resemblance to Cuthbert's coffin. The date of 870 has been incised on the left end, which suggests someone wanted to mark the slaughter.

Offa had adorned this monastery with gold, silver and gems as a shrine to Oswiu, so it must have been a prize for someone. Crowland abbey was attacked and the abbot with 70 members of the community were killed. Similarly, Evesham abbey had its shrine stripped by the Danes.

The *Great Heathen Army* of 865 was now reinforced by the *Great Summer Army of 871.* A determined conquest took place. In 871, they occupied London and this removed a large source of revenue from the Mercians. Strategically, this was a critical event. By 872, they established control of a disunited Northumbria and then moved south into Lindsey again, which was Mercian territory. They overwintered at Torksey and recent excavation has shown the camp occupied a huge 55 hectares. Curiously, it did not have surrounding defensive ditches. This strongly indicates a very large force of several thousand and unafraid of being attacked. Stray finds also suggests trading, metalworking and ship repair occurred at the camp.

In 865, the Vikings had been paid to leave Kent, but then changed their minds and ravaged the eastern part. The Mercians tried to repeat this buy-off, but again it did not work.

In 873, the Vikings sailed the 60 miles (96km) along the Trent from Torksey to Repton and wrecked it. Its church was seriously damaged, a separate chapel was reused for burial, part of the cemetery was dug up to make a ditched

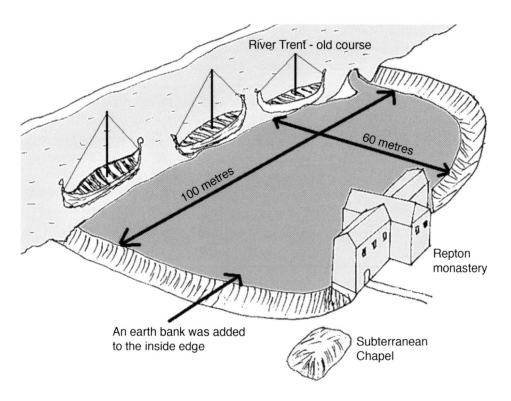

River Trent - old course

60 metres

100 metres

Repton
monastery

An earth bank was added
to the inside edge

Subterranean
Chapel

enclosure, a library disappeared and the monastic order terminated. A fortified area of around 1.5 hectares or 3.6 acres, with the church being its gate tower, was constructed with a v-shaped ditch about 4 metres deep and over 4 metres wide. This D-shaped camp extended between the church and the river protecting a harbour where up to 6 longships could anchor. Here they took *winter settle* in 873 to 874. If this fortified area was the encampment, a calculation estimates a force of 400 to 500 warriors. Very recently, evidence for buildings and metalworking outside the D shape has been found and it suggests there was a well-organised preparation for the next phase. Maybe, it was a greater encampment than has been previously thought.

Perhaps, there was a battle with the Mercian King Burgred which could explain the cremated remains of Vikings at Heath Wood, Ingleby, 2.2 miles south-east of Repton. Similarly, it would explain a mass grave at Repton with the remains of 200 to 300 warriors, with some bones recently carbon dated to around 875. Some have speculated that Ivarr the Boneless was a fatality; a special grave mound was uncovered by the church. The Vikings stayed for a year in the Repton area and, perhaps, they had to consolidate, or recover, their position. It is known the Great Army split up around this time. One faction then attacked Breedon Monastery, followed by destroying Modwenna's abbey at Burton. By following the River Trent, they reached and destroyed Tamworth in 874. At some point in this advance, it led to the Mercian King Burgred and his family leaving England for Rome, where he died soon after. It is unknown if this departure was a result of losing, or running away from a hopeless situation, or even an unrecorded battle.

Whatever happened beforehand, it is thought Lichfield and its cathedral suffered either despoliation or desecration in early 875. There was a suggestion the bishop Eadberht, Burgheard is another name connected to the cathedral at this time, finished in 875. By inference, the bishop was martyred. Typically, there was no record of what happened when the Vikings reached Lichfield. However, in 1992 during an excavation a burial was found with a charred stick on top of the remains. This is reminiscent of burial with a wand of hazel or poplar seen almost entirely in Scandinavia and points to a Viking corpse. No other bishop was linked with the cathedral until Wulfred 8 years later. The cathedral had 5 altars in the 850s being looked after by a bishop with around 20 prebendaries, half priests and half deacons, which with brethren would have meant a sizeable workforce under threat. It is plausible what happened at Repton was repeated at Lichfield. Anything suggestive of Christianity was desecrated, priests were hounded, or killed and wealth removed. Almost certainly, by the time the Vikings arrived at Lichfield it seemed there was no Mercian King and an army to defend the settlement. The breakup of Chad's shrine chest (a part is the Lichfield Angel) and its burial, together with finding burnt stone near the shrine and a possible Viking burial add to the notion of Lichfield Cathedral suffering desecration.

The absence of a king has been linked with the story of the Vikings choosing the next Mercian king, Coelwulf II, and making him a puppet; in a later Wessex chronicle, he was described as a *foolish king's thegn*. This does not concur with charters made by Coelwulf II, witnessed by Burgred's thegns, and with no reference to Viking overlordship. In 2015 at Watlington, Oxfordshire, a Viking hoard of silver was found including many coins depicting both Coelwulf and Alfred, including one showing the two kings sitting together. It was likely the Mercian king remained dominant, helped by a treaty with Alfred and Wessex. In 877, the Danes returned and made a treaty with Coelwulf in which greater Mercia was split along Watling Street into an eastern Danish region and a western Mercian region. Coelwulf had no alternative, but to accede territory. Coelwulf died or was killed, sometime between 879 and 881, possibly fighting the Welsh. If this was nearer the truth, it suggested Lichfield, together with the East Midlands, was abandoned being too difficult to defend once a fortified Viking base at Repton had been established.

Meanwhile January 878 was the low point for Alfred in a refuge surrounded by Somerset marsh having pursued ineffectually the Vikings around Wessex. By May, he gathered a very large army of 3000 and fought the disunited Vikings at Ethandum, Wiltshire (later identified as Edington). The remnants of the Viking army retreated to a fortified Chippenham, where they submitted after two weeks of siege and starvation. At a date sometime in the 880s, Alfred used the same tactic as Coelwulf to split his Wessex territory. He agreed with his Viking enemy to draw a line up the River Thames, along the River Lea and from the River Ouse to Watling Street. Alfred could not defeat the Vikings, but instead made treaties and then prepared for a second wave of battles. Between 892 and 896, he repelled a very large invasion attempt to take Exeter and was never troubled again until his death in 899. The Vikings had learnt Alfred was formidable.

There is a long list of churches, abbeys, monasteries and cathedrals being plundered and in some cases destroyed. Rochester was besieged in 885, but fought off the attackers and was probably the only Roman centre to do this. There was no repulse at Whitby 867, Bardney and Thetford 869, Soham and Reading 870, Dunbarton 870, Croydon and Wilton 871, Leicester 875, Hexham 875, Cambridge 875, Exeter and Wareham 876, Gloucester 877, St Davids and Chippenham 878. Important monasteries at Lastingham and Castor were at some point the attention of Vikings, but like many places, the dates were unrecorded. The east coast sees at Lindsey, Elmham and Dunwich disappeared. London was invaded many times, including by storm in 871 and 872, and St Pauls was destroyed in 962. York suffered damage in 866, 872 and 876 until the Archbishop made an arrangement with the Vikings. However, there was a vacancy between 900 and 925.

There was another campaign between 892 and 896. Targets were Appledore and Canterbury 892, Chester, Shoeburyness and Farnham 893, Mersea 894, Bridgnorth 895 and various places in the Midlands in 896. The Vikings avoided Alfred's Wessex and this was because of ramparts built around settlements turning them into fortified, small towns known as burhs. Rarely were they more than 20 miles (32km) apart, so maintaining communication. Furthermore, up to 27,000 men were conscripted into attending these garrisons. Alfred had half his army ready for action and the other half ready for defence. He also built a navy and made them ready to intercept. The Saxons, led by Alfred, were learning how to repel the Viking raiders. For this successful strategy, Alfred was described by his biographer as *Ruler of all Christians in the island of Britain, king of the Angles and Saxons*. In charters, he was *King of the English* and for the first time this epithet appeared on a coin. It was propaganda.

Alfred was succeeded by his eldest son, Edward *the Elder* in 899. He was crowned the following year at either Kingston upon Thames or Winchester. Over two decades he, together with a separate Mercian campaign, pushed the Vikings back. A massive defeat of Northumbrian Vikings and other rivals near Wednesfield, possibly followed immediately by a following encounter at Tettenhall in 910, meant the Danish Midlands were retaken. However, Dublin based Norse Vikings regained York and Northumbria in 919. By the end of Edward's reign, 924, he had secured all of England south of the line from the Mersey to the Humber and was overlord of the north, including Scotland. Edward's victories gave England almost 3 decades of freedom from serious Viking attacks. He was the first king that could legitimately be called *King of England*. There is little known on his development of the church apart from reorganising the dioceses of Winchester and Sherborne with a new monastery built at Winchester, where he was buried in 924.

Aethelstan, second son of Edward and King of Mercia and Wessex, reigning 925 – 939, secured Northumbria by marrying his sister, Eadgyth (Editha) to the ruling Viking at York. This marriage took place at the church in Tamworth, now St Editha's, and was solemnised by the Bishop of Lichfield in 926. A year later Eadgyth was widowed and she spent the rest of her life as a nun at Polesworth Abbey, Warwickshire.

By 928, Aethelstan probably ruled Britain and had the title *Emperor of the World of Britain*. His kingdom was now extensive and this could be the reason for making an extra tier of administration known as an ealdorman, who later became earls, and giving them administrative control over part of a kingdom. Furthermore, Aethelstan moved his Councils around England, so all could see his governance.

The Vikings had now reached their low point, but they were not finished. It had taken 50 years for the Saxons to return in full.

During Aethelstan's reign, the church was thoroughly looked after. William of Malmesbury, c1095 – c1141, wrote Aethelstan never hoarded riches and gave much to the monasteries. He was humble and affable to the clergy, mild and pleasant to the laity, reserved to the nobility and kind and condescending to the lower orders. He showed magnanimity to his

Aethelflaed, Alfred's eldest daughter, and her nephew Aethelstan outside Tamworth Castle. Aethelflaed, known as 'Lady of the Mercians' had married into the Mercian royal family and she and her husband were styled 'Monarchia of the Mercians'.

vanquished. Exchanges between monks here and on the Continent promoted better understanding and consequently manuscripts were imported. Viking kings even sent their sons to Aethelstan's court to learn kingship. Peace and wealth returned to Britain, but it did not last long. For reasons difficult to understand, Aethelstan entered North Scotland by sea and land in 934. No battles were recorded, but clearly, the Scot's king had caused an upset. In the same year he visited Chester-le-Street and Cuthbert's shrine leaving gifts including two illuminated manuscripts. He also gave to Beverley and York to keep the Northumbrians pacified. In 937, a combined army of Irish under Olaf Guthfrithsson and Scots with possible help from North Welsh mercenaries, engaged in a fierce battle around *Brunanburh*, possibly the name of a hill. Where this occurred has been much conjectured with over 30 locations posited. One writer believed the Mercians fought the Scandinavians, whilst the West Saxons fought a combined army of Celts and it was not far from the River Don, South Yorkshire. If so, it was a bringing together of the two large kingdoms and from now on there was an English army. Many kings and earls were killed and Olaf returned to Dublin. Very little is known about this battle and yet it was described as a decisive win for the Saxons. Aethelstan was now the first legitimate *King of Britain*. It was short lived, for he died two years later (939). He was buried in Malmesbury Abbey which significantly was on the border of Mercia and Wessex. Alas, his tomb was later looted. Peace was also short lived for later that year Olaf returned. Detail is incomplete, but it is known the Vikings retook York and made a pact at Leicester in 939, with a division of England. Within two years they tore this up and took control of the *5 boroughs* of the East Midlands (Derby, Leicester, Lincoln, Nottingham and Stamford), only to lose them again in 942. In 943, Tamworth was devastated, Northampton and Leicester were besieged, and much of Northumbria regained in 947 – 48. Ripon was attacked in 948, Ely at some unknown date and East Anglia was invaded. Chronology, detail and locations of battles, in this 15-year time span, are uncertain, but by c954, much of the Midlands and the north had been recovered and the Viking leader killed. The Danelaw was finished.

A second reign of peace and consolidation of the kingdoms occurred with Edgar, 959 – 975. He was

Edgar. At his feet is a wolf's head which is a reference to his demand of a tribute of wolf skins from a Welsh king. At this time, wolves were common in Wales.

not crowned until 973 having waited until he reached 30 years, like a priest for ordination. When in a lavish ceremony at Bath, he became King of Mercia, Wessex and England, for the first time a Queen sat alongside. This Roman-like imperial ritual was repeated with public acclaim in Roman Chester. It gave a new model for coronation, a ceremony that could have originated in 7th century Mercia.

Edgar was taught by a monk in his early life so there is no surprise he reformed the Benedictine monasteries. Lay clergy were replaced by celibate monks lacking any personal wealth. Ways of worship and observance were enforced. More texts were written in Old English. Much new artwork appeared including sculptured motifs showing acanthus leaves and elongated figures clothed in flowing costumes. At a council at Winchester, a definitive way of living in a monastery was laid out for every religious house. Monasteries described as neglected ruins were rebuilt. Tamworth in 963 was a good example. Large amounts of land were taken from the nobility and given to the church allowing monasteries to become financially independent again. Libraries and archives of relics were set up. From now to the Norman period, most kings had and encouraged relic collections. Sainthood was elevated and Edgar even made saints of his mistress and his daughter by his mistress. Shrines and pilgrimage were promoted. The king became the patron and protector for all monasteries and the queen was the same for all nunneries. Wealthy individuals were ordered to pay tithes to the church. By the year 1000, new reformed bishops and abbots were in place in Southern and Middle England, but it took another 7 decades before the north was changed. This was a monastic reformation and it lasted until Henry VIII's policy, 1536 – 1541, of closing down over 800 monasteries, abbeys, nunneries and friaries as well as removing valuables from cathedrals and churches.

Edgar also instituted new laws and ways of administering a large kingdom. Shire courts were now regulated. A uniform coinage was introduced. Some writers have gone as far as stating this was the start of statehood, as we know it. Perhaps, his greatest achievement was to recognise the rights of all Danes who had settled in England. Maybe this tolerant kingship was the reason he never had to go to battle against a Scandinavian foe. It is why he was called *Edgar the Peaceful*. He was also connected by marriage to all the important royal dynasties in Europe. Probably, the first English king to have true allies abroad.

Once again, the golden age did not last too long after his death. A monk wrote Edgar's death threw the kingdom into confusion, bishops were agitated, abbots were expelled, monks became fearful and clerics with their wives returned. One problem was the large amount of land given to the monasteries had given them great wealth at the expense of ordinary landholders. These old landholders now claimed they were forced to give up their land and wanted it back. Settling old grievances brought upheaval. An anti-monastic rebellion took hold and by 975, there was almost civil war. Famine and inequality did not help. Favoured monasteries at Pershore, Evesham, Winchcombe and Deerhurst were destroyed during this civil unrest.

Aethelred II, c966 – 1016, took the crown in 978, probably after having his older half-brother murdered. He reigned for 37 years, but it was never free of trouble, invasion and internal division. He was given the epithet *Unready* by a later chronicler who was very unsympathetic and unfair. Aethelred survived for such a long time by obedience that comes with feudal lordship, homage and fealty and this conflicts with the image of a dithering and passive king. Judgement on his reign was tainted by its disastrous ending, and by the number of his enemies who ended up being maimed or murdered. Another problem was caused by Aethelred reversing his predecessor's policy of giving land to monasteries by giving it back to loyal supporters. He then reversed this and repented. One example was Burton Abbey, Staffordshire, re-founded in 1003.

The Vikings realised by the end of the millennium, it was a weakening kingship. They systematically planned a new invasion using a strongly disciplined army and navy operating from fortified bases. To begin with, Aethelred countered this new insurgency, but gradually he was beaten. The list of raids is incomplete. It is known Southampton was attacked from the sea in 980, Thanet 980, Padstow 981, Portland 982 and Watchet in 988. Parts of Cheshire were invaded at this time and so was Anglesey and Pembrokeshire. In 991, a fleet of more than 90 ships attacked Folkestone, Ipswich, and Sandwich before making an assault on Maldon. There were heavy casualties on both sides and this has been described as a turning point. From their base on the Isle of Wight, the Vikings harried the West Country in 994 and the south coast every year from 997 to 1001. Exeter Monastery burned down in 1002, Norwich with its many churches was burned in 1004 and Canterbury in 1011. In 1002, Aethelred ordered all Danish men in England to be killed on 13th November, St Brice's Day, and some massacres, such as at Oxford, occurred. Such ethnic cleansing brought Viking retribution a year later in the south and south-east, and again in 1006. Feudal bonds holding up kingship started to weaken, indeed some leaders changed sides. The Mercians appeared to keep away. Much tribute, the amounts appear suspiciously high, was paid to the Vikings to remain peaceful. Accounts tell of churches being stripped of their wealth and churchmen giving up on land. It has been estimated half the nation's wealth was handed over. Most of this payment, however, must have stayed in the country and in time recirculated. It only strengthened the determination of the Vikings.

The end game was not far away.

Desecration in France

Viking warfare was even more intensive in France. The first incursion, 799, was a fleet of Viking ships sailing along the West Atlantic coast of France. A monastery on an island in the estuary of the River Loire was plundered. In 834, the monastery became their base camp and they overwintered there in 843. Then they sailed along the Loire River attacking many places between 834 and 850. Attacks along the Seine River in 841, left desolation in many places including at Rouen and Paris and this was repeated several times. In 842, Quentovic, a centre of trading to Britain, was sacked. In 843, Nantes Cathedral was stormed and some clergy killed. It was attacked again ten years later along with Tours. In 845, Paris was thoroughly looted and ransom given to make them leave. In 854, places in Brittany were sacked and the Bishop and monks were captured. Churches were raided again along the Seine in 856 and 866 with much tribute paid to the Vikings to keep away. Le Man was raided in 865. Then came devastation in Normandy. Between 879 and 892, it was the turn of North-East France with Calais, Ghent, Tournai, Reims, Arras, Cambrai and Peronne being targeted. In 886, Nantes was again overrun. After a peaceful period between 892 and 907, Brittany saw sporadic attacks. Then between 914 and 919 a series of heavy raids were made and by 921, the Vikings controlled the whole province. Very many monasteries were desecrated and a migration of monks to England resulted. Only after many battles were the Vikings finally removed from Brittany around 937.

This is only a brief summary of the many skirmishes and battles. It does not include those encounters where the Vikings were repelled or beaten. No detail has been given on the background of the insurgents with a mixture of Scandinavian people involved. A good number of Viking conflicts also involved French forces in opposition and in collusion. It was much more than straightforward plundering and fighting between two opposing armies. Much the same story can be told for Holland, Belgium, Germany, Spain, Italy, Faroes, Iceland, Greenland and even Morocco.

Only a part of Normandy stayed in the control of the Vikings. The first settlers were led by a chieftain called Rollo. There is circumstantial evidence to show he was Danish and another account says he was a Norseman from the Orkneys. It is a myth the province was inhabited by Normans alone. There were citizens from across Scandinavia, Britain, Ireland and especially France. It only became Normandy with later conquests. The ancestry of William, Duke of Normandy, 1035 – 1087, was far more French than was Norseman.

Canada
In 1960, 9 walled structures and many artefacts were found at L'Anse aux Meadows on Newfoundland Island. Iron tools and figurines matched those found on Greenland. A radiocarbon date of c1000 was obtained. Whether or not these Viking explorers moved farther south or around the Hudson Bay has still to be proved.

Raiding in Wales
Many raids were made along the lengthy coast of Wales with most by Norse Vikings. Often they had sailed from their base in Ireland and Dublin in particular. Anglesey was attacked in 865, 903, 918, 971, 972, 979, 980, 987 and 993. Such was its vulnerability. Pembrokeshire received raids in 982, 999, 1001, 1073, 1080 and 1091 and again suffered from easy harbour and little defence. There were excursions along the River Severn in 988, 1039 and on many more occasions. The later raids were made with Vikings colluding with Saxons and Welsh princes. The destruction of Anglesey was exceptional, but it seemed the raiding elsewhere was minimal and recovery occurred. 11 raids on St Davids over 130 years indicated either, the resilience of the monastery, or little treasure was available and not much plundering happened. There is little evidence of Vikings settling in their acquired territory and it seems they were often moving on, or were forced to move on. The exceptions were around St Davids, Haverfordwest and the Gower. There are graves with Viking artwork on stone, but they are sparse and scattered.

The outcome of this European-wide chaos was many religious houses were finished, whilst others tried to repair and continue and most went into decline. The organisation of the church was fragmented, monastic life, especially in eastern England, was considerably reduced, the bishoprics of Dunwich, Lindsey, Elmham, Hexham and Whithorn disappeared and many like York were reduced to obscure poverty. The dearth of charters and documents in Northumbria, East Mercia and East Anglia in the two decades before Viking assault can only be explained by disruption or desecration of scriptoria. There are post-Viking references to farmlands needing to be restocked, fortifications needing repair and new bridges to be constructed. The Vikings destroyed many churches and the extent of this demise is still an open question.

Even the extent of a new beginning has been questioned. For example, Lindisfarne after evacuation was not mentioned again until the 11th century when a Flemish bishop with Norman support resuscitated monasteries on the north-east coast, then revived the Benedictine community at Durham and eventually restored a priory church at Lindisfarne based on Durham Cathedral. A demise that lasted around 300 years. A similar story was told at Hexham. The problem is a rebuilding is not the same as a restart for the church. It is just as possible a rump of a religious community was present and continuing to worship in an impoverished church building. Since the lands and buildings held by Lindisfarne were extensive, it is quite possible the religious community had moved elsewhere.

At Lichfield a bishop's name appeared 14 years after the Vikings onslaught and 13 more names are known before the see was removed from Lichfield to Chester, 1075, and then Coventry, 1086, and before it returns with a repaired cathedral in 1129; an apparent full recovery time of 250 years. Yet there is no hard evidence to say the religious community had lost their church and ecclesia. At York in 972, Oswald, bishop of Worcester, a man with Danish ancestry, became the archbishop and the two sees were combined intermittently until the mid-11th century. After the demise of the Leicester see in 877, Dorchester acquired all the land to the Humber and then it became part of Lincoln after the Norman Conquest. There were similar reshuffles in Wessex and the West Country, with some sees being large and difficult to manage. It is in the 10th century at York and the 11th century elsewhere when the office of Archdeacon was made to help manage the many estates. Similarly, the office of Dean in a cathedral does not become defined until after the Conquest and at Lichfield, the Dean only began to have a strong position in the late 12th to early 13th century. Rebuilding gave as much a mixed understanding as the onslaught had given.

Where the Vikings triumphed they often forced their captives into apostasy and where the homeland won they often formed a treaty in which the Vikings had to honour the Christian God. Belief was bartered. In contrast, where the Vikings settled there is no evidence they were fiercely antagonistic to Christianity. Indeed, some Danish leaders accepted baptism as part of their obligations. It is a mixed picture, also a confused picture. For example, Repton, after much bloodshed, was still able to continue as a religious centre and how this ever happened considering the destruction does seem inexplicable.

Despite this doubt, the overall picture looks as if East Anglia, the Fen counties south to London, Leicestershire, Staffordshire and the East Midlands suffered badly. The southern counties into the Thames heartland, Shropshire to Cheshire northwards and much of Wales received destruction which still allowed eventual recovery. Worcestershire and Gloucestershire came out of it relatively unscathed. South Wales, Scotland and the South-West had sporadic attacks along the coast, but much of the area inland appeared to have avoided encounters. It has been said the Vikings would not have wanted annihilation because it enabled a return visit, but places having repeated attacks might be centres where the monks stoically continued because it was central to their steadfast belief. The level of ferocity, resistance and rebuilding has caused division. Here are two measured views.

Frank Stenton (1989) wrote,

> *Throughout England the Danish raids meant, if not the destruction, at least the grievous impoverishment of civilisation.*

John Blair (2005) summed up evidence with,

> *The experience of most of the (religious) communities must have been more-or-less traumatic during c870 – 930; few can have preserved more than exiguous liturgical life, and some may have been temporary abandoned. But enough remained for the basic fabric of ecclesiastical centres and cult sites to emerge in recognizable form, if modified and extended, in an era of reconstruction.*

A probable indicator of Viking threat

In the gold hoard found at Hammerwich, in Staffordshire, in 2009, was an inscribed silver-gilt strip. It was the main stem of a cross with its side arms removed. In its folded shape it is 8.9cm long (17.9cm if unfolded), 1.5cm wide and weighs 80g. It has a Latin biblical text scratched noticeably on the outside and again on the inside. The inscription on the outside has been filled with silver sulphide, called niello, to blacken the writing and make it clearer. The text ends next to a figure of a serpent, or dragon's head, with almond shaped eyes, curling jaws and a threefold tongue. This appears on both sides and would have been at the base of a cross.

The Latin text was taken from the Jerome Vulgate Bible and is the same as Numbers 10.35 and very similar to Psalm 67.1. It translates as *Rise up, O Lord,*

Drawing of the straightened out strip and split to aid definition. To see the real image enter Staffordshire Hoard, Inscribed strip, K550, into your web server.

and may thy enemies be dispersed and those who hate thee be driven from thy face. This was repeated on the back with three extra words added in very light incision which appear to be *adiute nos ds*, or *help us God*. It is thought the text on the back or inside was a practice and the top outside was the finished statement. This was a real and considered message of anguish added to the soil with the rest of the hoard. It shows a frightened clergy. Only God could save them.

INIMICITU

The lettering on the strip is in the form of Insular Majuscule with letters having open serifs at the ends. The style of writing and the insertion of niello in the scratch marks poses an enigma. Some think it points to a date later than the artwork of the military pieces in the hoard, which is around the year 700. Comparison of niello filled incised writing on metal like this points to an 8th or 9th century. A recent book (2016) by the author detailing the hoard and its history suggested the inscribed strip was written around 875 when the Vikings approached the nearby cathedral at Lichfield. Clearly, the Saxons were frightened and indicated this in the message. Several thousand warriors were at one time camped at Torksey on the banks of the upper River Trent in 873 and later, considering the size of the camp. A large force of 400 to 500 might have camped at Repton. There were probably no more than 100 Saxons warriors at Lichfield in 875 and the odds were therefore frightening. So did someone take the hoard, it could be carried in two hemp sacks, away from the Lichfield area, head west and bury it in a border location, on the English side of the Danelaw boundary, with the intention of retrieving it at another time. The gold strip was an angst votive plea for God's help and it was buried so the barbaric Vikings could not gain from this emblematic mix of important Christian and Military pieces. The damaging of the hoard pieces, which was no more than slight, points to keeping these treasured items away from the Vikings.

The exodus of books and relics

Columba praying alone on Iona had a vision of *a line of foul, black devils armed with iron spikes and drawn up ready for a battle* and he realised this was a forewarning of an attack on the monastery. He thought the battle continued for a day until God's angels came to the rescue and drove the devils off the island. This kind of cosmic battle between unequal sides and needing God's intervention was a repeated theme throughout Europe. It draws on the battle between the Israelites and the Philistines and Egyptians with a subsequent exodus.

Almost 200 years after the death of Columba this cosmic battle on Iona started. In 795, came the first attack followed in 806 with desecration and around 70 monks being savagely killed. The island was too vulnerable so Cellach, its abbot, moved to the new monastery at Kells, near the centre of Ireland. There the monks continued to describe themselves as *abbots of Iona*. A few monks remained at Iona but there was further killing in 825 and this signalled its demise. Most of Iona's treasures, which included manuscripts and metalwork, were moved to Kells. If the Book of Durrow was written at Iona, sometime between 650 and 700 with a median of 680, and then moved to Kells, it must have by 916 been moved a further 80 miles (130km) southwards to Durrow. If the book of Kells, c800, was written at Iona, and this is the generally accepted notion, then it too was carried away around 806. The beautiful decorated pages could have been added after its arrival at Kells.

The monastery at Iona in the 10th and 11th centuries was left to become the burial place for the kings ruling over the joint Pictish-Scottish kingdom. At least 48 monarchs are known to be buried on the island. In 1200, Benedictine monks re-established an abbey on Iona and this effectively ended 600 years of Celtic inspired worship.

With the destruction of Botolph's monastery in Suffolk in 870, his relics were split up and sent to Ely, Thorney and Westminster Abbey for safekeeping. Almost every monastery had one or several relics and Botolph's story could be told everywhere.

The coffin of Cuthbert with Cuthbert's Gospel inside, the Lindisfarne Gospel and other treasures, including a stone cross, were removed from Holy Island by monks and given sanctuary at Chester-le-Street in 883. This was 7 or 8 years after Bishop Eardulf and his community had fled Lindisfarne following the Viking raid in 875. The journey of Cuthbert has been embroidered, but it is said to have travelled around Northumbria, resting at some point at Crayke Monastery in Yorkshire and Whithorn, Galloway, where it was considered it should be taken to Ireland for safety. There is a miracle story of the Gospel falling into the sea and being recovered unchanged. In 995, news of fresh Viking raids caused the treasures to be taken southwards to Ripon. A few months later it went northwards again to Durham. They have stayed in Durham ever since, apart, that is, from a brief excursion back to Lindisfarne in 1069 following the *Harrying of the North* by William of Normandy. 700 Normans were butchered in Durham so the relics went via Jarrow, Belington and Tuggal to Lindisfarne taking 4 days. They returned in March 1070. The new cathedral began in 1093 and 11 years later, the relics were in a shrine by the high altar. In the Reformation, 1539, the treasures of Cuthbert were examined, his coffin was broken up and his bones reburied behind the altar. It is thought the Lindisfarne Gospel was eventually taken to London.

The St Chad's Gospel is also thought to have also been taken from Lichfield cathedral sometime around the arrival of the Vikings in 875. By the 9th century, the Gospel was in Carmarthenshire, mid-South Wales. This was a far west part of Mercia having been secured between c850 and the battle of Conwy in 881. The Mercians now had overlordship of most of Wales with support from the West Saxons. Its arrival in outer Mercia was marked by local people making notes in spaces in the book when it was displayed on an altar. In the margin of page 141 at the end of St Matthew's Gospel is an entry in Old Welsh describing a land dispute between Tutfwlch and Elgu, the son of Gelli. It was settled when a horse, three cows and three newly calved cows were given to reach a settlement so that there was no hatred between them from the ruling till the Day of Judgement. It was now being used to record oaths and another 8 were written in the margins. The memorandum written in the Gospel margin is the earliest known Welsh writing; with Latin used for the legal wording. Another entry in a top margin records how Gelli, son of Arihtuid, bought the book from Cingal for the price of his best horse and gave the book, for the good of his soul, to be placed on the altar of St Teilo, now the church of Llandeilo Fawr. This could have been an act of atonement since Gelli had done a shady land deal. If this confession is believed, and there is some doubt, the book's ownership changed before it was returned to a church; probably a family church passed from father to son. Gelli, like many others, was probably trying to make reparation before his death. On the page of St Luke is a list of places within 15 miles of Llandeilo, including a farm thought to be in Ammanford, which has led to some thinking this was originally a Welsh Gospel.

Assuming the book was written at Lichfield, it does make sense to take it to one of the early churches set up by St Teilo for safekeeping. The churches were in the middle of South Wales, in a remote part of Mercia, away from the coast and therefore farthest from the raiding Vikings. However, if this was the intention, then somehow its journey has got to account for the activity of Gelli and Cingal before it reached the church at Llandeilo. Perhaps, Gelli obtained the book and genuinely returned it to the church. There is the distinct possibility these marginalia were copied from earlier oaths and therefore have little to do with the Gospel's travels. A date of 830 to 850 has been given for the land dispute which means it was possibly written later in the margin of the Gospel to ensure the contract was kept.

When the Gospel returned to Lichfield, the name of Wynsi was added to the first page. This is thought to be bishop Wynsige, 963 – 975. A Saxon became bishop of Teilo c930 and at some point the group of churches came under the authority of Canterbury and this might have been the spur to return the book. By 1000, the Teilo community was in decline.

What happened to the relics of Chad in the post Viking era is a complete mystery. They were listed in a cathedral indenture in 1345 with the skull in a painted wooden case, an arm also being listed and more bones were in a portable shrine shaped as a church. After the Reformation, 1538 for Lichfield, the relics were secretively removed from the cathedral and 6 remaining bones are now kept in Birmingham's Roman Catholic Cathedral of St Chad built in 1841. The bones were analysed in 1995 and radiocarbon dated. 5 were dated to the 7th century and it is presumed Chad is represented in the collection. There seems to be a minimum of bones from 3 individuals in the collection. A 12th century list of saints, and where they lay, has Chad, his older brother Cedd and an unknown Ceatta at Lichfield and they might be represented in the bones. Far too much has happened to have any certainty, but it would be expected such sacred treasure would have been well looked after. The bones are now venerated collectively.

In 909, the relics (body only?) of Oswald were translated from Bardney, Lincolnshire, to a mausoleum at Gloucester to be with the remains of Alfred's Mercian ally who died in 871 and his wife, Alfred's eldest daughter, who died in 918. Both were strongly connected with Mercia and the location shows both Repton and Tamworth had now been downgraded as Mercian centres. It also showed how

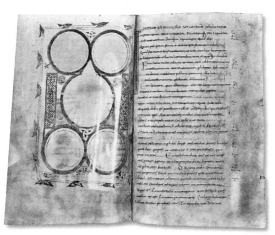

Oswald was still being venerated. The mausoleum became St Oswald's church. With much pilgrimage providing wealth, it soon became known as the *Golden Minster*.

In 981 Vikings attacked Petrocstow and burned the church. This was presumed to be Padstow in Cornwall. It was thought monks moved the relics of Petroc from

Replica page of the Bodmin Gospel shown at Bodmin church.

Padstow to Bodmin and kept them in an ivory casket. The British Library has the Bodmin Gospel thought to have been written in the late 7th to 9th century, possibly in Brittany.

Its decorated page resembles carpet pages seen in other Gospels. How it got to Bodmin church is unknown, but again it could have accompanied Petroc's relics from Padstow. In the margins, are manumissions listing slaves that have gained freedom, with some resident in Padstow.

In 984, Aelfheah became Bishop of Winchester and in the 990s had to deal with Danish Vikings raiding Wessex. He made treaties which were never kept and raiding persisted. In 1006, he became the Archbishop of Canterbury and brought to the Cathedral the head of Swithun for safekeeping. Peterborough Abbey had an arm and other monasteries had some bones. The Vikings reappeared in 1011 and ransacked Canterbury taking the archbishop for hostage. They demanded payment for his return, received some tribute, but then demanded more. This was not given and Aelfheah was martyred. An empty tomb of Swithun at Winchester remained a place for pilgrimage.

At sometime in the 9th century, the Vikings captured an illuminated Gospel known as the *Codex Aureus*. This was the first Gospel with illustrations in gold leaf. In a margin, was written how the book was retrieved with a ransom of gold. It was then donated to Christchurch, presumably at Canterbury, but it then fell again into the hands of the Vikings and today it is in the Swedish Royal Library.

The monks of Glastonbury claimed to have recovered the relics of Dunstan from Canterbury at this time and pilgrimage intensified at their abbey. What happened to manuscripts at Canterbury is unclear. It is known the scriptorium finished in the 9th century, but there must have been a large library for raiding when the Vikings arrived.

Relics and books were also transferred from one monastery to another in France as the Vikings moved around. For example, the relics of Martin of Tours were taken to Cormery in central France. The relics at Landevennec, Brittany, were moved in 912 when the monastery was destroyed. At the same time the relics of Samson were moved from Dol to Avranches in Brittany and then again to Orléans in North Central France. Later monks, relics and valuable items were taken out of Brittany and brought to England for safekeeping.

Almost all cathedrals and churches east of Watling Street lost their libraries and charter archives. Land titles had to be rewritten. In the 880s, King Alfred embarked on a project to replenish books needed for administration. He recruited at least 4 literate men from Mercia, one being the bishop of Worcester, and others from Wales, France and Germany. They set up schools of learning, wrote 120 chapters of law in the vernacular Old English, similarly translated *The*

Great Pastoral Care of Pope Gregory in order to train priests and produced the first history of Britain in English so all could know it. Alfred too helped to translate the Latin texts. All were written in clear vernacular handwriting. Alfred believed he had a divine responsibility to educate his subjects. It was also likely that Alfred from an early age had an intention to enter a monastery and his deeply Christian religiosity never left him. This strong care for the sacred and his subjects underlines why he was acclaimed *Great*.

The final onslaught

In 1005, there was a great famine and a pause in fighting. In 1007, a large force was bought off. Then in 1009, a huge Danish fleet landed at Sandwich, Kent, and over the next 3 years, Sweyn Forkbeard gradually conquered much of England and received considerable tribute. In 1013, Aethelred fled to Normandy and Sweyn declared himself king of England and made Gainsborough, Lincolnshire, his capital.

Many northern and East Midland nobles swore allegiance to Sweyn in disgust with Aethelred fleeing the country. Sweyn then moved southwards and attacked London and Bath. He died early in 1014 and Aethelred returned, but found he had minimal support. He did manage to drive Vikings from Gainsborough and he had two Mercian thegns killed for switching sides. The East Midlands were also recovered. However, Aethelred died in 1016.

All this turmoil induced Archbishop Wulfstan of York to deliver his *Sermon of the Wolf to the English* (Wulfstan was the Wolf) in which he stated the world was in haste and it neared the end; thought to be 1033, a thousand years from resurrection. He added it was because people were sinning every day by neglecting religion. In a later sermon Wulfstan claimed that with evil and deceit spreading widely throughout the world, there will come the greatest evil to men, the archfiend Satan himself. It was Revelation theology aimed at ordinary people including the invaders. If this sermon was carried around the churches, it showed the power of a top priest at a time of war weariness and absence of kingship. Government was now being directed by churchmen and apocalypse was the agenda and getting closer.

The end of pillaging and raiding ended on 18th October 1016 when Cnut (Canute) the Great, c990 – 1035, the son of Sweyn Forkbeard and around 20 years old, defeated a Saxon army at *Assandun* in Essex. Once again, the actual battle site is uncertain. The defeated Saxons were led by Aethelred's son Edmund Ironside, or King Edmund II. Many elite Saxons were killed. This date ought to be as familiar as 55BC and 1066, but 1000 years later, its marking passed with a few exhibitions only.

Cnut the Great. He is apparently looking to heaven and raising his foot because the sea is encroaching! A 12th century myth. He appears holding an orb and book showing Christian kingship.

In 1017, Mercia and other regions were purged of its leaders. Many of Aethelred's family were driven into exile.

Cnut eventually became the king of England, Scotland, Denmark, Norway and part of Sweden. He had close ties with Ireland and Germany. Cnut's swift and bloody conquest of England has many unknowns, but it ended the Saxon age, though it has been said ironically, Cnut was a better *Saxon* than previous Saxon Kings. Indeed, he married Emma, Aethelred's widow in 1017, having already married Aelfgifu, a Mercian from Northampton, probably in 1013.

Disputes in the Norwegian nobility forced Cnut to appoint his first wife and her son to be his governor in Norway, but it did not work out. Further Scandinavian disruptions caused him to divide England into 4 provinces and appoint trusted earls to rule whilst he was occupied elsewhere. Ironically, some, like Leofric the new earl of Mercia, were Saxon. Leofric founded new monasteries at Coventry and Much Wenlock.

Many laws from his predecessor were kept and Archbishop Wulfstan of York, 1003 – 1023, drafted new laws for Cnut. Wulfstan also told him to fear God constantly, to be in terror of sin, dread the Day of Judgement (thought to be only 16 years away) and shudder at the thought of hell. It appeared Cnut took note. It was likely Cnut would never have been accepted as king if he had not been a God-fearing Christian (having two wives was unimportant). Much of his reign was administered through the church. Only in his final years, after Judgement Day had failed to occur, did he appoint lay administrators.

Cnut the Great treated the church well and supported the bishops. Indeed, Cnut went to Rome and said it was to repent his sins, improve the conditions of pilgrims and establish the superiority of the archdiocese of Canterbury. To atone for killing Edmund, he built a large church for the monastery at Bury St Edmunds. For the battle at Assandun, he built a church at Ashingdon, Essex. It

Cnut and his wife Emma present the Winchester Cross to Hyde Abbey, Winchester c1030.
Cnut wears under a cloak a knee length tunic having decoration on the hem, trousers,
braided stockings and narrow shoes. Emma has a robe with headdress and she too has fine
pointed shoes. There is some evidence Viking clothing was dyed several colours. The
undergarment was probably linen and the outer tunic made of wool. It is the antithesis of
the unwashed and foul barbarian image given by several writers when describing the
Vikings. This is the only surviving image of Cnut and can be seen in the British Library.

was claimed he repaired all the churches and monasteries that had been plundered. Plus refilled their coffers. New churches were built and he was a generous patron of particular monastic communities. Cultural exchange with churches on the continent were encouraged. Cnut sent gifts of church books abroad and selective support was given to churches in Denmark and Norway. After a 19 year reign, Cnut died at Shaftesbury, Dorset, aged about forty, and was buried in the Old Minster, Winchester; later accompanied by Emma in 1052. His and her bones are said to be in a mortuary chest.

The rise of a new kind of monastery

The Augustinian mission, 597, brought in a form of worship known as Divine Office being used in the churches of Rome. It spread quickly throughout Britain and was widely used by the 8th century. Not much is known about it since no early Saxon service book has survived. It is known the day was divided into 7 times of worship that included sung prayers, chanted Psalms, hymns, readings, antiphons (call and response praises), perhaps a sermon or explanation of the reading and always a Eucharist. Maybe there was a diversity of services and it was not as rigid and regular as is often supposed. Churches with a lay community might have been very different. Rituals conducted in Latin would have been a great problem for lay worshippers. Communion would have been an annual privilege. They would be instructed to fast, remain sexually inactive for long periods, provide alms for the poor and weak and confess all sins. Pilgrimage would be expected. After death, burial would be in a separate area. A lay Christian was under a tough obligation. This goes a little way to explain the attraction for stone crosses and carrying relics; it was less demanding.

A generation ago, historians held Viking invasion and moral laxity caused this tradition of worship to completely disappear. It is now believed this form of worship was not entirely lost and there was some continuity. Indeed Alfred, 849 – 899, reinvigorated the old liturgy and introduced a new Gregorian style Roman Office.

In the middle of the 10th century, a group of reforming monasteries began to sing the Divine Office along strict Benedictine lines, which now had 8 services during the day. This gradually spread causing some monasteries to have to import books

Alfred enjoying his music.

and teachers from the Continent for guidance. This was the first time for using true Benedictine style worship in Britain and therefore the monasteries before this change cannot be compared with those that followed. Worship changed and so did the monasteries with a date of around 920 in England being quoted as the pivotal time.

The rise of the Parish Church

Prior to the arrival of the Vikings the early church had been organised and controlled by a select group of kings and nobility encouraged and administered by bishops and abbots in monasteries subjected to Benedict's Rules. The dynastic rulers financed the church and the clergy kept it spiritually correct. Some writers think the church was already showing decline by 820 and point to a decreasing output of artistic work and the selling of land to the nobility. If so, there was a weakness when the Vikings came. The mayhem of invasion meant much of the national wealth went to repelling or paying off the invaders. This occupied the kings and their relationship with the church deteriorated. Desecration of the cathedrals and monasteries meant the clergy moved around carrying as many portable objects as they could. There was a slow disintegration of the church over almost two centuries. In many places, Christian worship disappeared or was extemporaneous. In some locations, it was reorganised and a new church constructed, but that was exceptional. A few Cathedrals, Canterbury, York, Winchester, Worcester and the abbey at Bath, possibly continued for most of the time, but each centre had its own peculiar circumstances enabling adaptation in a time when the church languished. This, however, was in contrast to a great change in how people lived and worked.

Between the 8th and 12th centuries, farms and settlements began to be nucleated. By the millennium, it was widespread in Britain. Distinct hamlets and villages, often clustered round a green space, became the pattern of settlement. It allowed the outer fields to be demarcated and farmed as distinct units. Good and bad soils were shared and so was the water supply. There was a transformation in farming with the labourers knowing about their own patch and sharing ideas and tools with others. There began a cooperation with the work and a sharing of resources. Teams of oxen pulling mouldboard ploughs helped the communal cultivation of fields. Crop rotation with a fallow year when sheep were borrowed to manure soils helped fertility. Cereal production was better understood and a climatic warming helped this agricultural revolution. Reasons for this mutualism have been much discussed, but are not fully understood. Maybe the church, knowing they should be the stewards of the environment, drove this development. The outcome was more food and a growing population.

In time, the nobility turned their fields into enclosed feudal manorial estates and a small number of landholders slowly began to amass wealth. Around 5000 landholders were listed in the Domesday Book, compiled for 1066, and up to 100 had extensive lands. Historians in the past have ascribed the feudal system to be a key feature of post-Norman Conquest, but undoubtedly, its foundations were being laid in the 10th century. Holding evermore land as a way of social advancement was beginning. Dressing in style with elaborate clothing began to be used to show this advancement. Similarly, feasting with abundance on the table marked out the owner. Ostentation was appearing in people extra to the king, bishops and earls.

Every integrated settlement now had to have a church. Across Europe, a system of Parishes grew with each having a vicar who cared for his territory. Pastoral and spiritual care was being organised at a local level with the church positioned at the centre. Their prime pastoral responsibilities were to baptise new-borns and bury the dead. For this, their income drew on tithes and burial fees. This might have been the first time people were told where the dead could be buried, they had to have a presiding priest and it came with a cost. The churchyard was demarcated with the paupers usually buried on the outer north side, but this too had to be land consecrated by a bishop. This did not mean the local church was autonomous; the churches and chapelries remained under the supervision of a mother church. Recent research has revealed in some regions most of these mother churches were the pre-Viking establishments. For example, in the Gloucestershire and Worcestershire region 8 out of 10 areas were still being organised in the 11th century by a pre-Viking monastery. The new parochial system was a third tier answerable to the old monastery and cathedral. The Domesday Book, 1086, mentioned more than 2,600 local churches and this was only a fraction existing. In contrast, there were a mere 15 cathedrals.

As parishes increased, it was inevitable the Church demanded a tithe to sustain its new structure. For all men to give a tithe had been passed in 786, but there was no evidence it was enforced until Edgar, 959 – 975. A biblical tenth of farming produce became a new tax. Ordinary agricultural labourers now worked for and paid for the church. They joined the aristocracy in maintaining a Christian presence and this led to a great increase in revenue for the church. Conditions were then set for a new growth of the church and in return, every individual, down to the poorest labourer, had to be spiritually cared for. This new relationship transformed how people related to their church. The gap between the church and town narrowed until they were interdependent. Monks worked in the local community. In response, Lords on their manorial estates withdrew and built a private chapel. This must-have feature continued for the next three centuries. Withdrawal of legal protection and increasing taxation meant monasteries had to find new ways to fund their growing estates. Support from royalty and local benefactors had dwindled and with a few exceptions, their wealth now came from new resources. Gradually super monasteries began to appear founded on large-scale farming and land management. The 7th century to the 10th century monastery was no longer recognisable. In the Domesday Book, 1086, one sixth of valued land belonged to the monasteries.

Another apocalypse

Set against this great change with new growth of the church in Europe was the beginning of a second foreign nemesis, and this time it originated in the Holy Land. The unstable Caliph of Egypt ordered the destruction of the Holy Sepulchre in Jerusalem in 1009 and pilgrims reported damage being caused. In an unprecedented speech, the pope asked Norman recruits to kill those *alien to God* and they would be rewarded with their souls being cleansed. This later darkened to being rewarded with a promise of salvation. Jerusalem was retaken in 1099 in a second crusade. Atrocity in Antioch and Jerusalem, not always against Muslims for Jews were also demonised, meant the Papal church had now lost its fundamental core belief. It had become a warrior papacy. Correlations have been made with today's religious intolerance which is both wrong and a pity.

The Other World in the age of Vikings

Before the Viking raids, Christian centres around Europe were predisposed to Apocalypse and as early as the mid-8th century the Norse and Danes were given apocalyptic tags. One tract described the northern people as hardened by the most savage folkways, another called the people dog-heads, and a third described them as mother of dragons, scorpions, vipers and a lake of demons. Prophetically they warned *they (could) burst over the face of the earth and tear and devour everything like bread.* Some writers had guessed dramatically what was to come and the Christian language was aggressive and intolerant.

The first attack on Lindisfarne prompted Alcuin of York to claim the raid was a warning seen in Jeremiah 1.14 *Then the Lord said to me, Out of the north disaster shall break out on all the inhabitants of the land.*

Never one to miss an opportunity, Alcuin proclaimed the attack was a punishment for drinking, dressing up and generally poor behaviour. Other clergy joined in as one Viking raid followed another. It was an alarming sermon of repent before being killed by the barbarians. The Vikings had caused deep reflection and end-of-the-world fears with Christians, the righteous, being unjustly targeted.

The early Vikings relied on a pantheon of Gods, with much variation amongst the many different regions. Their ideas of the afterlife are not fully understood and much has been made from fragmentary sources. The dead rested in an underworld and it appeared to have been similar to the living world; death was an extension of life in another place. It explained the variety of grave goods buried with the departed. Male graves in Scandinavia contained tools, weapons and hunting dogs. Female graves had household implements, needlework, spinning and weaving artefacts, jewellery and lapdogs. There was no belief in a torment and no notion of forever living in bliss. This underworld came in various forms and where you went depended on your status and the nature of your death. It was overseen by certain Gods. Odin was the God of power, wisdom and battle and looked after kings and their elite warriors. He rode a horse with 8 legs called Sleipnir. He was also unpredictable. He appeared to be less important to those in Norway and Iceland.

Thor was the son of Odin and was the God of the environment. He had great strength and fought evil. He was reliable and looked after most Scandinavians. Frey and his sister Freyja bestowed peace and fertility. They were common in Sweden, but appeared in various forms throughout Scandinavia. There were other lesser Gods, giants, dwarves and elves, together with various beasts, that inhabited underworld communities. Communing with them occurred at certain locations in the countryside and within halls during feasting. Furthermore, a part of the dead could be revitalised and enter their descendants. The other world was never far from the living world.

Disposing of the body was also varied and could be an elaborate ritual. The Vikings quartered at Repton, Derbyshire in 873 to 874. A mass grave of 264

Sleipnir monument in Wednesbury.

skeletons, around 200 young men and 50 women, has been excavated and some had grave goods. The long bones, all small bones were missing, were piled neatly in a 2-roomed subterranean structure 4.5 metres square. It resembled a charnel house. 5 silver pennies date the burial to 873 or 4. It has been interpreted as a burial house for a Mercian Saxon king taken over by adding Viking bones from previous burials. They reused a Christian burial site to house their own relics.

Around 2.2 miles (3.5km) is Heath Wood, Ingleby, on a ridge overlooking the River Trent. Here 59 small burial mounds were excavated in the 1990s. Most contained cremations having burnt swords, buckles, nail and wire embroidery. It was thought many of the bodies had been burnt on boat planking. It was interpreted as a second Viking cemetery for the Repton area, but now using pyres to dispose of the body and treasured possessions. It has even been suggested it was the principal internment site for the Great Army and the battles around the year 874.

Other unusual ways of treating the Viking dead are known which have hindered a full understanding of their beliefs. Similarly, the low number of Scandinavian burial sites, no more than 40, hinders knowing their rituals of burial. Back home in Denmark and Norway, the conclusion is there was no distinct funereal tradition. Burial varied according to local practices. The burials in Norway of a queen and slave girl with abundant artefacts in the Oseberg ship, late 9th century, and a chieftain in the Gokstad ship were extraordinary.

Missionaries entered Scandinavia in the 8th century and some churches were built. However, the majority of people remained pagan until mid-10th century and then only gradually turned Christian. The Danes converted first, officially in 965, followed by the people of Southern Norway at the beginning of the 11th century. Sweden and Northern Norway were late in converting. It was not until the 12th century that an organised church was fully established. Under Cnut, English priests were given positions, especially in Denmark. British saints became popular folk heroes. New churches often incorporated English styles. In great contrast, the Dani who settled in Britain (an estimate of 15 to 40 thousand with a median of 25 thousand has been given) began to accept and follow Christianity within a relatively short length of time. The Northmen on various Atlantic islands converted at the end of the millennium. There never has been an inevitability about Christian conversion.

Jesus said to a crowd before crucifixion,

the light is with you for a little longer. Walk while you have the light, so that the darkness might not overtake you. If you walk in the darkness, you do not know where you are going. While you have the light, believe in the light, so that you may become children of light.

John 12.35-36

Chapter 9

STRUGGLE, SUFFERING AND IDENTITY – AN AFTERWORD

Among us, you will find uneducated persons, craftsmen, and old women, who, if they are unable in words to prove the benefit of our doctrine, yet by their deeds exhibit the benefit arising from their persuasion of its truth. They do not rehearse speeches, but exhibit good works; when struck, they do not strike again; when robbed, they do not go to law; they give to those that ask of them, and love their neighbours as themselves.

Athenagoras of Athens, c133 – c190,
in *A plea for the Christians*, written c177.

To take the first 1000 years of Christian history and determine its progression is very arbitrary. It is clear from humble beginnings a new religion was preached with great conviction by the early apostles. Various dialecticians and church fathers added early comments which gave perspective and proportion. Following many years of discourse and disagreement, an accepted testament and creed eventually were written. After the Romans made it their official Empire religion, bishops helped by abbots and monks began evangelising new countries. In countries bordering the Mediterranean and relatively close to the Holy Land, some were drawn to a church, were instructed in the faith and baptised. Merchants took the message to isolated settlements. This dissemination of the faith across Southern Europe, Northern Africa and into Asia was a complicated and extensive progression. In countries away from the Holy Land and on the fringes of the Roman Empire conversion was mediated through the conversion of the king and queen or taught by pilgrim saints. Local rulers often intervened, promoted, sometimes hindered and frequently made unholy trade-offs. They often subverted the affairs of the church to serve their ends. By the 8th century and in a piecemeal way, Christianity had been communicated to most of Europe, North Africa and many parts of Asia. It had become an established religion. Barbarians, as they were labelled, reversed its progress for a time, but they too were converted and convinced of its teachings. By the close of the millennium and in the wake of Viking desecration, churchmen became lawmakers and confidants of kings. The rise of the parish priest and church provided a local way of knowing God. Christianity became the centre of most people's lives. Probably around this time, the word *Cristendōm* was being used, originally meaning *Christianity,* but later coming to mean the lands dominated by Christianity. By the millennium, the western world, and much of the east, could claim to be a *Christendom.* This was the outcome of a long and tortuous history shaped by violence, suffering, struggle and argument, almost entirely involving priests collaborating with royalty, building churches and looking after communities. It started under Roman oppression and it finished with Viking and Fatimid Caliphate domination.

Sadly, it is often argued the growth of a religion with salvation at its core needed a background of hostility. Having a loving God in an unloving world provided hope, optimism and succour where little was present. It is easy to claim this is how individuals sought and sustained their faith. However, this is a modern interpretation from an age of plenty, some security and higher education and perhaps people of the darkest age did not see faith in this stark way. Struggle and strife were commonplace and, perhaps were not causal to becoming a Christian. It might have been the opposite; it led to faithlessness. It is the sentiment sometimes attributed to John Chrysostom, Bishop of Constantinople, 397 – 403.

The road to hell is paved with the bones of priests and monks, and the skulls of bishops are the lampposts that light the path.

The first millennium saw a new religion, based on how people behaved, thought and believed slowly evolve into an organised church which then aggrandized materially. Firstly, books, vessels for communion and hand bells appeared. Then came a building with an altar for Eucharistic celebration. Priests began to dignify the occasion with vestments and the church became furnished. Worship was ritualised, procession occurred and music accompanied and helped the liturgy. For some, the practices of the church distracted from knowing the very personal acceptance and renewal of faith. Its history hid from view how the ordinary individual responded to the complexity of the Biblical message. Consequently, the private journey of accepting God is missing in this story. Furthermore, the voice of women is largely absent in a history wholly dominated by men. All that can be said is individuals struggled with a difficult environment, were buffeted by local circumstances, had to be answerable to distant rulers and possibly faced threat. They might well have been subjected to a conversion founded on fear and distortion. Lay worship was demanding, probably unintelligible. Belief for many needed continuous reinforcement and spiritual rebirth was not a once in a lifetime event. In truth, steps taken to follow a Christian faith were unrecorded and are now virtually lost to any analysis. Those who claim to know how religiosity arose in this historic period are only guessing.

One rare personal struggle to faith was outlined by Augustine of Hippo in a book called *Confessions* written between 397 and 400. It was probably the first autobiography in the Latin Church and detailed Augustine following various beliefs and traditions in his early life until in his early 30s when he finally became a Christian. It was a collection of 13 books giving very personal confessions as to how he struggled to eventually become a priest aged 37. It became an exemplar for personal doubt, the testing of belief and final realisation. There is no doubt many of the early church leaders, including saints, went through this same personal struggle, even if their biographers would not want it known. The accusation from atheists critical of Christianity that it grew with ignorance at a time when people did not communicate and discuss much, might apply to isolated communities, but from early on, clergy were giving the detail and inviting individuals to find the truth. In an age of uncertainty, they too would be uncertain. Gaining a Christian belief was rarely spontaneous and often protracted, but it definitely was not borne from ignorance.

All this strongly infers the growth of Christianity was continuous and inevitable. By blurring periods, cherry-picking events and looking at changes at a national level it seems its spread was always outwards. This is illusory. The tight control of the Romans, the indifference to begin with of the Saxons, a geographical isolation with the Celts, the ransacking by the Vikings and the invasion of Muslims, together with local conflicts between rulers and spiritual arguments amongst the clergy all gave a discontinuous history. On many occasions, the shadow of barbarians reversed enlightenment. Seeing the light was punctuated by plunging into murkiness and sometimes it was extinguished. God's light at times only flashed.

Despite the many setbacks, the promulgation of Christianity was remarkable, even a miracle. It showed the teachings of Christ overcame all the hardships, attrition, impediments and heresies and many people glimpsed their value. It was tested with the years and evolved to become the force that shaped people's lives. It impacted on the law, questioned the right of kings, showed the mores of how to live, shaped our education and gave direction to how we all end up. Wherever Christians settled a learned tradition and cultural inheritance grew. Worship, prayer and penitence became an integral part of our behaviour. It shaped our soul.

In every generation, the question is asked, what exactly are our *Core Values?* Sometimes it is framed in nationalistic tones such as what makes us British. This has taken on a greater importance with the world now communicating globally and being more interdependent than ever before. Our culture is being immersed and hybridised in cultures from elsewhere and that entitles people to ask who are we? This struggle to define ourselves is being played out in all the fast media streams now open for individuals to make comment. Indeed, it has become an obsession. Simplistic labels such as stoic, reliable, fair-minded, open, democratic, welcoming, incisive and more play into the current horror of comparing one culture as sheep and another as goats. Paradoxically it is thought that by defining people and cultures, it will bring them together. Historically, it has emphasised division and led to terrible war and strife. Outwardly, we are all different and inwardly we are just as diverse. God's light has many colours. Let us hope and pray accommodating differences will mean the third millennium is better.

There is no better example of the expression of good values than in Jesus' parable of the Good Samaritan; a story deeply embedded in our collective understanding of what it means to be a good citizen, and which reminds us that our values have not emerged from a vacuum – but from the resilient and eternal structure of our religious, theological, philosophical and ethical heritage.

Archbishop of Canterbury in a speech in a
Lord's debate on UK values, December 2016

INDEX

213

By The Same Author

The Hoard and its History - Staffordshire's Secrets Revealed
Published by Brewin Books Ltd.
ISBN 978-1-85858-547-5
Price: £14.95

Available from www.brewinbooks.com